MW00827780

THE IDEOLOGY OF IMAGINATION

*Subject and Society in the Discourse
of Romanticism*

The Ideology of Imagination

Subject and Society in the Discourse of Romanticism

FOREST PYLE

STANFORD UNIVERSITY PRESS

Stanford, California

Stanford University Press
Stanford, California

© 1995 by the Board of Trustees of the
Leland Stanford Junior University

Printed in the United States of America

CIP data appear at the end of the book

Stanford University Press publications are distributed
exclusively by Stanford University Press within the
United States, Canada, Mexico, and Central America;
they are distributed exclusively by Cambridge
University Press throughout the rest of the world.

Original printing 1995
Last figure below indicates year of this printing:
05 04 03 02 01 00 99 98 97 96

To the memory of my father,
for the love of my family

Preface

On the back cover of *Arabesques*—Anton Shammas's fine and difficult novel about the politics of memory, language, and identity between Palestine and Israel—one finds among the enthusiastic notices the following excerpt from a review in the *Seattle Times Post*: *Arabesques*, writes Richard Wakefield, "is a triumph of the healing power of the imagination over the fragmenting force of politics."

The remark does not address the role of the imagination in Romantic discourse, nor does it tell us anything interesting about the role of the imagination in contemporary literature or culture. And readers of *Arabesques* will note immediately how the remark misses everything at stake in Shammas's compelling novel. But I preface my study with such a passage because of its value as a symptom: it demonstrates the tenacious purchase that the inherited notion of the imagination continues to maintain on our models of culture, interpretation, and evaluation. The imagination is often taken without question by the journalist or critic or teacher to be the guiding principle of literary production. Few received ideas of literary history have become more inflated by the nature of their circulation or have had a more mystifying effect than the "imagination," but its persistence as received idea is precisely a testimony to its ideological force, in this instance as a "healing power," as an agent of meaning and redemption.

This book examines the workings of the imagination in the texts of English Romanticism, those texts most responsible for its historical currency. While *The Ideology of Imagination* examines the English adventure of the concept of the imagination from the late eighteenth to the mid-nineteenth centuries, it is written with the sense that the Romantic legacy of that concept, however degraded or mutated, is still very much with us. By exploring the social as well as literary roles given to the imagination in Romantic texts, I believe we will be better positioned to understand the aesthetic tradition that makes the "imagination" into an agent that ostensibly redeems literature from the prosaic and divisive situation of politics and language. I should thus like to contribute through my readings of English Romantic texts a sense of the intractable and mutual pull of politics and language, which remains as much a legacy of Romanticism as the failed forms of redemption we encounter in concepts such as that of the imagination.

Those of us who teach Romantic and post-Romantic literature work with the burden and the charge of the imagination even when we choose to ignore it. I trace the impulse behind my study to two moments in the classroom. The first of these occurred in a sophomore survey of English literature at the University of Texas, where I was teaching Book VI of *The Prelude*. A group of skeptical undergraduates found Wordsworth's celebrated invocation of the "Imagination" thoroughly implausible: the poet addressed the imagination, they asserted, as if it were a strange but almost sentient thing, and not as a faculty that one possesses. Their curiosity about the passage interrupted the course of what had to that point been my primarily thematic and phenomenological interpretation of the poem and prompted me to consider what I would now identify as the rhetoricity of the imagination. I found myself compelled to attend to the strange figurative status of the imagination in the passage—the imagination as both "prosopopoeia" and "catachresis"—and to wonder whether the consequences of that figuration could be reconciled with the organicism of Wordsworth's stated project.

The second inaugurating remark now appears as a footnote to an essay by Gayatri Spivak, though I initially encountered it some years ago in her graduate seminar on Marxist criticism. She proposed there a distinction between a "strong" and a "weak" imagination in Romanticism, and she argued that in the *Defence of Poetry*, Shelley proposes an instance of the "strong" imagination: "a principle of irreducible alterity housed in the Self, which is directly opposed to 'the principle of Self.'" Spivak's sense of the Shelleyan imagination as the proposition of an insistent alterity that works against the "principle of Self" in which it is "housed" recovered a contradiction in the notion of the imagination: it opened the possibility of *reading* a term I had theretofore imagined as inherently and seamlessly idealist and, therefore, "ideological" in the most limited sense.

I recount these anecdotes because they mark the extensive debts this study owes to my students and teachers, and because they speak to the motivations for the book's critical orientation. From deconstruction I have drawn the imperative of "reading," of attending closely to the rhetorical operations at work in a text without regard to the "violence" this attention may inflict on a thematic or recuperative interpretation, even when that interpretation is proposed by the work itself. From Marxism I have drawn the imperative of considering how political desires and social agendas are written into the very structure and performance of the literary text. This book explores the workings of the imagination in Romantic texts in order first to understand the rhetorical machinations housed within its status as a prominent theme of Romantic discourse. I believe that such an exploration makes possible a second crucial dimension of understanding: namely, how the imagination, as figure, is invested with social and political—which is to say "ideological"—significance. To pursue such a double reading, the book turns often to the work of Louis Althusser, Walter Benjamin, and Theodor Adorno as well as that of Paul de Man and Jacques Derrida. And it draws upon the recent work of those who have pushed at the questions raised by deconstruction and of those who have pursued critically the intersections between post-structuralist modes of analysis and sociopolitical concerns.

That critical constellation is an extensive one, and my object in this book is not primarily to demonstrate the convergences or document the divergences between Marxism and deconstruction, but to consider how these discourses, and their (sometimes strained, sometimes unexpected) points of contact, open themselves to the ideological questions raised by the Romantic imagination.

The book has been some years in the making, and it bears the marks of many readings by and conversations with generous teachers, colleagues, and friends. I wish to thank my teachers from the University of Texas, John P. Farrell, Barbara Harlow, Wayne P. Lesser, Walter Reed (now at Emory), and Ramón Saldívar (now at Stanford). I am grateful to my colleagues at the University of Oregon for their readings, their conversation, and their support: Paul Armstrong, Kenneth Calhoon, Michael Clark, Suzanne Clark, James Earl, Joseph Fracchia, Linda Kintz, Randall McGowen, Steven Rendall, William Rossi, George Rowe, Kathleen Rowe, Cheyney Ryan, Steven Shankman, Richard L. Stein, Irving Wohlfarth, and Claudia Yukman. I am also fortunate to feel myself a part of a more extensive community of friends, mentors, editors, and colleagues whose readings and comments at stages both early and late have been indispensable to my writing and thinking about *The Ideology of the Imagination*: Nancy Armstrong, Ian Balfour, Ann Cvetkovitch, Deborah Esch, Fredric Jameson, James Kavanagh, Thomas Keenan, David McMurray, Eric Mendelsohn, Bradford K. Mudge, Michael Taussig, and Richard Terdiman. Helen Tartar has been a brilliant editor: patient, demanding, supportive, and always a *reader* in the fullest sense of the term. Ellen F. Smith has devoted scrupulous attention to the manuscript, and Nancy Young did a splendid job of copyediting. Lee Taylor lived with this book during its conception, its making, and its revision: the book and its author are deeply indebted to her love and support.

Finally, I wish to thank my mentor and friend, Gayatri Chakravorty Spivak: she taught me what I know about reading, and she taught me to read. It is to the gift of her teaching that I owe this book.

Portions of the Introduction and Chapter 4 have appeared in *Studies in Romanticism* (Spring 1994) under the title "Keats's Materialism." I am grateful to the editor, David Wageknecht, and to the board of *SiR* for their reading and support at a crucial stage of the project. A shorter version of Chapter 5 has appeared in *Novel: A Forum on Fiction* (Fall 1993): 5–23, under the title "A Novel Sympathy: The Imagination of Community in George Eliot."

Contents

THE IDEOLOGY OF IMAGINATION

Subject and Society in the Discourse of Romanticism

The imagination may be compared to
Adam's dream—he awoke to find it truth.

—Keats, letter to Benjamin Bailey (1817)

Of Imagination and Ideology

The term "imagination" is invested with such poetic, philosophical, and even political significance in Romantic thought that it is tempting to regard Romanticism itself as an effect of "Adam's dream," as the proper name for imagination's ascendancy. Taking as its starting point the claims made by the poets for the imagination's "truth," this book proposes to read English Romanticism's figuring of the imagination. It is my thesis that the imagination is given a social and political assignment as much as a poetic or philosophical one: the imagination is the figure by which Romantic texts address the disjunction between subject and society as well as that between spirit and matter. The Romantic imagination is thus assigned what traditions of social theory after Marx would identify as ideological tasks. But, still more importantly, politics and society cannot be regarded as the explanatory *context* of the Romantic imagination: I hope to demonstrate that social and political matters are inextricable from the imagination's poetic performances or philosophical assertions. The binding of imagination and ideology, a binding that occurs throughout Romanticism, means that a reading of the Romantic imagination can teach us something about the very notion of ideology with which we would presume to understand it.

The task of *defining* the Romantic imagination has proved to be notoriously difficult, in part because the term is such a mercurial one, in part because it is invoked in a variety of contexts to different ends, and in part because so many influential Romantic texts find it necessary to speculate on the nature and workings of the imagination. Its well-documented variability is, as historians of ideas have noted, something inherent in the concept itself.[1] In the Romantic imagination we discover that we are not dealing with a stable property of mind or a concept of selfhood but with a matter of discourse, with a figure. Learning the rhetorical status is the inaugural point for any sustained study of the imagination in Romantic discourse, because the figure of the imagination is consistently called upon to perform tasks in Romantic texts that its figural status cannot sustain. But to stress the figurality of the imagination is but to begin the necessary critical work, and I intend here not merely to demonstrate the rhetorical shapes of the imagination but to explore the crucial ideological fate of this *particular* figure in Romanticism.

The imagination can be figured as "another name for absolute strength of mind" (Wordsworth), as "the great instrument of moral good" (Shelley), as the sign of a meaningful connection between spirit and matter, or as the symptom of a disturbance in culture and society. To attend to the figure of the imagination in Romanticism, to explore the nature and significance of its appearances and disappearances in Romantic texts, demands the exertion of a textual analysis that is unlikely to yield any conclusive or consistent definition of the term. Nonetheless, I believe it is possible to begin with a provisional understanding of what the imagination is called upon to *do*: throughout its adventures in Romantic discourse, the imagination is assigned the responsibility of making a linkage, an articulation. Whether it is a matter of articulating "pure" with "practical" reason in the architecture of Kant's critiques or of linking subject with society in the organic "weaves" of George Eliot's narrative community, the imagination is designated the site or the agent of such a proposed articulation. I understand the task of articulating in both senses of the word: a linking, for instance of subject with society, as well as the language articulated by such a linking, for instance the language of "community." This means that the imagination, as it undertakes an articulation or tries to speak the language of community, necessarily points to the prior existence of a rift, a fissure, a disjunction that must be crossed or healed.

When we read the articulate language engendered through the figurings of the imagination—as the "growth of the poet's mind," for instance, or as the "repetition in the finite mind of the infinite I AM"—we encounter a language in which the imagination is thoroughly implicated with ideology. The intrication of imagination and ideology demands that we think of ideology as something more than the mystifications of "false consciousness" and more than a coherent body of ideas: it demands that we begin by conceiving of "ideology" as the fundamental necessity of a representation of the social. This is what John B. Thompson, following Marx, calls the necessity for a society to "forg[e] a representation of its unity,"[2] a unity that is not empirically present and that must thus be *re*presented. It is in this sense that the imagination in Romantic discourse is ideological: in its tasks of articulation, it addresses the fissures of the social and governs the attempted representation of their coherence. The inseparability of the social from its representations not only means that we must explore the social destination of ideas, but also demands that we consider the inscriptions of the social in all forms of representation, including those of the imagination. Recent studies of ideology—by Louis Althusser, Etienne Balibar, Claude Lefort, Slavoj Žižek, and others—have explored in various ways and to different ends the irreducibility of representation from our collective or individual negotiations with the social.[3] And from Marx to the present, such a conception of ideology is always linked, as Thompson tells us, "to the dimension of the imaginary" (*Studies*, 16). One cannot, in other words, hope to understand ideology without something called the imagination.

To make the intersections between imagination and ideology worth exploring, there must be something more at issue than the by now predictable revelation that the imagination is "ideological." For after Althusser—indeed, after Marx—how can we imagine a product of language or activity of *mind* that would not be ideological? It is my thesis that a reading of "the ideology of the imagination" not only sheds light on the imagination but in turn reflects upon the very workings of ideology. To examine the ideology of the imagination in Romantic discourse means to explore critically the nature of their co-implication. For not only is the imagination "ideological" in the most restricted and schematic sense of that term (a theme of literary and philosophical discourse, an element of the "superstructure"), but further the imagination is the vehicle by which Romantic texts address the problem posed by ideology. The project charged to the chapters that follow is to read for both terms, ideology and imagination, and to pursue the fate and consequences of their relationship in Romantic texts. My project is motivated by the conviction that considerably more is on the line in such an undertaking than an *explication* of the Romantic imagination in its more or less canonical appearances. From the perspective of contemporary literary and cultural studies, these texts on the imagination are of more than archival interest if they can be understood not merely as the records of a concept that has long since receded to the "history of ideas" but as documents that speculate in theme and by performance upon the operations of ideology. By this I mean that their speculation extends beyond the historically specific "ideology" of the age to the ideological operations through which our relations to language and society continue to be formed. But the imagination cannot be distilled from the texts in which it appears, and thus a reading of the imagination teaches us in the first instance about the workings of such texts. In particular, a reading of the imagination in Romantic texts reveals the mechanisms by which those texts present and occult their relationships to language, subjectivity, society—in short, their ideological condition.

Though the book identifies the imagination as the common figure through which Romantic texts confront their own ideological status, the individual chapters address the specific and often varying forms of these confrontations. To return to my earlier metaphor, the chapters explore the particular languages pronounced by the articulation of ideology and the imagination.

Chapter 1 is concerned with the "instituting" of the imagination at work in Coleridge's critical writings, an imagination that, once instituted, is expected to address England's fundamental social antagonisms and secure the narrative of national unity. The status of English cultural representation is also at issue in Chapter 2, which treats the narratives of the imagination in *The Prelude*, paying particular attention to the "dream of the Arab" in Book V. Both readings reveal the crucial ideological work in these formative poet-critics to be that of an "instituting" (Coleridge) and an "enshrining" (Wordsworth) of the imagination.

The third chapter, a reading of *The Triumph of Life*, marks a departure of sorts, in both direction and tone: *The Triumph of Life*, I argue, delivers us to the "ends" of the imagination, and in the process produces nothing less than an "epistemological break" in Romantic discourse, one that is not unrelated to that which Althusser describes in Marx. The demands of describing what happens in Shelley—of describing the poem's singular attempt to theorize the permanently ideological nature of representation—supplies the occasion for the book's most overt examination of the juncture between Marxism and deconstruction, in this case between Louis Althusser and Paul de Man. A consideration of the critical possibilities held out by this juncture is necessary, I argue, to begin an exploration of the deep and decisive faultline that emerges in Romantic discourse with Shelley's last great poem.

By marking *The Triumph of Life* as the site of an epistemological break, we gain a new recognition of the tension present within Shelley's work, a tension that runs throughout Romantic discourse and that opens a different perspective on the split between the first and second generations of Romanticism. To pursue some new implications of that split, Chapter 4 proposes a reading of the "materialism" I believe to be at work in Keats, a materialism that emerges in the resistance of "things" to "thought": in poems such as "Dear Reynolds" and *The Fall of Hyperion* this resistance appears in the wake of the imagination.

The novels of George Eliot are not often considered in the context of Romanticism; but I conclude my study with a reading of her early novels because I believe that Eliot's narrative project—her "narration of sympathy"—constitutes the most sustained and sophisticated Victorian effort to address the implications and reverberations of Romanticism's epistemological break. Chapter 5 demonstrates how the formal and thematic principle of "sympathy" in Eliot belongs to the expansive pedagogical aims of her novels: sympathy is the narrative response to the

Romantic legacy of the imagination, a response that speaks to the deep desires for community.

In each of the chapters, the appearances of the imagination reveal something more than a prominent theme or idea in a period of literary history. The imagination is the figure that emerges from the ideological situation of Romanticism, and it is this very situation that the figure of the imagination is in turn given the task of understanding and resolving.

The focus of the book is, clearly, a canonical *English* Romanticism and its Victorian aftermath. From the outset, however, in the work of Coleridge, we are made aware both of the "nationalist" project prescribed for the imagination and of the porousness of the national context. Coleridge demonstrates that the very possibility of an *English* Romanticism rests as much on the labors of translating as it does on the efforts of defining the imagination. It is striking that the invocations of the imagination throughout English poetry and criticism of the period often accompany and perhaps require invocations of foreign sites: France, Spain, "Asia," an "Arab Desert," classical Greece, and, most prominently, Germany.

The significance of Germany is however of a different order altogether. The English discourse of Romanticism is closely bound up with its German exchange, one that for Coleridge and for Eliot assumes an explicit activity of translation, such as that of finding for *Einbildungskraft* a properly English idiom. For Coleridge, the German point of departure is of course Kant, for whom the imagination holds out the promise of bridging reason and sense, establishing the link between world and mind, and abolishing the "immeasurable gulf" between the true and the good. In *The Critique of Judgment* the imagination is situated between the mind's faculty of reason, the noumenal domain of concepts, and the phenomenal world of sensory perceptions.[4] Generations of interpreters have documented the oscillations in Kant between the "empirical" and the "transcendental" moments of the imagination. If the oscillation is never fully stabilized or "harmonized" by the imagination, it is precisely because oscillation is the imagination's condition, its situation *between* sense and reason. Even in the rigors of the Kantian critique, the imagination, to borrow James Engell's comparison, functions as "a rare radioisotope, [which] sheds an eerie glow and seems to change its form into different elements" (*Creative Imagination*, 129). Kant ascribes to the imagination, "as a productive faculty of cognition," the power of "creating another nature, as it were, out of the material that actual nature gives it" (*Critique*, 157). The imagination does not treat nature itself but the "material" "supplied us by nature" that "can be worked up into something different which surpasses nature" (157). In this labor of transformation, the imagination mimics reason, which it can never match: the imagination "emulates the play of reason in its quest after a maximum" and strives "to go beyond the limits of experience" (158). The passage is a chronicle of the nonadequation between these faculties and is exemplary of the condition and the work of the imagination in Kant: the imagination remains caught between a "nature" that it exceeds and the play of a "reason" that it emulates but cannot realize.

The "Analytic of the Beautiful" calls for a judgment that proceeds "just as if it were a definite cognition" (*Critique*, 52). We have learned, however, to attend to the persistence and precariousness of the "as if" that remains here and throughout the third *Critique*: the condition of a judgment that "rests" on the "indeterminate but . . . harmonious activity" of the imagination and understanding.[5] However tenuous the conditional collaboration of faculties in the analytic of the beautiful, contemporary theory has most often turned to the Kantian sublime, for it is there that the "mutual agreement" between faculties disappears.[6] In the "mathematical sublime," for instance, the imagination is animated through its relation to reason; and this animation results not in cooperation but in "want of accordance" (96).[7] Over the last decade, critical and rhetorical readings, particularly under the rubric of deconstruction, have demonstrated the threat posed by the Kantian sublime to an "aesthetic ideology."[8] I refer to this widely rehearsed topic in order to note that it is the *failure* of the imagination, its "inadequacy" for "presenting the ideas of a whole" (*Critique*, 91), that results in the discomforting affective economy of the sublime and provokes, in turn, the "deconstructive" reading. The point to be stressed is this: in the third *Critique*, a founding text of modern Western reflection on the aesthetic, the activity of the imagination, while acknowledging the necessity of a link, an articulation, becomes instead the site of a decisive disarticulation.

The disclosures of such fundamental disjunctions (between theme and trope, between statement and performance) have been a principal topic—and, on occasion, an end—of post-structural analysis. In the texts of English Romantic poetry and criticism, the visitations of the imagination certainly endorse such an analysis, given the many forms, both structural and thematic, of their division. My interest here, however, is not primarily to document, much less to celebrate, the instances of the imagination's failures and the resulting disarticulations, but to explore how the failures themselves become the material for a renewed if anxious consideration of the ideological rift that reasserts itself in the wake of the imagination. If the reassertion of the rift is not always acknowledged thematically, it registers itself textually: in the widening gap between story and discourse, for instance in Eliot's late novels, or in its destabilizing effect on Keats's poetry. Such examples suggest that the "failure" of the imagination to accomplish the task of articulation does not mean that the rifts between mind and spirit or subject and society are left as they were "before"; rather, they reveal those rifts to be both necessary and inevitably "worked on." But if the rift *in* the social is best understood as irreducible and even constitutive *of* the social, that rift can be explored through the very concepts that have addressed it, such as that of the imagination. The imagination, for authors as disparate as Kant and Keats, finds itself "in a strange sort of purgatory blind" (Keats), in a curious "contact with nature" (Kant) that yields affect but no knowledge.

The following chapters tell the story of an imagination that is preceded by its demand, the demand to fill a need, to "harmonize" difference, to restore something lacking. For Kant, the imagination, unlike reason or sense, is primarily an effect of the structure, the filling in of a necessary and absent link within the architecture of the *Critiques*. The imagination is called on to fill in the gap opened between transcendental principles of reason and the empirical orientation of the senses, a project of linking that might best be described as "translation." The "task" of the imagination, as Paul de Man characterizes it, "its labor," may be "precisely to translate the abstractions of reason back into the phenomenal world of appearances and images whose presence is retained in the very word *imag*ination, *bild* in the German 'Einbildungskraft'" ("Phenomenality," 137). When de Man describes the "task" of the imagination in Kant as one of "translation," we are likely to notice the reference to Walter Benjamin's essay on the "task of the translator," a reference that renders the prospect of any successful translation doubtful from the start.[9] In the act of translation, according to Benjamin, the "transfer" from the original to the translation "can never be total." But the economy is not one of pure loss; Benjamin is interested in the strange, secondary effectivity of translation. For him, the translation itself bestows upon the text it translates the sense of its originality and hence its severance and its distance from the translation: "In translation the original rises into a higher and purer linguistic air" ("Task," 75). The act of translation produces a "disjunction" between texts which "prevents translation and at the same time makes it superfluous" (75).

Given the significance of German texts for English Romanticism, the disjunctive effects of translation are bound to extend to much of what takes place in the name of the imagination. In the case of Coleridge, for instance, this involves the English translation of *Einbildungskraft*, but it also includes the comprehensive translation of a *philosophical* concept into a principle of literary composition and evaluation and, more ambitiously still, into a political and pedagogical institution. This form of translation is not, of course, limited to English cultural thought; Schiller's *Letters on an Aesthetic Education* is premised on a "translation into practice" of Kantian "theory."[10] The accent of this Schillerian model is retained not only in Coleridge but also in George Eliot, whose own version of an "aesthetic teaching" calls for the translation of the Romantic concept of the imagination into a Victorian idiom of "sympathy," a translation that is made possible through its *transfer* to novelistic discourse.

The emphasis on translation in English Romanticism is not, however, the exclusive province of German themes or ideas: Shelley's translations of Plato come to mind, and we will consider what it means in the *Defence of Poetry* for Shelley to "translate" the imagination into the historical agent of cultural and political transformation. When Wordsworth refers in Book VI of *The Prelude* to the "Imagination" as "the power so-called / Through sad incompetence of human speech," he identifies the imagination as a fundamental problem of translation.[11] The translation of "Power" into "imagination" is necessarily a failed translation, one that reveals the "sad incompetence of human speech." The sublime appearance is necessarily mistranslated as "imagination," a mistranslation that conforms to Benjamin's model as it is translated in turn by de Man: by translating "Power" into language with the name of the imagination, Wordsworth points to the disjunction between the comprehension available through "human speech" and the "Power" that always exceeds and deforms it.[12] This fundamental misnaming makes of the imagination a figure, and more specifically that figure of figures, a "catachresis," a misnaming for which there exists no proper name in "human speech."[13]

Throughout the discourse of English Romanticism, the imagination is repeatedly assigned the work of translating or articulating, though such work is assigned to a figure that can never properly fulfill the terms of these assignments. The readings that follow explore the double logic of an imagination that is invoked to translate or articulate but that discloses or even effects a more fundamental mistranslation or disarticulation. To say this is to restore Hegel's awareness in *Faith and Knowledge*, for instance, that the imagination is itself the site *and* source of the diremption between subjective and objective worlds.[14] Deployed as a principle of coherence, an agent of linkage, or a medium of translation for the discourse of Romanticism, the imagination is simultaneously a principal site of its division and disjunction.

But in the readings that follow, I also attempt to describe the *outcome* of the imagination's double logic, an outcome that, given the significance ascribed to the term, has considerable social as well as philosophical implications. For if the imagination does not denote a process of mind and is more accurately regarded as the figural juncture of forces in conflict than as a consistent activity, if the imagination refers both to the necessity of linking mind with nature, spirit with matter, subject with society *and* to the formidable resistances to all such linkages, then the imagination, as well as the efforts to read it, should be understood as ideological in the most extensive sense of that term. When Romantic texts take up matters of perception, cognition, reflection, composition, affect, or judgment, they refer to the imagination: when the imagination appears on the expansive horizons of Romantic discourse, linked as it is to matters of seeing or knowing or judging or feeling, it bears within it deeply ideological inscriptions. To pursue a reading of the imagination in Romantic discourse, in short, is to confront the meaning and matter of ideology.

It is likely, however, that no term in modern social theory is as vexed, or as indispensable, as "ideology." Both the vexation of this term and the extent of the term's significance will be apparent from a cluster of related questions: By what means does a society represent itself? What roles (constitutive, regulative, legitimating) do these representations play in the reproduction of society? To the general questions of social theory we can add those raised more locally for literary studies by the question of ideology: What is the role of "literature" in social self-representation? What significant roles, if any, do literary texts (their production, reception, transmission) play in the reproduction of society? The phrasing of this knot of questions may be recognized as "Althusserian," but the questions are those raised in one vocabulary or another throughout contemporary social theory (Lefort, Bourdieu, Castoriadis, Giddens, Habermas, Laclau and Mouffe); and they are questions inaugurated in a critical fashion by Marx and addressed throughout the "Western" Marxist tradition (Lukács, Gramsci, Sartre, Adorno, Williams, Althusser). And in the chapters to follow, I contend that these are questions invited by English Romantic texts.

What distinguishes the Marxist analysis of ideology from competing models of analysis, and what makes it most pertinent to the concerns of this study, is its materialist insistence on forms of determination that disclose the nonidentity of things to themselves. Marx's own theorizing of ideology arises from and addresses the contradictions between matter and spirit, and thus returns us "in a materialist way" (Macherey) to the very divisions—between matter and spirit, for instance—addressed and thematized by the Romantic imagination.[15] While Marx acknowledges the worldly effectivity of ideas, his writings stress the determination of ideas by "non-ideas." Ideas, as we learn from *The German Ideology*, are insufficient to themselves: there obtains to the idea a material otherness that cannot be accounted for in the idea but that nonetheless exerts some form of determination over the idea.[16] *The German Ideology* insists on the "burden" of matter that German philosophy habitually denegates: "the 'mind' is from the outset afflicted with the curse of being burdened with matter" (43–44).

The characterization of the "material" as a curse to the life of spirit or mind is a prominent motif of English Romantic poetry, as in the famous opening lines of Book V of *The Prelude*, and it is the imagination that is often presented as the object threatened by material affliction. For the Marx of *The German Ideology*, ideology is both a consequence of the discrepancy between matter and spirit and an *inevitable* denial of that discrepancy in the name of the spirit. According to Marx, ideology arises from the fundamental separation between "consciousness" and "life" and then works to invert their determination: ideology functions by blocking knowledge of the social production of consciousness (44), by an "inversion" that represents "life" as if it were "determined by consciousness" (37). As a consequence, the ideological inversion is necessarily lived as if it were true. Thus, the famous analogy with the *camera obscura*: "If in all ideology men and their circumstances appear upside-down as in a *camera obscura*, this phenomenon arises just as much from their historical life-process as the inversion of objects on the retina does from their physical life-objects" (36).

While the reference to the optical effects of the *camera obscura* is often interpreted as the revelation of illusions to be dispelled, Marx asserts that the ideological "phenomenon" is not simply a mistake but the effect of "historical life-processes." Stephen Heath's gloss of the passage stresses the apparatus of ideology and thus recovers the sense in Marx that ideology is more than ephemeral, that it obtains in the real itself:

> As the individual faces the screen of ideology, . . . he or she sees a real image, in true, aligned, and him/herself in position with it, screened too, presented and represented. There is no turning round (or back) to reality as to a direct source of light, no putting the eye to a hole so as to see the world outside. Ideology arises from the historical life-processes taken up in it, the struggle is in reality which includes ideology as a real component of its presence, historical, social, and subjective.[17]

To say that "the struggle is in reality which includes ideology" is to assert the antagonistic, fissured nature of reality in which ideology is a "real component." Heath's account of the passage is important for its emphasis on the "screening" of ideology; I want to draw attention to the faculty necessary for the screening to "take." When Marx describes the ideological inversion-effect, he makes reference to the space of the imaginary and to the activity of the imagination: "If the conscious expression of the real relations of these individuals is illusory, if in their imagination [*Einbildungskraft*] they turn reality upside-down, then this in its turn is the result of their limited material mode of activity" (40). Marx *needs* the reference to the imagination in order to give an account of the *effects* of ideology. I note the reference not to point out the residues of idealism in the young Marx but to indicate how the imagination, far from being a mere ideological *symptom* of the contradiction between matter and spirit, instead both bears that contradiction within itself and reproduces it. Without imagination, ideological misrecognition could be construed only as simple illusion, as mistakes that could then be corrected by empirical reference. We are thus close to Althusser's important formulation of ideology as "active" in the mutual "overdetermination of the real by the imaginary and of the imaginary by the real" (*For Marx*, 234).

This is not yet a definition of ideology of course, much less a definitive account of the relationship between ideology and the imagination. But it may well be the case, as Etienne Balibar suggests, that Marx's speculations on ideology in that founding text of "historical materialism" do not propose a definition of ideology but rather elicit the *problem* of ideology.[18] To approach the problem of ideology in this way permits us to think the *necessity* of a representation of the social that—owing both to the vehicle of representation (in the case of Romanticism, the figure of the imagination) and to the fundamental noncoherence of the social—inevitably takes the form of a "misrepresentation." It may thus appear that "ideology" has as a concept been divested of any critical function, that it no longer serves the demystifying function undertaken by Marx. But as my reading of Shelley in Chapter 4 demonstrates, one's faith in the prospect of demystification is shaken rather than confirmed the closer one attends to the workings of the ideology. This is not to say that we cannot—by reading Shelley, for example—learn a great deal about the workings of ideology. But as Althusser insists, ideology is not "dissipated by a knowledge of it: for the knowledge of this ideology, as the knowledge . . . of its specific logic and of its practical role, within a given society, is simultaneously knowledge of the conditions of its necessity" (*For Marx*, 230). This is the charge of reading the ideology of the imagination in Romantic texts: discerning its "specific" logic and its "practical role" within the maintenance of nineteenth-century English society means exploring the "conditions of its necessity."

All of which is precisely what we lose in the solutions proposed by *The Romantic Ideology*: the *problem* of ideology itself. By returning the literary text to the social discourses of its historical moment, by reconstructing archivally the scene of its production and reception, a historicist critic such as Jerome McGann hopes to elude the ideology of the text and to achieve a position of genuine knowledge. McGann claims to demystify Romanticism by revealing the social conditions that are obscured or effaced by what he calls a "textual idealism," "an uncritical absorption in Romanticism's own representations."[19] However important such historical research may prove to be for an understanding of the poem's social context, and however much it has invigorated Romantic studies, it does not solve the problem of ideology, which is both more pervasive and more extensive. Ideology is not merely the gap between the literary and the social that gives rise to misrepresentations which might be rectified by empirical reference: as Heath's reading of Marx insists, the ideological gap is active in the real itself.

It would be a mistake, however, to discount the appeal of McGann's project of a "literature of knowledge," a project that promises to demystify "the romantic ideology." McGann's project is made still more attractive if we accept his assertion that the Romantic critical tradition has demonstrated an "uncritical absorption in Romanticism's own self-representations" (*Romantic Ideology*, 1).[20] While no literary critic *wants* to believe that he or she remains "uncritically absorbed" in the literary object of investigation, the difficulties of getting outside ideology, of avoiding "Romanticism's own self-representation," cannot be overestimated, not least of all because the means of escape entails another form of representation, one that may well turn out to be "Romantic." But such is precisely the force of McGann's claim: one can, and should, elude this abyssal and *Romantic* effect by reference to the "specific socio-historical circumstances" of the text's composition: "Poems are, first of all, acts of representation; as such, they can only be read when the entire facticity of those acts is raised into consciousness. The acts of poetry are begun and carried in specific socio-historical circumstances."[21] In his efforts to break the "closed circle of reflection," McGann turns not to the material properties of poetic discourse but to the "dominion of experience": "The cognitive dynamic played out through poetic discourse is not confined, however, to the closed circle of Hegelian, or Socratic, reflection. The dynamic involves real, objective knowledge because the poetic field remains, finally, under the dominion of experience and not consciousness" (*Knowledge*, 133). We gain knowledge of the "dominion of experience," according to McGann, when "we make our factive explorations through the literary archive" (133). But it is far from self-evident why the "dominion of experience" is, in the last instance, the privileged locus of *poetry*; nor is it clear that the "dominions" of "experience" and "consciousness" can be rigorously separated; nor, for that matter, is it at all clear that "experience" might not be but another name for ideology.

Nor is it the case that McGann's subsequent appeal to Keats clarifies matters: "When Keats distinguished the 'poet' from the 'dreamer' in 'The Fall of Hyperion,'" asserts McGann, "he made a comment about the archival, factive, dimension of art" (*Knowledge*, 156). But when we turn to the moment of the poem in which that distinction is posited, the "comment" made there is not the sort that propels us "towards a literature of knowledge" or the sort that returns us to the "archival, factive, dimension of art." The poem attends to this distinction between "dreamer" and "poet" at two crucial points: in the long exchange between the poet and the goddess Moneta (I.136–215), and in the poet's reflections in the opening stanza (I.1–18).[22] McGann attributes to Keats the Goddess's response to the poet's queries:

> The poet and the dreamer are distinct,
> Diverse, sheer opposites, antipodes.

> The one pours out a balm upon the world,
> The other vexes it.   (ll. 199–202)

The sentiment expressed in the lines is confirmed by the reference, here and elsewhere in Keats's poetry, to the "humanist" mission of the poet, as "physician to all men" (l. 190). But it will be recalled that the distinction takes place in the "rehearsing" of a dream, and, as the opening lines warn us, "fanatics have their dreams and who alive can say / 'Thou art no poet; may'st not tell thy dreams'?" (ll. 12–13).

The *question* is indeed an ideological one, and I will explore its ideological implications more fully in Chapter 4. Here it suffices to note that the lines ask for the difference between the "fanatic" and the "poet" without restoring any "factive dimension" by which we might answer with assurance—without, in other words, securing the distinction between a true and a "false consciousness." What we find in the lines are two modes of dreaming, and it remains impossible for the dreamer to know "whether the dream now purposed to rehearse" is ascribable to "poet" or "fanatic." If the "answer" proposed in subsequent lines is an "archival" one, it invokes an archive that does not lend itself to historicization:

> Whether the dream now purposed to rehearse
> Be poet's or fanatic's will be known
> When this warm scribe my hand is in the grave.
>   (ll. 16–18)

The promise of the knowledge will be made good, these rather haunting lines assert, only when "this warm scribe my hand is in the grave," when the literary archive turns, literally and materially, to the bones of the poet.[23]

But if a reading of Keats's poetry is unlikely to endorse McGann's version of the archival imperative, I believe that there is nonetheless something crucial to be gleaned here: the disjuncture between what McGann calls "consciousness" and what he calls "experience" is indeed another name for the ideological disjuncture (between spirit and matter, between "consciousness" and "life") that it is the object of the Romantic imagination to address. But the *problem* of ideology is not solved by the empiricist turn to "experience" or by the historicist turn to the archive. Such is the predicament not solely of McGann's work but of much that goes by the name of the New Historicism in Romantic studies.[24]

But it is often the case when a set of prevailing critical methods is displaced by another that the most telling questions derive from the assumptions that motivated the displacement in the first place: namely, why the displacement is deemed necessary, what critical problems it is expected to solve, what insufficiencies ("historical") and excesses ("theoretical") it addresses, how the displacement is to be achieved, and— from the new perspective of the ascendant methods—what has been displaced. New Historicist critics have been in fact unusually attentive to the disciplinary lineage of their method of study, and they do not hesitate to remark on the historical necessity of their enterprise: a turn or return to history after the textually oriented formalism they tend to associate with deconstruction. In this regard, Marjorie Levinson's work is especially notable for its provocative reflections on this historical juncture of criticism. The essays collected under the title *Rethinking Historicism* attempt, Levinson asserts in her Introduction, "to avoid the post-structuralist pitfall as well as the more obvious mimetic danger."[25] In what has become a familiar complaint, Levinson identifies the "post-structuralist pitfall" in Romantic studies as "Yale's present-mindedness," its formalism. What plays "Scylla" to this formalist "Charybdis" is the "extensive and binary contextualism" of traditional historicism, which could include certain variants of Marxism. Though that opposition certainly stands in need of closer critical scrutiny, I am interested here in remarking how the presentation of such an opposition becomes necessary as a founding gesture for the New Historicism.

It is my contention that in order to consider the ideology of the imagination, we must "rethink" the very juncture that motivated the New Historicism to begin with, the juncture that critics such as McGann and Levinson claim to have navigated successfully. It means returning to the Scylla of Marxism and the Charybdis of deconstruction, for I believe that these fateful monuments loom ahead of as much as behind any critical enterprise.[26] Carolyn Porter's suggestion that the New Historicism "would actually benefit from a closer scrutiny of Marxist critical theory" is thus very much to the point.[27] According to

Porter, the problem with the New Historicism "is not that it is Marxist [as Edward Pechter had complained], but on the contrary that it has
seemed at times remarkably inattentive to the theoretical and methodological issues that Marxist critical theory—especially in its more recent forms—has raised regarding the historicization of literature" ("Historical Yet?" 30). These are questions that I address in the following
chapters, regarding the ideologies of literary history (Wordsworth,
Keats) and the ideological role of the imagination in the discourses of
social history (Coleridge, Shelley, Eliot), and they are questions for
which the turn to the (assumed) transparencies of "experience" and
the "archive" are inadequate to the ideological opacity posed by the
problem of history.

   Within the Marxist tradition, one could turn to Theodor Adorno
—frequently and favorably referred to by McGann—to recognize the
inadequacy of the historicist gesture that, according to Adorno, results
in blindness to "genuine historical content": "[W]orks of art," writes
Adorno in *Aesthetic Theory*, "are . . . unconsciously the historiography
of their own epoch; history is not the least form of knowledge they
mediate. *That is precisely why they are incommensurable with historicism*,
which seeks to reduce them to a history external to them rather than to
pursue their genuine historical content."[28] The turn to the archive, to
the "factive," is thus from Adorno's perspective paradoxically the refusal to engage the historicity inscribed in the very constitution of the
work. In this vein, McGann's historicism and recourse to the "dominion of experience" are still harder to reconcile with his approving references to Louis Althusser. Perhaps no Marxist critic is more resolutely
incompatible with historicism than Althusser: "Marxism," he declares
with a daring polemical flourish in *Reading Capital*, "is, in a single
movement and by virtue of the unique epistemological rupture which
established it, an anti-humanism and an anti-historicism" (119). The
"first still uncertain strokes" of the "epistemological rupture [*coupure*]"
are, Althusser says elsewhere, "inscribed in *The German Ideology*." But as
an event, the "break" or "rupture" cannot be historicized in any strict
sense for the very reason that "we are still inscribed in the theoretical
space marked and opened by this break" (*Lenin and Philosophy*, 39, 40).

   The work of Althusser does not authorize a New Historicism, but it is indispensable to any materialist analysis of the problem of ideology. The currency of Althusser's name has diminished dramatically over the past decade, at least in part because of his refusal to retreat from a commitment to Marxism.[29] I contend that, however unseasonable, Althusser remains the starting point for any consideration of ideology, of ideology's relationship to literature, and of the institutional disposition of ideas—all of which are central concerns of my study. Two of the following chapters explicitly take up Althusser's work: In my opening discussion of Coleridge's project of a "national clerisy," I refer to Althusser's understanding of the "ideological state apparatus" and the ideological functioning of "literary culture." And in my reading of Shelley in Chapter 3, I turn to Althusser's account of the specular nature of ideology, to his thesis regarding ideology's *permanence*, and to his understanding of the Marxist "epistemological break."

Here it will suffice to introduce two prominent elements of Althusser's work that make it particularly suited to an exploration of the Romantic imagination's ideological functioning. The first is Althusser's insistence that ideology cannot be reduced to "false consciousness," and that this is due to the "active" functioning of the "imaginary": the mutual "overdetermination of the real by the imaginary and of the imaginary by the real."

The second aspect of Althusser's work that should be stressed here regards the *institutional* nature of philosophy and the mechanisms by which it poses and addresses social and political problems. As Althusser formulates it in his essay "Transformation of Philosophy," "philosophy produces . . . theoretical figures that serve as mediators for surmounting contradictions and as links for reconnecting the different elements of ideology" (*Philosophy*, 259). Such an observation is crucial to an understanding of the tasks assigned to the imagination in Romantic discourse; although—and here we are obliged to turn in a supplementary fashion to deconstruction—imagination's status as "figure" does not, as I have suggested above, necessarily accommodate the "theoretical" (much less "practical") mediation it appears to promise.[30] I should like to take from Althusser this sense of the ideological activity of philosophy—"a kind of theoretical laboratory in which the fundamentally political problem of ideological hegemony . . . is experimentally perfected in the abstract" (*Philosophy*, 259–60)—and extend it to the domain of Romantic literary discourse.

While the pertinence of Paul de Man's work for any study of Romantic poetry stands in little need of justification, my contention that de Man's work is critically turned to the workings of *ideology* is likely to be met with skepticism. But I would insist that de Man's work is consistently about the problem of ideology, and that it opens nothing less than a materialist analysis of the linguisticity of ideology.[31] The most important elements of that analysis, however, are not to be found when de Man refers to the term "ideology." De Man's *references* to ideology, most famously in "The Resistance to Theory," regard it as a first-order "confusion" "of linguistic with natural reality, of reference with phenomenalism" (*Resistance*, 11), a confusion that can be (theoretically if not practically) "demystified." But it is precisely where de Man abandons the term "ideology" that his texts open themselves to its workings and its inevitability. In de Man's attempts to confront the necessary entanglements of language with action or reflection or cognition or judgment, we find indispensable theoretical work on the ideological predicament.

One could find elements of this work in many of de Man's diverse analyses: the undoing of "image" by "emblem" in Yeats, the homologous disallowal of "symbol" by "allegory" in English Romanticism, the sense of irony as permanent parabasis, the aporetic intertwining of constative and performative aspects of language, the rhetorical defacements of theme. Instead, I want to allude briefly to the topos of "materiality" stressed in de Man's late essays. In his readings of Hegel, Kant, Kleist, Baudelaire, and others, de Man returned to what in the essay on Kant he calls "the prosaic materiality of the signifier." We often encounter the assertion of a "materiality" at the end of the late essays, as if materiality itself was to have the last word. This last word is repeated, moreover, in essay after essay in the late period, as if repetition is precisely the mode in which materiality must be confronted. De Man discloses the reiterated, perhaps inevitable disarticulation between structures of meaning (spiritual, historical, ethical, aesthetic, hermeneutic) and the materiality—the blank force and positing power—of language.

The redemptive gestures or recuperative structures inevitably fail to account for the "prosaic" materiality of language, which is both productive of and incommensurate with those structures and gestures.

This is where we find de Man's work contending with the questions of ideology and converging with materialist criticism: what we call ideology here can be characterized as (1) the disjunction between a linguistic materiality and the spiritual, redemptive forms of meaning and culture and (2) the process by which that disjunction is produced and reproduced. To give the process in shorthand narrative form, a linguistic positing (subjectless, meaningless, contingent, accidental) is followed and effaced in a recuperation (by intention, by meaning, by aesthetics, by ethics) that involves the same linguistic elements of the founding gesture, and that fails nevertheless: the repetition of the pattern is constitutive of both signification and ideology.[32] Rodolphe Gasché has discussed this aspect of de Man's "formal materialism": "Considering the sheer arbitrariness and intrinsic senselessness of the material and signifying agencies of language, the randomness of their individual occurrences, . . . and the opacity of their literal materiality, all experiencable meaning appears *superimposed* on them."[33] The aesthetic "meaning" that appears "superimposed" is, nevertheless, bound to occur, and this inevitable and inadequate "meaningful" occurrence takes place by forgetting the "originary" materiality.[34]

We thus find ourselves once again unexpectedly close to *The German Ideology*, where Marx stresses that the "burden" imposed by matter on spirit extends to language. The materialism of de Man's practice of rhetorical analysis converges here with the demonstration opened by Marxist theorizing of ideology: the determination of the "idea" by the "non-idea," by the blank, material substratum that resists accommodation to the spirit, to consciousness. It is, moreover, an act of "violence" that is at work not only in the primary disfiguration of language but in the aesthetic gesture of recuperation itself: "Aesthetic education by no means fails," asserts de Man in "Aesthetic Formalization in Kleist"; "it succeeds all too well, to the point of hiding the violence that it makes possible" (*Rhetoric*, 289). If the aesthetic is, in other words, an inadequate response, a cover-up of the brute, nonhuman aspects of lin-

guistic power, it is nonetheless a violent act that has political consequences, for as de Man argues in "Kant and Schiller," the aesthetic *state*
must be understood politically.[35]

My readings of the Romantic imagination find their point of departure in the relationship between de Man's "formal materialism" and
the historical materialism of a critical Marxist tradition, a relationship
invited by de Man's own invitation in "The Resistance to Theory" to
read *The German Ideology*. To determine what can be made of that relationship for an exploration of the imagination's ideological importance to English Romanticism—its importance to the relationship between aesthetics, politics, education, and the state—is the burden of
the chapters that follow.

To establish the vocabulary for such an exploration, we should return once again to Althusser, to his stress on the "materiality" of ideology, the *force* of institutions ("Ideological State Apparatuses") such as
that of education. "Ideology always exists in an apparatus, and its practice, or practices," asserts Althusser, and "this existence is material"
(*Lenin and Philosophy*, 166). It is important to keep the Althusserian
thesis in mind, for throughout the Romantic tradition, the imagination refers to the ideological inscription of things in thought, to the
ideological moment constitutive of the subject's relationship to society, and to the construction of an ideological project that I call the instituting of imagination.[36] In the texts of Romanticism, the imagination
and its translation into social "sympathy" serve as governing or articulating ideas that institute and organize "Romantic" cultural practices
as diverse as the formation of a "national clerisy" (Coleridge) and the
reading of a novel (George Eliot). The "institutional" moment of the
imagination should not be regarded as secondary to its more explicitly
theoretical presentations. For what we have called the ideological instance of the imagination within Romantic discourse is, among other
things, the irreducible inscription of an "institutional" and material
moment in the formation of ideas.

The institutional moment cannot be translated into a stable political position inherent in the imagination; the ideological orientation
of the concept of imagination cannot be judged in advance of a reading
of its textual inscription. The imagination in Romantic discourse is as

likely to be placed into the service of conservative, even "counterrevolutionary" cultural and political agendas as it is to be invoked in the critical or even revolutionary project of a Shelley. Of course, the politics of nineteenth-century British cultural discourses are notoriously contradictory and unstable, a "nebulous compound," as Terry Eagleton describes it, of "Burkean conservatism and German idealism."[37] Romanticism, insofar as it announces the withdrawal of God and the internalization of spirit in the principle of subjectivity, is another name for the critical and crisis-ridden passage, the "precarious transition from the institutions of religious and political coercion to the apparatuses of moral-psychological consent."[38] Eagleton is describing, here with reference to George Eliot's use of "sympathy," the sociopolitical process Antonio Gramsci called "hegemony."[39]

The ideological function of the imagination extends to the cultural formation of narratives of the nation organized around the themes and figures of "community." On this topic my readings converge with recent work on nationalism, with an understanding of the nation as, to recall Benedict Anderson's helpful term, "imagined communities."[40] From Coleridge and Wordsworth to George Eliot, a principal assignment of the imagination (or "sympathy" in Eliot's translation) is to secure (or restore) access for the subject to an "organic" form of social relations that can be called an English "community." The imagination thus becomes formative for the (ideological) construction of nationalist narratives that might preserve English cultural representation from what Wordsworth, with reference to the French Revolution, calls "the o'erpressure of the times." The imagination holds out the promise of a meaningful articulation of poetic, philosophical, and political discourses at the moment when their reconciliation carries a sense of *national* urgency, implicating what Coleridge calls the "constitution of church and state." If the exiles of the second generation tell different stories, they are stories that explore in a critical fashion the relationships between the imagination and society, stories that become "materialist" only once the imagination has been taken to its breaking point.

I am interested in examining the constitutive ideological roles played by the imagination in the development of an "aesthetic education" and in national self-representation. To this end the texts I read

are both *moments* of and *monuments* to the imagination: Coleridge,
Wordsworth, Keats, Eliot, and even Shelley have become principal texts
of an Anglo-American and Commonwealth cultural education, canonical markers and agents of the ideologically sanctioned tradition of English literature.[41] To invite once more a return to these texts, in spite of
the most stringent precautions, is to reinvest in the cultural authority of
that tradition. But the contemporary crisis over the status of the canon
in literary or cultural studies, a crisis that often revolves around the
questions of exclusion or inclusion, is symptomatic of a deeper ideological crisis regarding the formation, transmission, and function of cultural value in Western societies during the era of late capitalism.[42] Culture is never a simple matter of preservation, of course, and even in
their most conservative moments, the texts of Coleridge and Wordsworth and Eliot demonstrate an awareness of the historical constitution of cultural value. The imagination is understood by Coleridge,
for instance, to institute a grounding principle of national culture by
which the very "constitution" of church and state may be preserved.
Each of the texts I have chosen to read conducts its own speculations on
canon formation and, more broadly, on the constitution of cultural and
social value. In other words, I am interested in these texts not simply
because they are sanctioned products of the elaborate ideological machinery of cultural and literary value—"the aesthetic ideology"—but
because for each of these texts the institution of cultural value becomes
a crucial formal and thematic issue around the status of the figure of
the imagination. In other words, the *teachings* of the imagination in the
texts I have chosen give ideological lessons, in part about the reading
and teaching of literature and its cultural and political value.

　　To undertake such an exploration of the cultural, institutional, national—that is to say, ideological—stakes for the Romantic imagination requires modes of reading sensitive to the co-implication, or better still, to the "constellations" of imagination and ideology. Theodor
Adorno found in Benjamin's notion of the constellation a morphology that allows us to discern signs of the object in thoughts and concepts, a morphology that can no longer be claimed by the opposition
between positivism and idealism. "The subjectively created content,"
says Adorno, "the 'constellation' becomes readable as sign of an objec-

tivity: of the spiritual substance."[43] Through the constellation we de-cipher the inscriptions of materiality in the forms of thought—the signs, in other words, of ideology. When imagination and ideology form a constellation, we find not *the* ideology, the ideological truth of the imagination; rather, without primary and secondary positions, each term takes shape through its implication with the other. As in a stellar constellation, the connections between these moving points of illumi-nation give them a shape, a figure that makes them readable. As with stellar constellations, we read in these connections between ideology and the imagination a different figure at different moments, a figure that may in certain seasons and under certain conditions vanish from sight. "By the force of imagination," Coleridge says in his 1818 lec-tures on Shakespeare, "we see in the constellations, brought close to the eye, a multitude of worlds." To read for these constellations also risks confronting, as Coleridge also recognizes in his remarkable late poem "Coeli Enarrant," not a "multitude of worlds" but their inverse, "one large black letter": to embark on such a reading risks our being stranded without "reading aright." We have often construed from the apparently blank and meaningless motions of these stellar constellations meaningful and even mythological narratives that, no less than Adam's dream, are understood to explain truthfully the course of worldly events. And since we have long invested in heavenly constellations—those random arrangements of stars in the night—stories of our pasts and our futures, might we not assume the task of what Keats called "keen-eyed astrologers" and when gazing at this Romantic constellation of imagination and ideology, imagine something other than what we see, something other than a map of our thoughts, the hieroglyphs, per-haps, of a materialism?

CHAPTER I

COLERIDGE

The Institution of Imagination

"Revolution in Philosophy"

About midway through Chapter Nine of the *Biographia Literaria*, Coleridge, acknowledging his intellectual debts, pays Kant the following tribute: "The writings of the illustrious sage of Königsberg, the founder of the Critical Philosophy, more than any other work, at once invigorated and disciplined my understanding. The originality, the depth, and the compression of the thoughts . . . took possession of me as with a giant's hand."[1] The "writings of the illustrious sage of Königsberg" provoked nothing less than a genuine "revolution in philosophy," one that, Coleridge asserts, has been "completed" by the work of Kant's followers. "To Schelling" in particular "we owe the completion, and most important victories of this revolution in philosophy" (1: 163). Coleridge follows this tribute with an accounting of his "obligations" to the "system" of "Critical Philosophy" and a declaration of his enlistment in this revolutionary campaign: "To me it will be happiness and honor enough, should I succeed in rendering the system itself intelligible to my countrymen, and in the application of it to the most awful subjects for the most important purposes" (1: 163–64). Coleridge thus dedicates himself to the importation of this "revolution in philosophy" to England, to the English translation and "application" of "Critical Philosophy." Guided, or rather "possessed," by the "giant's hand" (i.e., Kant), Coleridge assumes the role of an English Schiller.[2] Though he does not spell out the terms of the "most awful subjects" and "most important purposes" to which the "system" will be applied, it is evident—here and elsewhere—that Coleridge believes that nothing less than the meaning and fate of the country is at stake.

This chapter is about the fundamental role Coleridge assigns to the imagination in a project that is jointly political and philosophical. I argue here that we should read Coleridge's speculations on the imagination in the *Biographia Literaria* and elsewhere as an attempt to "institute" the imagination, and by way of this "institution" to secure the subject of the English nation. The project, already under way in the autobiographical writings and, significantly, in the poetry, reaches its culmination in the important late essay *On the Constitution of Church and State*. This is not to say that Coleridge approached the imagination and its Kantian provenance as a direct instrument of nationality or tool of the nation-state. Rather, I will argue that according to Coleridge a philosophical grounding is necessary to ensure the basis of society and only the concept of the imagination can achieve such a ground. In the process, the imagination can be made to resolve what Coleridge recognizes to be the divisive historical antagonism at the heart of English society.

Thus, by the "institution" of the imagination, I mean in the first instance the role the imagination plays in Coleridge's thinking about social and political as well as philosophical institutions. But reading Coleridge's speculations on the imagination should demonstrate something more: the material (and institutional) provenance of such ideas and their political (and institutional) effectivity. To understand Coleridge's writings as the "institution of the imagination" is to understand the imagination both as an instituting idea and as the material institution, the "apparatus," through which the imagination produces and reproduces its effects. As I see them, these are the methodological implications of such a reading: that a philosophical and poetic concept such as the imagination is for Romantic discourse intimately bound up with political and social institutions and, moreover, that the concept serves as a materially instituting idea. This is something other than a traditional idealism, for it makes no claim for the autonomy of the idea or for the idea as a final determinant. I would claim the method as "materialist" in that it argues for the inextricability of social and political matter within the *textual* production of ideas.[3] The stress on the "textual" should not be misconstrued: it does not mean a reduction of worldly activity to the formal constraints of the book but rather an attention to the material conditions and operations of language in philosophical and political thought. My point is that to read for the imagination in Coleridge, to read for the imagination *in a materialist way*, requires something other than situating these theoretical and poetic texts within their institutional or archival context; it means exploring the instituting or positing force at work in an idea such as the imagination.

Instituting is, moreover, a feature of language; by way of language's power to posit or to institute (a power to be distinguished from its capacity to refer), ideas and beliefs come into existence that have no prior empirical status. We will only begin to approach the position Coleridge achieves once we understand the linguistic operations at work in the acts of instituting the imagination.[4] For this reason, the poetry is crucial to our understanding of the ideological activity of the imagination in Coleridge, not merely as a practical example of his theoretical speculations but also—in the case of the late poem "Constancy to an Ideal Object"—as a "theoretical" medium of its own, a medium that sheds light on the workings of ideology, including that of Coleridge's own nationalism. To explore the linguistic intertwinings of imagination and ideology requires close attention to the imagination's textual production and to its role not simply as concept but as rhetoric, in the sense of persuasion and of figure. In the case of Coleridge, the fate of the figure is indeed tied to the fate of a nation and is thus understood by this Romantic poet and critic to have very real political consequences. This is not, therefore, so much a "revisionist" interpretation as it is an attempt to restore some of the institutional significance already at work in these texts.

We find the mutual implication of rhetoric and political history, for instance, in Coleridge's references to Kant, where the historical events known as the "French Revolution" permit, or require, the former "Jacobin" to characterize his project according to a *rhetoric* of revolution. That Coleridge should represent his undertaking with the rhetoric of revolution should come as little surprise, for the *Biographia Literaria* is written in the shadow of Napoleon's defeat. We cannot, in other words, read what Terry Eagleton has called Kant's "Copernican Revolution" outside the historical drama of that other revolution.[5] For Coleridge as for Schiller the "eyes of the philosopher are fixed as expectantly as those of the worldling upon the political arena where at present, so it is believed, the high destiny of mankind is being decided."[6] No European philosophical discussion or literary self-representation can expect to extricate itself from this arena, and even aesthetic theory unavoidably if implicitly contributes to the commentary on the revolutionary scene.

The inflection of Coleridge's revolutionary commentary and commitment is, of course, politically "counterrevolutionary": only the importation and institution of a German Revolution can prevent the seditious importation of a more specifically French Revolution.[7] Nothing is "apolitical," therefore, about the turn to Kant; Coleridge's Kantian declaration speaks to his awareness of the entanglements of philosophy and politics, and to his efforts to appropriate a revolutionary rhetoric. The passage demonstrates that for Coleridge, philosophical speculation on subjectivity becomes the "laboratory," to use an Althusserian formulation, for an inquiry into politics.

The enduring political significance, the "peculiarity," as John Stuart Mill called it, "of the Germano-Coleridgean school" resides in the nature of Coleridge's turn from France to Germany.[8] The meaning of this turn is most productively approached as an articulation of politics and philosophy: far from securing the autonomy of the aesthetic, the imagination in Coleridge represents an attempt to lend political theory and practice the rigors and security of a formal philosophical system. The terror of the French Revolution, according to Coleridge, was the monstrous issue of a philosophy organized not by "first principles" but by "democratic fanaticism," the nightmarish ideological effect of an unsound philosophy (*Biographia*, 1: 199). *Politics must henceforth be instituted through the imagination.* Only the cultivation and institution of philosophical principles—precisely those that Coleridge finds in Kant and Schelling and that cohere in the concept of the imagination—can effectively govern both nation and individual. The imagination, ostensibly a principle of self or faculty of mind, thus assumes in Coleridge's work a public, institutional role in the securing of the nation. This is, in part, the imperative that Coleridge translates (or appropriates) from Schelling: "[P]hilosophy in its first principles must have a practical or moral, as well as a speculative side." But the passage of the imagination from private faculty and philosophical concept to a political and hence public principle is further complicated by the *Biographia Literaria*, for it turns out that autobiography is not merely the setting or the record but the *agent* of that political and philosophical articulation. To gain access to the social and philosophical meaning of the nation, in other words, one must read a very peculiar autobiographical narrative. Coleridge's ambitious analogy, of a piece with his emphasis on the trope of synecdoche, directs his understanding of the conjunction of politics, philosophy, and the imagination: "it is with nations as with individuals." Thus the quite considerable pressure on the vehicle of this articulation, the story of a "literary life."

"Biographia Imaginatio"

For Coleridge, the institution of the imagination is an autobiographical *activity*: the theoretical speculation on the faculty of the imagination in the *Biographia Literaria* is important not only as the exposition of a theme but further as performance, as an instance of self-production and self-representation. The story Coleridge writes of himself is intimately bound to the narrativity of the imagination. And, conversely, Coleridge's theory of the imagination, drawn though it is from "Critical Philosophy," is imbricated with his narrative of self-formation. Coleridge's autobiography is more than the record of his efforts to define the imagination, for the theorizing of the imagination as it is enfolded in the life story plays a crucial narrative role in the making of the "literary life and opinions" of this Romantic poet and critic. The *Biographia* presents the imagination as both a formal and a thematic concern of subject-making, and this dual function earns it a doubly ideological promise. In the theoretical sphere, the imagination must link politics with philosophy and in the process establish the coherence of the autobiographical and theorizing subject. We should read the ambitions of the "literary life" in this light: the *Biographia Literaria* proposes a theory of the imagination that it would institute through the act of autobiographical narration. But the ambitions of the project are more expansive still: for the theory of the imagination should not only establish the principles of poetic composition and evaluation (such as we find in the second volume of the *Biographia*), but should secure those "first principles" of philosophy and politics that could serve as the new foundation for English subject-making. "Without the philosophical organ" supplied by the imagination, asserts Coleridge, "philosophy is the mere play of words and notions" (*Biographia*, 1: 251). Small wonder that the theory of the imagination should figure so prominently in the telling of a "literary life."

Everything in the first volume of the *Biographia* comports itself toward the revelation of the imagination: the early "chapters" of the life—the formative education, the engagement with "Associationist" philosophy, the early enthusiasm for democratic principles, the decisive introduction to German transcendental philosophy—are interpreted in light of the imagination's appearance as a meaningful story of growth and development. We are invited to read the entire second volume of the autobiography as the product of the theory of the imagination: we could scarcely imagine, for instance, the extensive evaluations of Wordsworth's poetry and poetics without the governing critical principle of the imagination.[9]

The break between the two volumes of the *Biographia*, announced by the disclosure of the imagination, repeats at the level of publication the formal gap inherent in autobiographical narration between the narrating subject and the narrated subject, between the "I" of the present who tells the story and the "I" of the past who belongs to the story as a character. Structuralist narrative theory has demonstrated that the distinction featured in autobiographical discourse between the narrated and narrating subjects is present in any text. The subject who orders and tells the story belongs to the *discours* (or discourse) of the text, while the subject about whom the story is being told, the "life" that is being narrated, belongs to its *récit* (or story).[10] Though this division may be operative in the discursive structure of any narrative, the epistemological and ideological problems it generates are perhaps more difficult to conceal or to control when, as in autobiographical narrative, the story is about the "self" who authors it. In his reading of Wordsworth's *Essays upon Epitaphs*, Paul de Man describes, by way of Gérard Genette, the split between the two subjects of autobiography and pushes at the more radical implications of structural narratology:

> We assume that life *produces* the autobiography as an act produces its consequences, but can we not suggest, with equal justice, that the autobiographical project may itself produce and determine the life and that whatever the writer *does* is in fact governed by the technical demands of self-portraiture and thus determined, in all its aspects, by the resources of his medium? And since the mimesis here assumed to be operative is one mode of figuration among others, does the referent determine the figure, or is it the other way round: is the illusion of reference not a correlation of the structure of the figure, that is to say no longer clearly and simply a referent at all but something more akin to a fiction which then, however, in its own turn, acquires a degree of referential productivity? (*Rhetoric*, 69)

The doubled subjects of autobiography are caught up in this mirroring, the familiar *mise-en-abyme* structure, an "illusion of reference" that, as de Man goes on to assert, refuses epistemological certainty, including knowledge of self. The point is not merely that the relation between life and portrait is undecidable but that undecidability is "productive" and, moreover, productive of referential effects. It must be stressed that for de Man this abyssal structure *discloses* rather than disrupts the ideological condition of subjectivity. It is a disclosure made in the reading of any autobiographical text, and as we shall see, it is a disclosure that Coleridge acknowledges as his own theoretical point of departure. To assert, as de Man does here, that the figure cannot be derived from the referent is to suspend epistemological foundation. But the assertion is not to be taken as a nihilistic gesture on the part of the critic; it reveals rather that "something more akin to a fiction" has "in its turn" acquired "a degree of referential productivity" that, while producing the referent as its effect, *persuades* us of a referential primacy. Thus, in the terms of our argument, the "mode of figuration" called autobiography *institutes* the referent retroactively as its source. Our subsequent and pervasive confusion of figure and referent is, as de Man would describe it in *The Resistance to Theory*, "what we call ideology."

Coleridge's literary autobiography offers an exemplary lesson on the complicity between "figure" and "referent" and its ideological consequences, for few life stories are more indebted to what de Man calls "the resources of the medium" or have been more plagued by the notorious "charge of verifying the authenticity of the signature and the consistency of the signer's behavior" (*Rhetoric*, 71).[11] At the same time, Coleridge speculates in the *Biographia* on the very duplicity that would deprive the text of its epistemological moorings, and what he sees in the mirroring of his self-reflection is not the threat of the subject's undoing but the very elements of subject-making.

The formal division is duplicated in spirit if not to the letter by the two volumes of the *Biographia*: the first volume is devoted primarily to the development of a critical consciousness in the discovery of philosophical principles, while the second volume is, with notable exceptions, devoted to the present expressions of literary "opinions" and models of literary evaluation made possible by his philosophical education.[12] The ten Theses of Chapter Twelve, drawn extensively from Schelling, are presented as the theoretical conditions for the "deduction of the imagination" that concludes the first volume and establish the basis for the "principles of production and of genial criticism in the fine arts" featured in the second volume (*Biographia*, 1: 264). Thus, for the text to become an autobiography, it needs the imagination. The revelation of the imagination demands that Coleridge reinterpret his former philosophical, political, and literary positions, and moreover, from the perspective of the story's narration, the imagination bestows upon the earlier chapters their narrative meaning and coherence. By this reflection, the story Coleridge tells of his "literary life and opinions" is less the source for than the consequence of the imagination. Only by virtue of the imagination does Coleridge's story qualify as a "literary life": the imagination promises the coherence between the two subjects of narration (he who writes, he who gets written). Not only is the imagination the focal point of the *récit*, but it also organizes the *discours* and guarantees their narrative coherence.[13] The imagination is what would allow Coleridge to make his life story, so full of the words and thoughts of others, his own. Within the paradigm of auto-biography, the revelation of the imagination functions as Coleridge's "conversion" experience: its location in the narrative suggests this trope, as does the theological language Coleridge employs to define the "primary imagination." From the autobiographical perspective, the imagination is as much an *event* as a theme, perhaps the event that, like the moment of conversion, becomes *more* than an event, the "necessary point of view" (Weintraub) that confers on all other events their meaning and that makes this a genuinely *spiritual* autobiography.

But when it finally arrives in the last pages of Chapter Thirteen, the much anticipated and celebrated definition of the imagination does little to fulfill the promises of reconciliation and guarantees of coherence it had prompted. What one finds in the definition is the disclosure of a new and singular division within the faculty itself:

> The IMAGINATION then I consider either as primary, or secondary. The primary IMAGINATION I hold to be the living Power and prime Agent of all human Perception, and as a repetition in the finite mind of the eternal act of creation in the infinite I AM. The secondary I consider as an echo of the former, co-existing with conscious will, yet still as identical with the primary in the *kind* of its agency, and differing only in *degree*, and in the *mode* of its operation. It dissolves, diffuses, dissipates, in order to re-create; or where this process is rendered impossible, yet still, at all events, it struggles to idealize and to unify. It is essentially *vital*, even as all objects (*as* objects) are essentially fixed and dead. (*Biographia*, 1: 304)

We are compelled to return to this passage in spite of the amount of commentary it has accumulated, but not solely because of the canonical position it has achieved as a definitive statement of the English Romantic imagination—though its ideological role in Anglo-American literary history certainly warrants examination. More importantly, we should *read* the passage because it is more than an expression of a particular aesthetic ideology: within the vocabulary of Romanticism, it is an investigation of the structure of ideology itself. This means that we must understand how the suddenly doubled imagination both *fails* to fulfill its narrative expectations and simultaneously *succeeds* in proposing a model of subjectivity to be instituted on the basis of a "fundamental" division.

We might begin exploring this double logic by considering how the passage opens itself to two divergent critical traditions. We could trace a long tradition of interpretation—one diverse enough to include I. A. Richards, M. H. Abrams, and Jerome McGann—that has regarded the passage as the presentation of Coleridge's ideas about the faculty of the imagination. These critics belong to this tradition because, whether in veneration or denunciation, they have taken the passage as an institution. Another tradition—one associated with post-structuralist theories of reading but extending to those who have by a variety of methods attended to the performance of the passage—has engaged the implication of the divisive elements in the imagination's presentation: it has, in other words, treated the passage as a narrative act of instituting. I identify this opposition in the critical tradition not in order to declare an allegiance but to indicate how both traditions are provoked, or instituted, by the passage itself. To read the passage is to encounter a division in the very faculty that is being called upon to unify, a division moreover for which there is no preparation or explanation in Coleridge's work. At the same time, the passage that calls for this reading has itself acquired the status of an institution of the imagination, and such institutionality is neither secondary nor mistaken; it is, in fact, a primary project of this Romantic critic. In that double gesture and in the doubling of the imagination resides the condition of ideology.

What Coleridge calls the "primary IMAGINATION"—the "living Power and prime Agent of all human Perception"—is posited as the nonsensual, nonempirical, nonsubjective force that is *constitutive* of seeing.[14] The "primary IMAGINATION" exceeds the purview of the "conscious will" and as the "repetition in the finite mind" of the "infinite I AM" is the condition of worldly being. Arden Reed's account of the workings of the primary imagination is particularly relevant: "The primary imagination is a continuous, and eventually an almost unconscious part of everyday experience."[15] Paraphrasing Christian von Wolff, Coleridge describes the ubiquity of this aspect of the imagination in his 1818 *Lectures on European Literature*: "in omnem actum perceptionis influit imaginatio" ("the imagination is involved in every act of perception").[16] This deep "involvement" makes it clear that for Coleridge the primary imagination is not an exclusively *poetic* imagination. Indeed, Coleridge's accounts of the poetic imagination as such—here and throughout his work—are much closer to what he identifies in the *Biographia Literaria* as the secondary imagination: an "echo of the former [i.e., primary imagination]" "co-existing with conscious will."

One could identify Coleridge's undertaking—his definitions and distinctions of the imagination—as "ideological" in the most restricted sense, as the idealist and mystified investment in a divine power of mind, the spiriting away of worldly being by the "eternal act of creation in the infinite I AM." But more is gained, I believe, for an understanding of the ideology of imagination when we read Coleridge's work as an effort to address what he already *recognizes* to be an ideological condition of subjectivity. Coleridge's text takes on the effort of exploring the doubleness of the imagination through which the subject is constituted and situated. Ideology resides in and through this double structure: what, following Arden Reed, we call the "unconscious" and what Coleridge calls the "divine" (because divinely based) activity of perception forms the primary imagination, that which makes possible its conscious "repetition" or "echo" in the subject.

The critical distinctions that produce the theory of the imagination extend beyond the account of the imagination proper. The definitions of the dual properties of the imagination are themselves fashioned on the basis of a strict distinction from "fancy": "The Fancy is indeed no other than a mode of Memory . . . blended with, and modified by that empirical phenomenon of the will which we express by the word CHOICE. . . . It must receive all its materials ready made from the law of association" (*Biographia*, 1: 305). Coleridge's distinction between "fancy" and "imagination" can be interpreted as the attempt within his theorizing of the imagination to account for what Marxist theories of ideology would, with different reference and to different ends, call "false consciousness": "fancy"—that which belongs to mere "memory," that which has no creative powers of its own and which "must receive all its materials ready made from the law of association"—is relegated in Romantic discourse to the status of *false* consciousness.

What Coleridge calls the "secondary" imagination derives its significance not only from its relationship to the "primary imagination" but also from its critical relationship to "fancy." The "secondary imag-

ination" is itself given a double movement: a conscious critical "desyn-
onymizing" that "dissolves, diffuses, dissipates, in order to re-create."
The "secondary" imagination possesses, moreover, the power to demystify: as Coleridge describes it in reference to Wordsworth's contri-
butions to *Lyrical Ballads*, this imagination has the capacity to awaken
"the mind's attention from the lethargy of custom" and to remove from
perception "the film of familiarity" (*Biographia*, 2: 7), such as that which
characterizes the "associative" faculty of fancy. It will take a Shelley to
invest the critical function of the imagination with a radical political
and poetic orientation, one not tethered to divinity. With Coleridge,
the critical aspect of the imagination remains "secondary," its "vital-
ity" dependent on its connections with divinity, "the eternal act of creation."

This is why the *gesture* of distinguishing between imagination and
fancy is of such significance for Coleridge. We have long recognized
that the values of the distinction between "fancy" and "imagination"
are often if inconsistently acknowledged in eighteenth-century poetic
and aesthetic texts.[17] But Coleridge declares that to read Wordsworth is
to experience the necessity of a rigorous separation between the two
concepts. He recounts that in his "repeated meditations" on the "excel-
lence" of Wordsworth's "writings" and "mind," he "first suspect[ed]"
and was soon charged with the conviction "that fancy and imagination were two distinct and widely different faculties, instead of being,
according to the general belief, either two names with one meaning, or
at furthest, the lower and higher degree of one and the same power"
(*Biographia*, 1: 82). Coleridge attributes the historical confusion of these
two faculties in part to "accidents of translation" that must now be critically disentangled or "desynonymized" (1: 83, 82). Once it has been
"fully ascertained" that "this division" is "grounded in nature," the
"theory of the fine arts, and of poetry in particular" will "derive some
additional and important light" (1: 86, 85). Aesthetic theory will be illuminated by the distinction, by the critical operation of "desynony-
mizing" that, Coleridge hints, is already under way in Germany (1:
85–86). To authorize these distinctions and definitions, Coleridge links
the opposition between fancy and imagination to the corresponding
differences, established throughout the early chapters and duplicated

by the itinerary of his autobiography, between the mechanistic "associative" philosophy of Locke and Hartley and the "transcendental" philosophy of Kant. Thus, unlike fancy, with its limited, associative capabilities, the imagination is ascribed "a synthetic and magical power" that "blends and (as it were) *fuses*" (2: 16). The "magical" power of the imagination is capable of the "reconciliation of opposite or discordant qualities" (2: 16). Coleridge states in his 1808 *Lectures on the Principles of Poetry* that the imagination possesses the "power" of "fusion," by which it can "*force many into one*" (*Lectures* 1: 81). Invested with such power, the imagination can fulfill what Coleridge, following Leibniz, describes as the "criterion of a true philosophy." Such a philosophy "would at once explain and collect the fragments of truth scattered through systems apparently the most incongruous. The truth, says he [Leibniz], is diffused more widely than is commonly believed; but it is often painted, yet oftener masked, and is sometimes mutilated and sometimes alas! in close alliance with mischievous errors" (*Biographia*, 1: 244–46).

The task of the philosopher, according to Coleridge, is to recognize the "truth" in its "painted" or "masked" or "mutilated" guises in order to disclose what, translating Schelling, he calls a "truth self-grounded, unconditional and known by its own light" (1: 268). But in the case of the imagination, these stringent theoretical requirements are difficult to meet: the "truth" of the imagination cannot be known "by its own light," according to the *Biographia*, because the powers of "synthesis," "fusing," and "reconciliation" belong to a different order from the primary imagination, defined by Coleridge as "the repetition in the finite mind of the eternal act of creation of the infinite I AM." As an "esemplastic" power, the *secondary* imagination is assigned an ideological project of another sort, the task of reconciling a *prior* contradiction. Such an activity is not "identical in kind" with that of an imagination existing in the form of a "repetition": the primary imagination has the effect of introducing the gap between the "finite mind" and the "infinite I AM," between the human and the divine, a gap only emphasized by the figure of "repetition."

The distinction between the primary and the secondary imagination, as Thomas McFarland explains it, appears without preparation in Chapter Thirteen and is never again pursued.[18] But the textual performance of the argument, the doubling of properties at such a crucial point in the presentation of the theory, is nonetheless significant, in part because it runs counter to the declared intentions of Coleridge's philosophical undertaking: a "science of ultimate truths" determined to overcome "arbitrary dictation" and to establish "fixed canons of criticism." Coleridge's narrative of the imagination, in other words, introduces the very division that the faculty is expected to resolve.[19] If the secondary imagination—which "dissolves, diffuses, dissipates, in order to re-create"—is, as McFarland asserts, the version of the poetic imagination that Coleridge returns to throughout his criticism, the status of the primary imagination remains uncertain and unacknowledged. It remains uncertain, for instance, whether this divided ground of the imagination can manage either to fulfill the "criterion of a true philosophy" or to secure the coherence of a scattered autobiography.

We might address these problems by proposing to read once again the narrative of Chapter Thirteen, by attending to the story of the imagination's appearance. It is, to be sure, a curious narrative, punctuated by postponements, withdrawals, apologies, disavowals, and, most notoriously, an interruption: a letter sent by a "friend" who turns out to be "Coleridge."[20] The "friend," who has read the entire manuscript on the imagination, urges Coleridge to "withdraw the chapter from the present work, and to reserve it for your announced treatise ['announced' but never written] on the Logos or communicative intellect in Man and Deity" (*Biographia*, 1: 302). The letter continues: "Imperfectly as I understand the present Chapter, I see clearly that you have done too much, and yet not enough. You have been obliged to omit so many links from the necessity of compression, that what remains looks . . . like the fragments of the winding steps of an old ruined tower" (1: 302–3). A "still stronger argument," the "friend" goes on to say, is that the chapter, which is bound to exceed "a hundred pages," will "greatly increase the expense of the work." Yet another objection is added to the problems of composition and high cost: the chapter—itself but a part of the *Biographia*, which is itself designed only as an introduction "to a volume of miscellaneous poems"—will be received as an "imposition" by readers who are "neither prepared or perhaps calculated for the study of so abstruse a subject so abstrusely treated" (1: 303). Coleridge is only too willing to subject himself to the judgments of the "friend," to heed his most "judicious" advice—it "produced a complete conviction in my mind"—and to content himself with "stating the main result of the chapter" (1: 303). The "real" "Chapter on the Imagination" is "reserved" for a "future publication," a publication that, of course, never appeared.

The passage functions as a kind of litmus test for the pattern of interpretation I have outlined above: for those who make a critical investment in the theoretical *statement* of the imagination, the story is likely to be regarded as a nuisance, if it is heeded at all. It is possible to ignore this infamous narrative of promises, withdrawals, and postponements, or to view the interlude as a typical Coleridgean eccentricity that does not however interfere with the "main result."[21] Though the letter may block the chapter, it does not similarly prevent the presentation of a formal definition of the imagination. But to pursue the meaning of the imagination in this way, to read for the "main result," is to repress the repeated instructions and requests that insist on the obstacle of the letter.[22] Near the beginning of Chapter Twelve, for instance, Coleridge, admitting to an "anxiety of authorship," presents his "unknown reader" with the following request:

> that he will either pass over the following chapter altogether or read the whole connectedly. The fairest part of the most beautiful body will appear deformed and monstrous if dissevered from its place in the organic Whole. Nay, on delicate subjects, where a seemingly trifling difference of more or less may constitute a difference of *kind*, even a faithful display of the main and supporting ideas, if yet they are separated from the forms by which they are at once cloathed and modified, may perchance present a skeleton indeed: but a skeleton to alarm and deter. (*Biographia*, 1: 233–34)

If we read only for the "main and supporting ideas," the "body" of the text will appear disfigured, the lurid image of a "skeleton" that will only "alarm and deter." "A lurid thought," writes Coleridge in the late poem "Limbo," is "growthless dull Privation" (l. 35), the mutilation of the organicism to which the critic as well as the poet must aspire.[23]

Coleridge delivers the request "to read the whole connectedly" with urgency and at the expense of "various" other requests. The request to read the chapter according to the model of a living human body is of a piece with the rhetoric of organicism that remains a principal ideological legacy of the *Biographia*. Given its prominence in this "chapter of requests and premonitions concerning the perusal of omission of the chapter that follows," we have no indication that we are not to take the request seriously. The decision made in "the chapter that follows" to withdraw that chapter and to leave in its place only the "main result" cannot thus be made to square with the demands of Coleridge's organicism. If followed to the letter, Coleridge's instructions to "read the whole connectedly" make a strict interpretation of Chapter Thirteen, or what is left of it, impossible. In view of the elaborate preparation of Chapter Twelve, the performance of Chapter Thirteen—its interruptions, withdrawals, and postponements—seems to be deployed to bar our access to the theory of the imagination. Rather than dismiss the process or the outcome, we should regard the moment as one of genuine crisis, the crisis of theory and crisis *as* theory. The appearance of a fragment when a fragment cannot be allowed should be read as the text's symptomatic admission of such a crisis.

What we *are* granted admission to under the title "Chapter Thirteen" is little more than an introduction and a "main result," with "not so little as a hundred pages" of argument canceled by a brief letter. Only a fragment remains of the "theory of the imagination," a theory that is itself already a fragment: "the fragments of the winding steps of an old ruined tower." "I see clearly that you have done too much, and yet not enough," writes the "friend" whose judgments govern the fate of the theory. A fragment of a fragment, the "dissevered" result of a work already excessive *and* deficient: Coleridge's "definition" of the imagination is, by the aporetic logic of its own narrative, doubly "deformed and monstrous."

The persistent doubleness that characterizes these two central chapters of the *Biographia Literaria* is never reconciled in the text. We are met with a text that insistently proclaims its desire for identity, for knowledge, for the "organic whole" but that is beset and even propelled by images of deformity, mutilation, and ruin.[24] We encounter in the *Biographia Literaria* a text that announces that "it is the essential mark of the true philosopher to rest satisfied with no imperfect light, as long as the impossibility of a fuller knowledge has not been demonstrated" (1: 242), but that at the very point where it is to secure its entire philosophical project "rests satisfied" with the "imperfect light" of a fragmented theory.[25] Such difficulties run deeper than thematic inconsistencies, for the trajectory of the autobiographical narrative is propelled by the cancellations of Coleridge's stated project. Of course, no one is likely to accuse Coleridge of the strictest philosophical rigor; lapses of consistency in the *Biographia* do not have the same status they would in such systematic philosophers as Kant and Schelling. At the same time, the lapses or maneuvers in Coleridge's account are not merely mistakes to be revealed; for they are taken up by Coleridge himself and, once "worked on," become in turn the basis for his theory.

What results is an irreconcilability that, casting its shadow back and forth over the entire text, puts the very premise of the theory of the imagination in an "imperfect light." "All knowledge," Coleridge asserts, "rests on the coincidence of an object with a subject" (*Biographia*, 1: 252). This coincidence, which must be broken up in the course of philosophical "explanation," is ultimately to be resecured by the imagination. But the text introduces the prospect that the originary coincidence may be the *effect* of "a *surreptitious* act of the imagination" (emphasis added), an act of imagination that, as Coleridge points out in the second "Thesis" of Chapter Twelve, conceals the absence of a central and unifying principle.[26] The "surreptitious act of the imagination" is capable of misrepresenting a discontinuous "series" as a "continuous circle." The mystifying property of the imagination is an agent of "mischievous errors," one that manufactures the illusion of identity. Though Coleridge will assert that the imagination is "a torch to light us whither we are going," he nonetheless acknowledges its potential deviousness as "a Jack O'Lanthorn to lead us out of the way." If the "office and object" of the philosopher is "to demonstrate the identity" of the subject to its object, the difficulties our philosopher experiences in satisfying this demonstration (which force him first to pass over an originary indeterminacy and then to take the "groundlessness" of the subject as "the ground of all other certainty") might well be attributed to the mystifying work of the imagination. By the light of the *Biographia*, as much "Jack O'Lanthorn" as "torch," readers of Coleridge are confronted with the prospect that the presumed coincidence of subject and object, on which "all knowledge rests," and the promised unification of the two subjects of autobiography are but the illusory effects of a surreptitious desire.

Ideology and "Ideal Objects"

In the case of such an "unmethodical" a thinker as Coleridge is so often presumed to be, a concept as variegated as the imagination may find adequate expression in the poetry alone, which can tolerate and even benefit from its mobility. This is, for instance, Stephen Prickett's interpretation of Coleridge's "imagination": "over and over again," writes Prickett, "we find that it is only in his poems that he can adequately relate the central ideas with which he so vainly seems to be struggling in his prose" (*Coleridge and Wordsworth*, 78). Prickett locates such an expression in Coleridge's remarkable late poem "Constancy to an Ideal Object."[27] The poetic object of constancy is not, Prickett contends, "an abstract concept, but is the creativity of the Imagination which manifests itself in our most everyday perceptions" (203). These conclusions are particularly suggestive for the connections they draw between the imagination and "our most everyday perceptions," precisely those that Althusser would identify as "ideology."

The poem does indeed open with a deliberation on the limitations of "everyday perceptions" inasmuch as these are subject to contingency and mutability, to what Coleridge describes as "a world of change":

> Since all that beat about in Nature's range,
> Or veer or vanish; why should'st thou remain
> The only constant in a world of change,
> O yearning Thought! that liv'st but in the brain?
>
> (ll. 1–4)

Given the insistence of worldly mutability, "the only constant" belongs not to the empirical domain but to "yearning Thought! that liv'st but in the brain." The force of mutability is such that even "Thought" is but a remainder, something left after everything "in nature's range" "veer[s] or vanish[es]." As the site and source of constancy, "thought" is characterized emphatically as a "yearning": desire itself thus becomes "the only constant in a world of change," a desire that perpetually posits the lost "ideal object." In the lines that follow, "Thought," by the structure of address and as if by the force of its "yearning," has shifted to the position of an *object* of endearment: "Fond thought!" (l. 7). The titular "constancy" that the poem purports to describe is thus not a grammatical feature of the poem itself, since the poem permits and promotes the interchange of subject and object positions. The "constancy" narrated by the poem, as many readers have noted, is the constancy of a lover in mourning: "Fond thought! not of all that shining swarm / Will breathe on thee with life-enkindling breath" (ll. 7–8). The "ideal object" remains inaccessible to worldly animation or the "life-enkindling breath" and is thus strangely preserved from "that shining swarm."

The "ideal object" to which the poem dedicates "constancy" can only grammatically be identified as "thought." By force of desire and by linguistic effect—by that which is often called imagination—a "fond thought" appears "*as though* some dear *embodied* Good" (my emphasis):

> Still, still as though some dear embodied Good,
> Some living love before my eyes there stood
> With answering look a ready ear to lend,
> I mourn to thee.   (ll. 13–16)

The lines reproduce the "strange" effects of the "self-power of the imagination," such as Coleridge describes it in his 1818 lectures, "when painful sensations have made it their interpreter": O, strange is the self-power of the imagination— . . . —strange is the power to represent the events and circumstances, even to the anguish or the triumph of the *quasi*-credulent soul, while the necessary contingencies, are known to be in fact quite hopeless. . . . And yet the effect shall have place, and substance, and living energy" (*Lectures*, 2: 208). The "self-power of the imagination" is "strange" in part because it is—like the power of language to posit without reference, or the power of language to *insti-*

tute—the power to misrepresent "events and circumstances" and, as the poem demonstrates, to make a "thought" appear as if it were "some living love before my eyes" or as if it were a capable interlocutor:

> I mourn to thee and say—"Ah! loveliest friend!
> That this the meed of all my toils might be,
> To have a home, an English home, and thee":
> Vain repetition! Home and Thou are one.
>
> (ll. 16–19)

A "vain repetition" indeed: according to the syntactical logic of the poem, "home" and *thought* "are one." By this perhaps brutally literal reading, a "home," *particularly* an "English home," is only "thought," for without "yearning" or "fond" thought, what we call "home" is but a "becalmed bark," adrift in *inconstancy*, on "an ocean waste and wide" (ll. 22, 23).[28]

The first section of the poem concludes at this point, and its relation to the subsequent section appears to reside in nothing more than the "ideal" object of address. "And art thou nothing?" the poet demands of his "ideal object." The narrative that answers this question has been understood—by Stephen Prickett, for instance—to "resolve" by "poetic insight" the impasse reached in the opening section. Such a resolution would reconcile the apparent disjunction of the two sections and give the poem formal unity.

> And art thou nothing? Such thou art as when
> The woodman winding westward up the glen
> At wintry dawn, where o'er the sheep-track's maze
> The viewless snow-mist weaves a glist'ning haze,
> Sees full before him, gliding without tread,
> An image with a glory round its head;
> The enamoured rustic worships its fair hues,
> Nor knows he makes the shadow, he pursues!
>
> (ll. 25–32)

The story of the "rustic's" sighting of the "image with a glory round its head" is corroborated by Coleridge in a footnote to the poem as a "phenomenon, which the author has himself experienced." However we interpret the poet's corroboration of the phenomenon of the "brocken spectre," the scene of the "woodman" represents a significant shift in focus. But Coleridge does not, here or elsewhere, identify the "rustic" as possessing a privileged access to reality or to the imagination. In the scene, the "woodman" lacks what Coleridge always found lacking in the "rustic": "a certain vantage-ground" (*Biographia*, 2: 44).[29] Only from the "vantage-ground" can we make out the Romantic ideology of the "rustic" at work; for the figure of the rustic is the very effect of such a critical and poetic "vantage-ground," a figure both exploited and explored by Coleridge's poem. It is precisely such a "vantage-ground" that makes it possible to see the "enamoured rustic" as another "ideal object" of Romantic desire, a necessary projection. And only from the perspective of this "vantage-ground" can we see that such a scene is a repetition of Plato's parable of the cave. The "enamoured rustic," not "know[ing]" that "he makes the shadow," blindly "pursues" the "image with a glory round its head." The illumination is, moreover, in no sense an enlightening one: "a glist'ning haze" woven by "viewless snow-mist."[30] The "glory" of the image that the "enamoured rustic worships" is the effect of the elaborate work of mystification: in this "vain repetition" of Plato's parable, we find the "glist'ning haze" woven by the "viewless" "mist" of ideology. The "woodman" "worships" and "pursues" by his imaginative and perhaps unavoidable misrepresentation of the "ideal object." The "surreptitious" power of the imagination creates these ideological effects, generating illusions and constituting belief.

If "Constancy to an Ideal Object" is about the "Imagination which manifests itself in our most everyday perceptions," it is about the ideology of that imagination, about the inevitable misrecognitions produced by the "self-power of the imagination." These ideological effects are far-reaching enough to mystify contemporary readers who take the poem to demonstrate the "poetic insight" of the imagination. But of more significance to what concerns us here, the "self-power of the imagination" that we witness in the poem extends to the discourses of the social as Coleridge conceived them. For if the "self-power of the imagination" as we see it functioning in "Constancy to an Ideal Object" is a mystifying power, it is at the very same time and for that very reason a *necessary* and *instituting* power: a power necessary for the

"Constitution of Church and State," a power necessary for producing belief in such "glist'ning hazes" and "ideal objects" as an English nation.

The Cultural Constitution of a National Subject: "It Is with Nations as with Individuals"

Published in 1829, only months after the passage in Parliament of the Catholic Relief Bill, *On the Constitution of Church and State* begins by addressing the question of Catholic emancipation, the issue whose parliamentary debate alone spans the first three decades of the nineteenth century. The parliamentary resolution to the problem offers Coleridge, an opponent of the Relief Bill, the occasion to speculate at length on the matters of church and state. What results is Coleridge's most sustained and coherent piece of critical writing, an essay in which he proposes nothing less than the guiding principles of the narrative of English history, principles that are linked theoretically and institutionally to the concept of the imagination.

The issue of Catholic emancipation—which is to say the "imperial" issues of Ireland and of English colonialism—represents for Coleridge a genuine crisis of the *English* Church and State. The crisis is not restricted to its parliamentary details; for Coleridge it implicates the very meaning of England and prompts his genealogical examination of the philosophical and historical foundations of "Church and State."[31] As the point of departure in his search for instituting principles, Coleridge takes up the "Idea of a Constitution."[32] Unlike the mere "conception" of a constitution, which is bound to empirical constitutions and therefore always bears the vicissitudes of "a world of change" ("Constancy to an Ideal Object"), the "ever-originating idea" of a constitution is the sign of both origin and *telos*. Within the space of this idea runs the course of history itself; the "*idea* of an ever-originating social contract constitutes the whole ground of the difference between subject and serf, between a commonwealth and a slave-population" (*Constitution*, 15).

But as Coleridge pursues the idea of the constitution, it turns out that what we had supposed to be the origin is instead the *effect* of another idea: "But a Constitution is an idea arising out of the idea of a state" (19). This idea, Coleridge tells us, is founded on an antagonism: the state arises from the tension between "two antagonistic powers or opposite interests, . . . those of PERMANENCE and of PROGRESSION" (24). By these allegorical stage-names Coleridge designates the aristocracy and the bourgeoisie as the principal players in the historical drama of the state. The maintenance of the state, the *constitution* of the state, depends upon the reconciliation of this antagonism, on the alliance between aristocracy and bourgeoisie. But it turns out, not surprisingly in such an extended chain of references, that the idea of the state is another effect, the effect of the idea of the nation. We find in the "idea" of nation the unifying principle, the "ever-originating idea," that informs both constitution and state. In a discarded manuscript note, Coleridge remarks that the nation "is the Unity of the successive Generations of a People. A *State*, again, is the conservative Form (therefore, at once the Form and the Power) of the unity of a People" (24 n. 2). Thus, the nation is in Coleridge's words "the magnet" (31) that draws together and unifies the conflicting interests or powers within the state. The nation thus possesses the capacity of instituting or "self-power" that Coleridge attributes to the imagination: the power "*of fusion to force many into one*" (*Lectures*, 1: 81). This is an "idealism," of course, but one that was to have, and that continues to have, material effects; and it is precisely as Coleridge understood such idealisms. The half-title Coleridge added for the second edition of *On the Constitution of Church and State*, "According to the Idea of Each," alludes to the historical effectivity that Coleridge understood ideas to possess.

That Coleridge would take a historical contradiction for a perpetual and constitutive tension is itself a symptom of the "peculiarities" of the English "version" of a bourgeois revolution that Marx later characterized as "aborted." British historian Perry Anderson has argued that though the revolutionary transformations generated by the events of 1640–88 are "capitalist," they are not, strictly speaking, bourgeois: in other words, the effects of the revolution are, according to Anderson, to be measured primarily in economic and not in political or ideological terms. While the events of the revolutionary period opened the way for "the development of a dynamic capitalist agriculture and the rise of a mercantile imperialism," these transformations were achieved, Anderson argues, "by profoundly transforming the *roles* but not the *personnel* of the ruling class."[33] Anderson underlines what he identifies as the singular significance of England's deviation from the classical paradigm of bourgeois revolution: "*There was from the start no fundamental, antagonistic contradiction between the old aristocracy and the new bourgeoisie. English capitalism embraced and included both. The most important key to modern English history lies in this fact*" ("Origins," 31). During the course of the next two centuries, it was the ideological and institutional project of the English ruling bloc to "weld" or "fuse" aristocracy and bourgeoisie together in "a single social bloc" (38).

The preservation of this contradictory and fragile alliance became increasingly tenuous during the early decades of the nineteenth century. The issues Coleridge customarily refers to by their official parliamentary designations—Catholic Relief, Corn Laws, Reform Bill—were, among other things, the signs of a deep ideological crisis of the English nation-state.[34] Coleridge recognized the crisis of the English state in the 1820's as the expression of the antagonisms within the ruling bloc, antagonisms between the "principles" of "permanence" and "progression." But this state crisis could not be resolved by either the aristocracy or the bourgeoisie because, according to Coleridge, the state is merely the "form" of the unitary idea of the *nation*, and the nation in turn presupposes a "third estate," which is "the ground, the necessary antecedent condition of the former [two estates]" (*Constitution*, 42). The principle represented by the third but "necessary antecedent" estate is "civilization," which Coleridge understands as the active and harmonizing process of cultivation: "the harmonious development of those faculties that characterize our humanity" (43). Civilization, Coleridge elaborates, is the name for the historical narrative that "binds the present with the past" and "connects the present with the future" (44). This is a continuous narrative process, in which the story of the nation is produced and reproduced, a national story that in turn informs and secures the constitution and the institutions of the state.[35]

Both the production and the dissemination of this narrative of national civilization—what we might today call an official history—must be entrusted, Coleridge argues, to a "permanent class of order," a class whose allegiance belongs neither to the aristocracy nor to the bourgeoisie, but to the idea of the nation itself.[36] There is, of course, nothing "disinterested" about the "permanent class of order," one that withdraws from local parliamentary disputes in order to serve and preserve the nation-state. This cultural and pedagogical project—assigned traditionally to the "National Church" and operated there solely as a theology—must now be delegated, according to Coleridge, to a marginally more secular "national clerisy."[37] That such a "class of order" or "national clerisy," what Gramsci might call a "permanent intelligentsia," did indeed exercise "a pervasive power . . . upon civil society at large" and play "an unusually central and political role in promoting social integration" confirms the significance of Coleridge's speculations on the role of the intellectual.[38] The British historian Tom Nairn argues that the English "clerisy" was "neither a state-fostered technocracy (on the French model) nor an alienated intelligentsia (on the Russian model)," but a "class" formed, much as Coleridge outlines it, by "civil society itself, not the state."[39]

For the national clerisy to perform the indispensable cultural and ideological tasks of "social integration," historical education, and political reconciliation, it must be grasped, Coleridge asserts, that the origin of the nation, like that of the constitution, is not a "historical fact" but a "pure fiction" (*Constitution*, 14). Far from undermining the status of "nation," the admission of its pure fictionality demonstrates precisely the ideological effectivity Coleridge ascribes to the idea of the nation and speaks more generally to the effectivity of what we call ideology. The governing "*idea*" of the nation precedes and informs all empirical nation-states: the maintenance and reproduction of that idea by the "national clerisy" is, therefore, an indispensable political function.[40] Coleridge conceives nationhood as a fundamentally imaginary relationship and the nation itself, to use Benedict Anderson's term, as an "imagined community."[41] This "home," this "English home," is thus nothing more but nothing less than a thought, a "yearning thought," an ideological projection.

"Civilization," then, is to be understood as the perpetual unfolding of the national story, a story that must designate a shared and consistent territory and that must bind this imagined space temporally with a mythic past and an expansive and imperial future. The historical narrative of English civilization must cultivate a deep temporal connectedness that, within the imagined collective space of the nation-state, will give rise to a shared national consciousness.[42] Coleridge understands the imagination to be the faculty necessary for such a *social* activity, one that is ideological in the most extensive sense of that term: it is this social role of the imagination that makes it possible for the state to secure, in Althusser's words, the means of "reproducing its own conditions of existence." When Coleridge assigns his national clerisy with the "preservation of the treasures of past civilization" (*Constitution*, 43), the work of such preservation is by no means mere guardianship: it is the institutionalized cultivation of a national memory through which the "ever-originating idea" of a nationhood can be perpetually reformed. By presiding over and preserving cultural continuity, by making and remaking that notion of culture, by writing and rewriting the "pure fiction" of the nation, Coleridge's national clerisy might in the short run "harmonize" the two class factions which comprise the ruling bloc and for the long run secure the legitimacy of the state and the permanence of its constitution.[43]

Coleridge's ambitious ideological project was to be implemented within the institutional framework and practices of schooling. By assuming the pedagogical responsibilities traditionally assigned to the church, Coleridge responded to the sense of a crisis in the role of higher education pervasive in the early decades of the century by proposing that the national clerisy should provide "the main aids, instruments and materials of NATIONAL EDUCATION, the *nisus formativus* of the body politic, the shaping and informing spirit, which *educing*, i.e. eliciting, the latent *man* in all the natives of the soil, [training them as] citizens of the country, free subjects of the realm" (*Constitution*, 48). Not only does the educational program supply the means for the deployment of "civilization," but, according to Coleridge, it is the very site of a very specific subject-making process: from the "soil" of England, the "native" is formed into an English citizen, a "free subject of the realm." What Coleridge calls English civilization and what we have identified as the historical narrative of a national culture works when, by its insertion in the "main aids, instruments and materials of NATIONAL EDU-

CATION," it functions as "the shaping and informing spirit" for the formation of English subjectivity. This understanding of the significance of education for the preservation of the state is indeed one of Coleridge's principal legacies: as John Stuart Mill describes it, Coleridge demonstrates that "a main essential ingredient" of a "*system of education*" is "*restraining discipline*" (*Mill*, 121). Coleridge's investment in the role of the national clerisy confirms Althusser's understanding of the multiple ideological articulations of a "literary culture" within the education system:

> The literary culture that is dispensed in the teaching of schools is not simply an academic phenomenon; it is one moment among others in the ideological education of the people. Through its methods and effects it overlaps with others that are deployed at the same time: religious, legal, moral, political, etc. These are all so many means of ensuring the hegemony of the leading class, grouped around the state in which the dominant class holds power.[44]

Coleridge ascribes a crucial social significance to the place and function of a "literary culture," but it represents for him more than "one moment among others in the ideological education of the people." As he conceives it, the institution of education—the "literary culture" in the broadest sense of that term—provides the indispensable point of coherence for the ensemble of ideological practices. Stephen Prickett confirms the significance of these implications: for Coleridge's readers, writes Prickett, "the real message of his work seemed clear: the Church of England, properly endowed, and with its privileged status in the universities unchallenged, was the best bulwark there was against social change and reform."[45]

We might recall here the route that culminates with this pedagogical program. Coleridge identifies as the occasion for the composition of his essay the national crisis produced by the Catholic (Irish) question. He proceeds from this topical concern to what he conceives of as the fundamental and fundamentally historical idea of nationhood as the "purely fictional" grounds that must be perpetually reproduced by the institution of a national clerisy. Coleridge reads the Catholic question as the displaced symptom of a generalized crisis of the national consciousness, and of a more specific deterioration of the educational system intended to form national subjects. *On the Constitution of Church and State* concludes an ideological project Coleridge initiated as early as 1816 with the publication of *The Statesman's Manual*, an essay that proposes the principled interpretation of Scripture as the "guide" to political judgment. From its very inception, the explicitly ideological project of teaching, civilizing, subject-making is linked to Coleridge's efforts to uncover the "first principles" of philosophy: these principles must inform the discourse of the nation through the cultural and pedagogical institution of the national clerisy. The "criterion of a true philosophy" is for Coleridge the imagination, and it is by way of the imagination that the idea of the nation can take form and be maintained. We can thus begin to calculate the nature of the political and social—or ideological—investment in this philosophical concept: Coleridge's many returns to the imagination represent the attempt to ground, formalize, and institute (Tory) politics through philosophy.[46]

Coleridge's definition of the imagination in *The Statesman's Manual* corresponds closely to the formulations of the "secondary" or "esemplastic" imagination developed in the *Biographia*: "[The Imagination is] that reconciling and mediatory power, which incorporating the Reason in Images of the Sense, and organizing (as it were) the flux of the senses by the permanence and self-circling energies of the Reason, gives birth to a system of symbols, harmonious in themselves, and consubstantial with the truths, of which they are the *conductors*."[47] The spirit if not the letter of the Kantian *Critiques* is imprinted in the first portion of the definition, but when Coleridge introduces the metaphor of childbirth he begins to deviate considerably from the function of the imagination as it is formulated by Kant. Once the imagination is assigned the role of "giving birth" to a harmonious "system of symbols," the imagination is no longer merely a bridge between reason and sense, no longer only a "mediatory" or "reconciling" but a feminized productive power. The passage reveals the doubleness that is a consistent feature and burden of the Coleridgean imagination: to reconcile *and* to produce.

This doubleness, always unacknowledged and at least potentially contradictory, is nonetheless necessary for the imagination to be effective as a political principle. We have already noted how the imagination, understood as an agent of "reconciliation," promises not only to resolve the antagonism between "reason" and "sense" but also to reconcile what Coleridge identifies as the homologous antagonism between "Progression" and "Permanence." To authorize his invocation of the imagination as a political "first principle," Coleridge refers to Scripture and asserts that at the origins of European culture, the imagination, at present obscured by the "contagion" of "mechanistic philosophy," was rightly regarded as the true source of politics and history: "The histories and political economy of the present and preceding century partake in the general contagion of its mechanistic philosophy, and are the *product* of an unenlivened generalizing Understanding. In the Scriptures they are the living *educts* of the Imagination" (*Statesman's Manual*, 28–29). The *Statesman's Manual*, in which this famous definition of the imagination is proposed, is conceived explicitly as an ideological training manual "addressed to the highest classes of society" (3). In *The Statesman's Manual* and throughout Coleridge's mature critical writings, the imagination is both the philosophical or poetic foundation and the ideological *model* for the political work of culture and education. The imagination is intended to perform a function directly analogous to that assigned to the national clerisy: the power of the imagination, the harmonizing third term, reconciles reason and sense and thus mirrors the duties of the national clerisy, itself the "third estate," to forge on the basis of the "idea of the nation" a sustainable alliance between landowners and bourgeoisie. Moreover, for the imagination to be established as a governing social principle in the interests of the nation, it must be "educed" through the national clerisy, through the pedagogical and administrative offices organized in the "civil service."

Coleridge is not, of course, the sole author of the cultural program of an English civilization or even of this project of a national clerisy. What distinguishes Coleridge's version of such a conservative cultural and political agenda from those of Burke and Arnold and what links it to George Eliot is Coleridge's importation of the "German Revolution in Philosophy" as the foundation and model for an English subject-making process, a process that takes as its starting point, moreover, not a presumed unity of self but a division and specularity understood to be the condition of subjectivity and society.

The "power of truth," Coleridge writes early in the *Biographia*, is "obtained by contemplating the subject in the fontal mirror of the idea." Although truth itself is, according to Coleridge, "divine" and therefore unavailable as such to the human subject, truth's *power* may be "obtained" by "contemplating" the image of the subject as it is captured and reflected in the "fontal mirror" of the idea. Thus, the power of truth resides in between subject and mirror, in the story of a reflection. Here, the subject, far from being identified as the source of truth or origin of knowledge, sees itself caught in an elaborate structure of specularity. On just these grounds, Coleridge objects to Hartley's model of subjectivity: it fails to account for the double and specular subject, reducing the subject to "the mere quick-silver plating behind a looking-glass" (*Biographia*, 1: 119). The doubleness that Coleridge sees, the specular double scene of the subject and its reflection, is a textual feature of autobiographical discourse, one that Coleridge appears to mimic formally in the organization of the *Biographia*. The passage suggests the extent of Coleridge's philosophical interest in the workings of specularity, which is at the heart of the ideological workings of subjectivity.

Coleridge's project of designing the governing narratives of a national subject is to be performed by virtue of such division. The imagination in Coleridge can thus be understood as an ideological activity in which the division inherent in the subject—the infinitely repeated division in the "I am"—simultaneously provides the imaginary conditions of its coherence. The psychoanalytic notion of "suture" offers a suggestive analogy for this process.[48] Suture, as Stephen Heath summarizes it, "names not just a structure of lack [in the subject] but also an availability of the subject, a certain closure" ("On Suture," 85). The suturing process is performed by way of the very division inherent in the subject as conceived by psychoanalysis, and it manufactures a sense of "pseudo-identification," the sense that the "I" is joined to the "symbolic." In Heath's words, "the stake is clear: the 'I' is a division but joins all the same, the stand-in is the lack in the structure but nevertheless, simultaneously, the possibility of a coherence, of the *filling in*" (86). We have seen that the imagination in Coleridge issues from a fundamental division in the subject, and *simultaneously* "fuses" the sense of coherence. And since for Coleridge "it is with nations as with individuals," the imagination's activity is a social one, generating the "pseudo-iden-tification" with that "ideal object" called the nation.

The power and difficulty of Coleridge's theory of the imagination is that it does not *presume* the unity of either subject or nation; it takes the divisions of both as the starting point of its ideological work. Coherence is not, in other words, a condition of the process but an imaginary outcome. Admitting the fictionality of the nation for Coleridge does not constitute an act of demystification that would of itself threaten the dissolution of the nation. Implicit in Coleridge's work is an understanding that ideology operates on the basis of such doubleness and specularity. Far from spelling its undoing, the revelation of the nation's "pure fictionality" is the very condition of its ideological effectivity. Taking into account the "pure fiction" of the nation, Coleridge finds in the imagination both the condition of perception and social being *and* the principle of an *eventual* cohesion that can make the nation. Thus, the "idealism" of Coleridge's theory enables the ideological purchase of the imagination. This is the significance of his "constancy": England can function only as an "ideal object," but as such it achieves its greatest ideological power. We have already seen that Coleridge conceives the project of the national clerisy as the preservation and cultivation of a continuous narrative of English civilization, an official history of the nation that, once institutionalized in the system of education, furnishes the ideological anchoring for the state. For Coleridge, the imagination institutes the process by which divisions inherent in subjectivity—divisions reproduced in the formal doubleness inherent in autobiographical discourse—are "reconciled" or "harmonized" as the subject is, by virtue of its "training" in the systems of education, "sutured" or written into this national narrative.

By treating what Coleridge calls the imagination—philosophical concept and subjective faculty—as the instituting of an ideological process, we are closer to the understanding apparent in those "Anglican divines and Tory politicians," as Jonathan Arac refers to them, who read Coleridge with such interest throughout the nineteenth century.[49] What they found there, what has made his body of work repeatedly attractive to conservative theologians and intellectuals, poets and politicians, is an ideological theory of the imagination that holds the promise of real social and political effects. We need only recall John Stuart Mill's reckoning of Coleridge's formative influence on the development of English social and cultural thought: "the existence of Coleridge," he declared in 1840, "will show itself by no slight or ambiguous traces in the coming history of the country" (*Mill*, 99). Coleridge's theorizing of the imagination has indeed "shown" itself: as the point over which politics, philosophy, and poetry converge, as the agent of a powerful model of ideology, as the "institution" of a "revolution in philosophy." This should demonstrate why, after a century and a half, the ideological effects of the imagination and the ideological effects of Coleridge's own critical project continue to "show themselves by no slight or ambiguous traces" in the disciplines of literature and the canons of cultural value.

CHAPTER 2

WORDSWORTH

The Poetry of Enshrinement

"Enshrining, / Such is my hope"

Towards the end of a passage that has become one of the most visited shrines of a great Romantic monument—the celebrated "spots of time" passage in Book XII of *The Prelude*—Wordsworth, after admitting the persistent disjunctive effects of time, declares the "hope" of his poem:

> The days gone by
> Return upon me almost from the dawn
> Of life: the hiding-places man's power
> Open; I would approach them, but they close.
> I see by glimpses now; when age comes on,
> May scarcely see at all; and I would give,
> While yet we may, as far as words can give,
> Substance and life to what I feel, enshrining,
> Such is my hope, the spirit of the Past
> For future restoration.—Yet another
> Of these memorials.[1]

Wordsworth sees something more than the general truth that past events exceed the grasp of memory to recover them, that memory is incapable of claiming the positivity of the past. What is revealed to him is

59

memory's shutter-effect: "the hiding-places of man's power" "close" upon approach, and they necessarily, even constitutively, resist recuperation as positive, empirical phenomena. The work of memory's shutter-effect, in other words, *confirms* the past's inaccessibility. The passage concludes by presenting, as a consequence of this disclosure, one important version of the work of Romantic poetry: the act of "enshrinement." What remains unavailable as an empirical past may through "enshrinement" be made available as "spirit" for "future restoration." "Such is my hope," says the poet. The implications are considerable: all internal "feelings" and thoughts called up by remembrance and reflection, produced by an unrecoverable "source," must be externalized, given, "as far as words can give, / Substance and life," *enshrined* through their translation into poetic language. The passage is a significant one, not only for what it says about the field of memory and the path of "internalization" but—crucially, I believe—for what it suggests about the role of that particular Wordsworthian version of "internal thought" called the imagination.

I begin with the thesis that "enshrinement"—the poetic act of preservation and celebration—may well be another name for poetry as Wordsworth conceives it. Enshrinement is for instance a way to characterize what takes place in "Tintern Abbey" or "I Wandered Lonely as a Cloud," where the poetic act of revisitation both preserves and celebrates the spirit; and I propose in the present chapter to read the poetic enshrinement of the imagination featured in *The Prelude*. But we need only to recall Wordsworth's critical interest in epitaphs to recognize the instability of this mode and to be reminded of the proximity between writing as *enshrinement* and writing as *entombment*. The imagination makes its appearances in *The Prelude* in ways that make it difficult finally to distinguish enshrinement from entombment. Indeed, it is in the name of the imagination that interruptive forces threaten—as in the "dream of the Arab" in Book V—to "engulph" the English poet and to entomb "spirit" itself. Thus, to read for the imagination in *The Prelude* is to encounter what is perhaps best understood provisionally as the dialectic of enshrinement and entombment, though the details of our reading will complicate that dialectical model.

The aims of my reading are not, however, merely to reveal the implication of enshrinement and entombment in Wordsworth, but to consider the *ideological* effects such intertwining exerts in the poetry. For I would argue that "enshrinement" offers the means by which we can best approach the ideology of imagination in Wordsworth: enshrinement, and its implication with entombment, is the mode by which the imagination is figured in *The Prelude*; and if the imagination in Wordsworth often appears as "another name" for ideology, it is by means of its enshrinement that its ideological effects can be achieved. By way of the poetics of enshrinement, we can discern the role of the imagination in the intertwining of poetry and politics in Wordsworth, an imagination that must pass through "oriental" visions to culminate in national dreams.

The ideological effects of this "enshrinement" within the literary and cultural tradition are considerable, for if Coleridge institutes an imagination to which we still adhere in our conventions of interpretation, no text has more enshrined the imagination as the governing faculty or "guiding idea" of Romantic poetry than *The Prelude*. "Imagination having been our theme," Wordsworth asserts near the end of his autobiographical poem, "This faculty hath been the feeding source / Of our long labour" (XIV.206, 193–94). *The Prelude* is itself a shrine or, more precisely, an extended memorial, an autobiography written in memory of the imagination, enshrining the imagination for "future restoration," preserving "man's power" from deluge, sheltering it in the crypt of the poem from which it can be resurrected as a monument of English poetry.

If the imagination is both "theme" and "feeding source" of *The Prelude*, and if the imagination must withdraw from the "o'erpressure of the times," the "way" of the imagination—the course of its enshrinement—ultimately leads from the "element of the nature's inner self" to "love of humankind" (1805, VIII.514, 518). As it is narrated in *The Prelude*, "love of humankind" is "another name" for "sympathy," a term that identifies the imagination's spiritual as well as social capacity as Wordsworth inherited and developed it.[2] Sympathy, as James Engell summarizes it, is "that special power of the imagination which permits the self to escape its own confines" and to establish genuine intersubjectivity; sympathy could thus "be considered the cohesive force behind an organic view of the universe."[3] At the level of society, sympathy is the "cohesive force" that underwrites organic notions of community.

To this end, the poetics of "enshrinement" provides the means to reread "internalization," the Hegelian trope by which the imagination—and indeed Romantic poetry—is canonically interpreted. That interpretation is further complicated when we consider that "entombment" in Wordsworth may be "another name" for what we in our Hegelian heritage call "negation." But most importantly, the pattern of enshrinement and entombment visible in *The Prelude* makes it possible to understand the ideological dimensions of internalization as something considerably more complicated, and something considerably more powerful, than a mystified withdrawal from the social and political world. To make good on the promise of enshrinement would mean to achieve the full ideological effects of sympathy: to make the "way" of the imagination pass from its necessarily internal course to a worldly "love of mankind" that can sustain a genuine sense of community. Moreover, *The Prelude* as Wordsworth conceives it would not so much describe as perform this enshrinement, making of itself the cultural shrine it has indeed become. The imagination's enshrinement in *The Prelude* retells the story of internalization and, in the process, prompts a visit to another great Western shrine of the dialectics of "spirit," Hegel's *Aesthetics*.

Imagination's Lodgings

Near the beginning of "Sign and Symbol in Hegel's *Aesthetics*," Paul de Man makes the following assertion regarding this powerfully canonical albeit, as de Man points out, largely unread text of aesthetic theory:

> Whether we know it, or like it, or not, most of us are Hegelians and quite orthodox ones at that. We are Hegelian when we reflect on literary history in terms of an articulation between the Hellenic and the Christian Era or between the Hebraic and Hellenic world. We are Hegelian when we try to systematize the relationships between the various art forms or genres according to different modes of representation or when we try to

conceive of historical periodization as a development, progressive or regressive, of a collective or individual consciousness. Not that such concerns belong exclusively to Hegel; far from it. But the name "Hegel" stands here for an all-encompassing vessel in which so many currents have gathered and been preserved that one is likely to find there almost any idea one knows to have been gathered from elsewhere or hopes to have invented oneself. Few thinkers have so many disciples who have never read a word of their master's writings.[4]

Much remains to be said about such a fascinating assertion, but I am interested here less in weighing de Man's claims about the reach of "the master's writings" than in considering the way the passage both represents "Hegel" and introduces the Hegelian thematics that it subsequently reads. The passage serves not only to justify de Man's return to this canonical text but to compel his readers to follow suit. No critique of the "aesthetic ideology" can hope to be successful, de Man implies, without the most searching consideration—without the *reading*—of Hegel. Such a reading is necessary because the name "Hegel" has come to stand for the very category of the aesthetic, and because, against the grain of the interpretive tradition in his name, the text of Hegel "upsets what we have taken for granted," according to de Man, namely, "the unassailable *value* of the aesthetic" ("Sign and Symbol," 766).

Hegel as "all-incompassing vessel" is another, and much more fragile, name for the notion of "totality" that we have come to associate with the German philosopher. Readers of de Man are also likely to be reminded of his lecture on "The Task of the Translator" and his reading of Benjamin's phrasing of the "vessel" of language, a vessel that is already broken and that we, often in the name of Hegel and the aesthetic tradition, struggle to keep intact. The mode of the vessel also announces a topic important in de Man's reading of Hegel and to our reading of Wordsworth: the Hegelian topic of *Erinnerung*, which de Man translates as "preservation and gathering within" and which is conventionally translated as "internalization." Hegel's *Aesthetics* offers at once a comprehensive theory and an exemplary model of the dialectics of internalization, the model most responsible for what Derrida has called the "conventional Hegelianism" that has in turn dominated the interpretation of English Romanticism.[5]

The imagination is pivotal to the story told in the *Aesthetics* of spirit's dialectical self-recognition, marking spirit's emergence from the undifferentiated state of nature: "at the stage of the *beginning* of art the urge of the imagination consisted in striving out of nature into spirit."[6] At the far end of Hegel's narrative, through the force of this desire, this "urge" and "striving," the imagination becomes enshrined in the interior domain of the spirit. In the Romantic world of lyric poetry, imagination has found its place in "the spirit's own *subjective* disposition": "Out of the objectivity of the subject-matter the spirit descends into itself, looks into its own consciousness, and satisfies the need to display, not the external reality of the matter, but its presence and actuality in the spirit's own *subjective* disposition, in the experience of the heart and the reflections of the imagination, and at the same time to display the contents and activity of the inner life itself" (*Aesthetics*, 1,111). If classical art is defined by the adequation between subject and object, Romanticism for Hegel *is* "the spirit's own *subjective* disposition." Characterized by the ascendance of the "principle of inner subjectivity," Romantic art expresses a new discrepancy between meaning and form, a "withdrawal" from exterior appearance: "At the stage of romantic art the spirit . . . becomes sure of its truth by withdrawing from the external into its own intimacy with itself and positing external reality as an existence inadequate to itself" (518). Once the spirit has withdrawn "from the external," however, the "true content" of Romantic art, "absolute inwardness," cannot be represented as such, cannot assume material form: "[A]bsolute subjectivity as such would elude art and be accessible to thinking alone if, in order to be *actual* subjectivity in correspondence with its essence, it did not then withdraw out of this reality into itself again" (519). What Wordsworth identifies in *The Prelude* as the "meditations of mankind" becomes by this narrative the object of aesthetic representation, "the main region" of poetic thought.[7] The result is a shuttling movement between the inner world and its contact with "external existence." The story of such contact is often told in Romantic texts through what Hegel calls "an infinitely enhanced wealth of inner and outer collisions" (526).

Though Hegel does not consider the imagination to be the property exclusively of Romanticism, it is only at this stage of art that the imagination, now "subjectively independent," becomes visible as both the agent and object of artistic representation: "[G]enuinely lyric poetry, as *art*, tears itself free from this already existent world of prose, and out of an imagination now become subjectively independent creates a new poetic world of subjective meditation and feeling whereby alone it generates in a living way the true contents of the inner life of man and the true way of expressing them" (*Aesthetics*, 1,127). From its "subjectively independent" position, the imagination marks the rupture between internal and external worlds and secures for poetic thought, and for philosophical speculation, the "world of subjective meditation" "torn free" from the "world of prose."

By mapping the trajectory of the spirit through the aesthetic, Hegel's lectures graph the appearance of the imagination and the development of the principle of subjectivity. But Hegel tells another story here, one of a necessary "entombing" of spirit in the Orient (India, Egypt, Persia) *prior* to its Western birth and development. In the Hegelian division of symbolic forms, Oriental art remains within the boundaries of the unconscious symbolic, the "forecourt" of art. Though the "pre-originary" space of the Orient is necessary for the appearance of both the idea of art and the principle of subjectivity, the art of the Orient "differs essentially" from that of the West in that an "individual consciousness does not disclose itself" in the former (*Aesthetics*, 355). Even in Egypt, Hegel's "land of the symbol," the spirit cannot "feel at home" since it "has still not really found its own inner life," it has yet to "speak the clear and distinct language of spirit" (374, 354).[8] The symbolic signification characteristic of Egypt can be traced to the pyramids themselves: "The Pyramids put before our eyes the simple prototype of symbolical art itself" (356). Through these massive funerary monuments, the spectacular representation of the dead, internalization is at work, an "inner meaning" first distinguished from an "external form" (356).[9] By marking the space of the dead with magisterial entombment, with the "perennial preservation of corpses," the Egyptians "made the transition of mind to its liberation, although they have only reached the threshold of the realm of freedom" (355). Thus, spirit can be born out of a prior death and entombment in a culture that, according to Hegel, preserves but cannot know it in its maturity.

Only with the decisive turn from East to West does "the truly inward . . . begin to wrest its way out of the natural" (*Aesthetics*, 348). By passing from the symbolic world of the pyramids to the sublimity of the Old Testament, from the monument to the word, or from tomb to shrine, "we find ourselves at once on a totally different ground on which we can feel at home, no matter how strange and different from ours the situations, events, actions, and characters may be" (374–75). The world of the Hebrew Old Testament introduces the "moment of the sublime" and establishes the passage in Hegel's narrative from East to West. The moment inaugurates spirit's westward journey and thus simultaneously constitutes retrospectively the world from which spirit has migrated *as* the "Orient."[10]

I am interested here in this strange trajectory, the logic of a story that places an entombment and a death prior to a birth, that builds shrines from tombs, and that needs its projected Orient to tell a Western story. It is a story that concludes, of course, with Hegel's version of spirit's enshrinement in the "subjective disposition" of Romanticism, and it is a story that will resonate with Wordsworth's "dream of the Arab" in Book V of *The Prelude*. Versions of the story get told repeatedly in Romantic and post-Romantic culture, if never again in the magisterial or encyclopedic form that Hegel gives. One compelling and pertinent version of the story is told by Georg Lukács in *The Theory of the Novel*, a work he would later characterize as "essentially determined by Hegel." *The Theory of the Novel* follows Hegel in describing the interiorizing experience of literary form in Romanticism as an experience of rupture with reality. For Lukács, the enshrinement that is definitive of Romanticism comes at the expense of life itself:

> In Romanticism, the literary nature of the *a priori* status of the soul vis-à-vis reality becomes conscious; the self, cut off from transcendence, recognizes itself as the source of the ideal reality, and, as a necessary consequence, as the only material worthy of self-realisation. Life becomes a work of literature; but, as a result, man becomes the author of his own life and at the same time the observer of that life as a created work of art.[11]

And it is precisely the project of *The Prelude* to fashion from the radical separation of self and world a "heroic argument," to produce with a lyric consciousness a work of epic or Miltonic scope that while "enshrining" life will avoid entombing it from the world (III.191, 104). In Book III, for instance, when Wordsworth "retraces" the object of the "glory" of his youth, he is moved to stress that the object of his "tale" is to be strictly distinguished from the world of "outward things":

> And here, O Friend! have I retraced my life
> Up to an eminence, and told a tale
> Of matters which not falsely may be called
> The glory of my youth. Of genius, power,
> Creation and divinity itself
> I have been speaking, for my theme has been
> What passed within me. Not of outward things
> Done visibly for other minds, words, signs,
> Symbols or actions, but of my own heart
> Have I been speaking, and my youthful mind.
>
> (III.170–79)

The poet must turn to his outside world for the language of this interior drama, but internalization changes the nature of the subject's disposition towards those "outward things" now irrevocably regarded as external and alien. Subjectivity becomes, as Lukács describes it, an "arbitrary conqueror" of the world from which it has withdrawn:

> Lyrical subjectivity has to go for its symbols to the outside world; even if that world has been made by subjectivity itself, it is nevertheless the only possible one; subjectivity, as an interiority . . . proceeds as an arbitrary conqueror, it snatches fragments out of the atomised chaos which is the outside world and melts them down—causing all origins to be forgotten—into a newly created, lyrical cosmos of pure interiority. (*Theory of the Novel*, 114)

For Wordsworth the name of the "arbitrary conqueror" is the imagination, defined in the Preface to the 1815 edition of his *Poems* as the "operations of the mind upon . . . [external] objects."[12] The imagination holds the alchemic power, according to Wordsworth, to "melt down" the fragments it takes from the outside world and to recast them into something "newly created": "These processes of imagination are carried on either by conferring additional properties upon an object, or abstracting from it some of those which it actually possesses, and thus enabling it to re-act upon the mind which hath performed the process, like a new existence" (*Literary Criticism*, 182). The "processes of imagination" make use of the discrepancy between self and world to confer or to abstract properties, and in their "re-action" describe what we call ideology: something is forged from the processes of imagination, a "new existence" that we believe in and enshrine as true. The imagination effects a withdrawal from the world of "external objects" into the dwelling-place of mind, a withdrawal that in its turn establishes not only the principles of poetic thought or lyric consciousness but also, ultimately, the ideological processes of representation.[13]

Though the imagination always refers to some version of the ideological relationship between self and world, in *The Prelude* the relationship is far from stable; as a result, the appearances of the imagination in the poem serve more as an index of its instability. In the course of this "philosophico-biographical" poem, the imagination serves as the object as well as the agency of the poem's narrative energies. These two narrative functions—the goal towards which the narrative comports itself and the subjective source of the poetry—are not necessarily compatible. As the contentious critical history of the poem demonstrates, the variability creates considerable difficulty for Wordsworth's readers, since interpretations of *The Prelude* often hinge on the interpretation of the imagination and since its various incarnations in the poem invite divergent interpretations.[14] We may, for instance, regard the imagination as an "auxiliar light" issued from the poet's mind that generates effects exceeding sensory perception, "bestow[ing] new splendour" (II.368–70). In the celebrated appearance of this "power" in the 1805 version of Book VI, "Imagination" is sublime:

> Imagination!—lifting up itself
> Before the eye and progress of my song
> Like an unfathered vapour, here that power,
> In all the might of its endowments, came
> Athwart me.   (1805, VI.525–29)[15]

In this apostrophic interruption, we find the imposition of an imagination that would undo most everything declared or asserted in its name, by Wordsworth for one, including much of his great poetic shrine. The passage forces us to apprehend an imagination that we cannot know or comprehend. Likened to an "unfathered vapour," the imagination invoked in the passage exceeds altogether subjective authority. Here the imagination appears as an autonomous "power" that, when exercising "all the might of its endowments," creates confusion and despair: "I was lost as in a cloud, / Halted without a struggle to break through" (1805, VI.529–30). Nothing about the hiatus should be read as tribute: in the shape of the sublime, the imagination poses a threat to narrativity itself, a moment of sublime blockage to the "eye and progress" of the poem itself.[16]

We might understand Wordsworth's considerable revisions of the passage to demonstrate the need to contain imagination's sublimity, to find lodgings that will preserve it from the threat posed by its "vaporous" appearances. If we follow the poem's narrative itinerary, we are likely to consider the sublime presentation of the imagination to be superseded by subsequent formulations. By this logic, Wordsworth's concluding designation of the faculty is the one we are most likely to regard as definitive:

> Imagination, . . . in truth,
> Is but another name for absolute power
> And clearest insight, amplitude of mind,
> And Reason in her most exalted mood.
> (XIV.189–92)

The lines restore the imagination as a power of mind, securing it as a principle of subjective sovereignty and realigning it with "Reason" itself. Far from an "unfathered vapour," the later account of the imagination reasserts the very powers of mind that are ungrounded by the earlier passage.

Wordsworth adds other "names" to this account of the imagination, however, and these amendments demonstrate that the variability and flux of the imagination in the poem are features of the *imagination's* own narrative movement. The following lines make explicit what is implied throughout *The Prelude*, that the imagination has all along been the agent as well as the object of the poem:

> This faculty hath been the feeding source
> Of our long labour: we have traced the stream

From the blind cavern whence is faintly heard
Its natal murmur; followed it to light
And open day; accompanied its course
Among the ways of Nature, for a time
Lost sight of it bewildered and engulphed:
Then given it greeting as it rose once more
In strength, reflecting from its placid breast
The works of man and face of human life;
And lastly, from its progress have we drawn
Faith in life endless, the sustaining thought
Of human Being, Eternity, and God.
                    (XIV.193–205)

At the moment of poetic summary, a retrospective consideration of the poem's itinerary, the dual *narrative* function of the imagination comes to light: the imagination is both the "feeding source" or, as the 1805 text has it, the "moving soul" of the poem's "long labour," and simultaneously the "stream" itself, the winding "course" of the autobiography. Without the imagination the poem is inconceivable, though the poem is itself the "tracing" of this "faculty."[17] The poetic act of "tracing" reveals that the "feeding source" springs from the darkness of a "blind cavern" and by its treacherous course threatens to "bewilder and engulph" the poem itself. Once the course of the imagination is contained, and the threat of its deluge diminished, it rises "once more / In strength," "reflecting" from its now "placid breast / The works of man and face of human life." De Man has taught us to attend to such instances of face-giving and to recognize the trope, prosopopoeia, or the conferring of a face, as the trope of autobiography.[18] Here the "face of human life" appears in the "reflection" of the "stream" called imagination, and the trope of its appearance demonstrates that for Wordsworth as for Coleridge, the imagination is constituted by a self-reflection. *The Prelude*, in other words, is an autobiography because of the course taken by the "stream" of the imagination. "The works of man" appear in the same reflection, one that thus connects through the imagination the making of the subject to the activities and products of social history. The course of the imagination progresses beyond this reflection to, "lastly," "the sustaining thought / Of human Being, Eternity, and God." Though the imagination leads from the world of the subject and history to "Faith in life endless," this "sustaining thought" does not derive from the imagination itself or its reflection but is "drawn" from the imagination's "progress," from its narrative movement. The "sustaining *thought*" "Of human Being, Eternity, and God" is an effect of the narrative progress of the imagination generated by the poem itself; and thus "Faith in life endless" is postulated not through the existence of God but through the specular appearance of self and history in the stream of the imagination. It is an imagination that promises, as Wordsworth writes in Book XI, to "teach" "truth" (l. 45).

The rewriting and rerouting of the imagination is the object of Wordsworth's poetics of enshrinement. Taking Wordsworth's cues, we might describe enshrinement as making a "sublime" imagination into a source of "beauty." The work of enshrinement is visible in the earliest compositions, even in the course of a single episode. The celebrated account of the ascent of Snowdon in the 1805 text is one such instance. Ascending the mountain on "a close warm night" (1805, XIII.10) and "hemmed round on every side with fog and damp" (l. 16), the poet is struck suddenly by a flash of light. At that instant,

> I looked about, and lo,
> The moon stood naked in the heavens at height
> Immense above my head, and on the shore
> I found myself of a huge sea of mist,
> Which meek and silent rested at my feet.
> A hundred hills their dusky backs upheaved
> All over this still ocean, and beyond,
> Far, far beyond, the vapours shot themselves
> In headlands, tongues, and promontory shapes,
> Into the sea, the real sea, that seemed
> To dwindle and give up its majesty,
> Usurped upon as far as sight could reach.
>   (1805, XIII.40–51)

"Usurped" of its power by the "huge sea of mist," "the sea, the real sea" seems "to dwindle and give up its majesty" to the spectacular and uncontrollable transformations of "vapours." The lines conform to nothing so much as our understanding of the "sublime," as that poetic representation of "boundlessness," of a magnitude that, "great beyond all comparison," "usurps" the "majesty" of empirical objects. The passage recalls the earlier visitations the imagination makes in Book VI as an "unfathered vapour" that, as in these subsequent lines, has the effect of ungrounding the poet. "And we stood," the poet continues, "the mist / Touching our very feet" (ll. 53–54). At this point of surveying the unreal sea, this "huge sea of mist," a break occurs:

> And from the shore
> At distance not the third part of a mile
> Was a blue chasm, a fracture in the vapour,
> A deep and gloomy breathing-place, through which
> Mounted the roar of waters, torrents, streams
> Innumerable, roaring with one voice.
>   (1805, XIII.54–59)

Without cause or warning "a blue chasm" appears, "a fracture in the vapour," and by the fracture alone is the "roar" exhaled. The "majesty" "usurped" from empirical reality, from "the sea, the real sea," is transferred by means of the "chasm" or "fracture" to "one voice" caught in awful stutter: "the roar of waters, . . . / . . . roaring." For Wordsworth, the inarticulate roar, made by the "fracture in the vapour," "that dark deep thoroughfare," points to nothing less than "the soul, the imagination of the whole":

> The universal spectacle throughout
> Was shaped for admiration and delight,
> Grand in itself alone, but in that breach
> Through which the homeless voice of waters rose,
> That dark deep thoroughfare, had Nature lodged
> The soul, the imagination of the whole.
>   (1805, XIII.60–65)

The scene that yields "the imagination of the whole" is not the "universal spectacle" "shaped for admiration and delight"; it is rather "in that breach"—what Wordsworth in his revision calls the "rift"—that "Nature lodge[s] / The soul, the imagination of the whole."

I am interested in this untenable lodging of imagination, the "breach" or "rift" that "shapes" the spectacle *other* than for "admiration and delight." The lines declare that access to the "soul, the imagination of the whole" is achieved not through the majesties of the empirical world but through acts of usurpation elicited by the figures of "fracture," "chasm," "rift," "breach." The significance of the passage is more than formal, for the last figure in the series, the "breach," is itself a figure for political rupture and theological violation: a transgressive opening, a "usurpation," the "breach" recalls the original "breach disloyal," "revolt and disobedience" that in Milton is the source of man's Fall.[19]

The poem breaks off here. The lines that follow the hiatus narrate the poet's "meditation," the act of contemplative reflection, a "recollection in tranquility," which revises the spectacle of the sublime as a testimony to the workings of the imagination as a power of mind, "the glorious faculty" (l. 89), "the perfect image of a mighty mind" (l. 69). Nothing in the scene proposed that "the imagination of the whole" belonged to the mind or could be so interiorized: the effects of a "breach" must be revised subsequently as a dedication to "the glorious faculty." "When the scene / Ha[s] passed away," "the perfect image of a mighty mind" takes its place. The philosophical meditation, chronologically subsequent, serves as a sort of "reaction-formation," the revisionary substitution of that poetic scene. This "meditation," already begun in 1805, characterizes the course of the poem's revisions until, in the last versions, the scene proceeds "with fit reverence" far from any "breach disloyal" to the pious application of "the words of Holy Writ" (XIV.125). By the meditation, imagination is "preserved, enlarged" (l. 121) and made the vehicle of a "genuine liberty" of the self (l. 122). The "preservation" and "enlargement"—or enshrinement—of a liberating imagination is created by the effacement of its antagonistic appearance "in the breach." The revisionary course of meditation enshrines the imagination in the poem's conclusive definitions of the faculty as

> another name for absolute power
> And clearest insight, amplitude of mind,
> And Reason in her most exalted mood.
> (XIV.190–92)

The pattern of enshrinement I am describing in *The Prelude* is not limited to the structure of specific scenes; it extends to the poem's dom-

inant images, most notably that of the "river." The image of the river
invites the promise of organic continuity and manufactures the illusion
of an unbroken passage from "love of nature leading to love of man."
The image of the river might thus appear to fill the "wide" "vacancy"
between the past and present and thereby dispel the troubling discrepancy between the two subjects or, as Wordsworth refers to them, the
"two consciousnesses" of autobiography:

> so wide appears
> The vacancy between me and those days,
> which yet have such self-presence in my mind,
> That musing on them, often do I seem
> Two consciousnesses, conscious of myself
> And of some other Being.
>
> (II.28–33)[20]

But the poem's images of the river often refuse the comforting sense of
continuity the river seems to promise: the recurrent and irreducible
difference of present and past in the poem is refigured by the image of
the river into an inability to fix origins, to assign sources:

> Who knows the individual hour in which
> His habits were first sown, even as a seed?
> Who that shall point as with a wand and say
> "This portion of the river of my mind
> Come from yon fountain?"
>
> (II.206–10)

In these two questions, the organic and temporal image of the "seed"
and its growth is displaced by the *spatial* images of the river and its
source. The organic phrasing of the earlier question is rewritten such
that the possibility of continuity dissolves. The image of the river in
the poem insistently raises questions of origins, inviting an understanding that the river's currents might connect past with present, only
to block such a passage, and prevent the resolution promised by organic models of continuity. The unavailability of any real sense of continuity, the impossibility of assigning origins, an impossibility learned
through the very act of recollection, make the prospect of "analysing

the soul" a "hard task" (II.232, 237) and make the work of enshrinement necessary.

The primary temporal motion of a river is not, moreover, from a
stable present to a past; the image of a river raises the prospect of a future, of a point toward which the currents flow. As it is figured in *The
Prelude*, the image of the river thus marks internally the disconsonance
between the progressive movement of narrative and the retrospective
force of memory. This disconsonance is registered in the opening lines
of Book IX:

> Even as a river—partly (it might seem)
> Yielding to old remembrances, and swayed
> In part by fear to shape a way direct,
> That would engulph him soon in the ravenous sea—
> Turns, and will measure back his course, far back,
> Seeking the very regions which he crossed
> In his first outset; so have we, my friend!
> Turned and returned with intricate delay.
>
> (IX.1–8)

The lines introduce a very different motivation for the role of memory
in the poem than the desire to restore continuity with the past.
"Swayed / In part by fear to shape a way direct," the narrative digresses
and diverts, postponing its encounter with the "ravenous sea." In any
autobiography the narrative dynamics that propel the story forward lead
to death; only by turning and returning "with intricate delay," only by
seeking again through memory "the very regions" "crossed" can the
poem manufacture the illusion of postponement. A circuit of images—
fountain, stream, river, sea—establishes the vocabulary of autobiography: from "fountain" to "ravenous sea," the narrative trajectory of *The
Prelude* is formed by the textual relation between two non-narratable
points. This is how the poem speaks of a condition inherent in autobiographical discourse: shuttling between "old remembrances" and "the
ravenous sea," poetic memory keeps death at bay.[21]

The trajectory of the autobiography is further complicated by the
fact that Wordsworth's life story is directed by the tracking of the imagination and intersected by the public history of the French Revolu-

tion. Moreover, the stories of poet, imagination, and revolution are all produced through the same circuit of images. The narrative "streams" of poet and imagination cross and are crossed by the threatening convulsions or "deluge" of the French Revolution. Deluge is not, of course, the only image used in the poem to depict the Revolution. In the stream of revolutionary events, as Wordsworth writes in *The Excursion*, his "troubled mind" "in a struggling and distempered world / Saw a seductive image of herself."[22] But this "seductive"—and gendered—specular identification must be resisted since the stream leads inexorably, as Wordsworth writes in *The Prelude*, to those "engulphing" rivers: a "river of Blood," a "deluge" spread "through the land" (X.480, 584).[23] Only his stabilizing return to "The tranquil shores / Of Britain" prevents Wordsworth from becoming implicated in "the exasperation of that Land" (*Excursion*, III.817):[24]

> The tranquil shores
> Of Britain circumscribed me; else, perhaps
> I might have been entangled among deeds,
> Which, now, as infamous, I should abhor—
> Despise, as senseless.
> (*Excursion*, III.812–16)

The return to the sure footing of the homeland prevents Wordsworth from becoming "entangled" in the "deeds" and "deluge" of revolution and prompts the poetic work of enshrinement.[25]

Recollection, by the "intricate delay" of its turning and returnings, would turn deeds into narratives that encase the past, thereby preserving the past from "deluge" and "ravenous sea" alike. Such is the internalizing form of recollection that Hegel calls *Erinnerung* and that I have described as enshrining, a recollection that removes experience from the order of deeds, stores and preserves it as memory. Safely enshrined, the spirit of the past might thus elude the ravages of time, what Wordsworth calls the "ravenous sea." It is the same transformative power of recollection, memory as a "creative force," that Georg Lukács identifies as the distinctive feature of "the Romanticism of Disillusionment": "Only in the novel and in certain epic forms resembling the novel does memory occur as a creative force affecting the object and transforming it. . . . The duality of interiority and the outside world can be abolished for the subject if he (the subject) glimpses the organic unity of his whole life through the process by which his living present has grown from the stream of his past life dammed up within his memory" (*Theory of the Novel*, 127). When Lukács refers to "certain epic forms resembling the novel," he could be describing *The Prelude*, a pseudo-epic that discards traditional epic themes for the distinctively novelistic story of an individual life narrated through memory. "The surmounting of duality," Lukács goes on to say, "makes this experience into an element of authentically epic form," for the persistent "duality of interiority and the outside world" is never surmounted. Though Wordsworth may well have dedicated the poem to the effort to glimpse "the organic unity of his whole life through the process by which his living present has grown from the stream of his past life" (and the language of the subtitle appended to the poem suggests that desire), the poem demonstrates that the inescapable "damming up" of memory blocks the poet's desire to see his life as an "organic unity." That blockage is not cleared in the poem, but it is the task of enshrinement to recast the inevitably discontinuous "internal thoughts," and to lodge them in a shrine that, by gathering and preserving, would make them available for "future restoration."

Shrine of Poetry, Tomb of the Other: The Dream of the Arab

For the imagination to be enshrined in *The Prelude*, it must pass through the dream of a desert wilderness, the apocalyptic "dream of the Arab" in Book V. In the book of the poem devoted to books and in the long dream sequence that opens it, the question of "internal thought" and its proper enshrinement provokes considerations of the formation of English and European cultural traditions and of the historical relation of these traditions to Europe's Others. The dream, in other words, introduces into the poem a new question of ideological value and power, one that again links it to Hegel. Moreover, if we accept Geoffrey Hartman's interpretation that "the dream is sent by imag-

ination to lead the poet to recognize its power," then the consequences
of the dream are considerable for the shape of the imagination and for
the fate of the autobiography.[26]

The dream is prefaced by Wordsworth's lament over the irreconcilability between the "deathless spirit" of the "meditations of mankind" and the frailty and impermanence of their material embodiment
as inscriptions in books:

> Oh! why hath not the Mind
> Some element to stamp her image on
> In nature somewhat nearer to her own?
> Why, gifted with such powers to send abroad
> Her spirit, must it lodge in shrines so frail?
>
>   (V.45–49)

Wordsworth does not condemn writing as the material contamination
of thought; he recognizes that the mind cannot go it alone, cannot
"send abroad" its powers without "some element to stamp her image
on / In nature." However, all forms of inscription or recording are incommensurate with the powers of the mind because, unlike "deathless spirit," matter must inevitably decay. The nonaffinity bemoaned by
Wordsworth between the products of mind and their material and mortal "lodgings" is another name for what we have called the persistence
of ideology. The scene of this ideological nonaffinity is the condition
faced by the imagination, shuttling between subject and object, between an assertion of the mind's power over the external world and
the visitation of a power over which the mind exercises no control. If
these powers of mind are indeed what Wordsworth has in mind as the
imagination, they are nonetheless at the mercy of their objectification
by "frail," worldly "shrines."

The dream is precipitated by the "sea-side" reading of *Don Qui-*
xote. After closing the book, Wordsworth muses on poetry and geo-
metric truth and their exemption from "all internal injury" until, seized
by sleep, he passes into a dream in which he finds himself on "a bound-
less plain / Of sandy wilderness, all black and void" (V.65, 67, 71–72).
Distress over his predicament is suspended temporarily when "an un-
couth shape" appears who seems to be "an Arab of the Bedouin tribes"

(l. 77). The "new-comer" bears with him a stone and a shell which, "To give it in the language of the dream," turn out to be the "books" of geometry and poetry (l. 87). The Arab presents the shell-book of poetry to the dreamer, "commanding" him to listen to its song. What Wordsworth hears "in an unknown tongue" that he nonetheless "understands" is

> A loud prophetic blast of harmony;
> An ode, in passion uttered, which foretold
> Destruction to the children of the earth
> By deluge, now at hand.   (V.93, 95–98)

The Arab confirms this interpretation, declaring "with calm look" that what had been prophesied would "come to pass" (V.99, 100). After proclaiming it his mission to bury the books, the Arab rides on to fulfill the "errand."

Once Wordsworth has learned the message of the prophecy, his attention turns again to the figure of the Arab, who, as the dream unfolds, undergoes a series of transformations. The first appearance of the Arab is greeted by Wordsworth as a sign of hope:

> At the sight
> Much I rejoiced, not doubting but a guide
> Was present, one who with unerring skill
> Would through the desert lead me.   (V.80–83)

Wordsworth's certainty is soon dispelled, however, as it becomes clear that the Arab will not perform the duties of a "guide" who will lead the dreamer through the desert of his dream. The Arab's message of an imminent apocalypse only renews Wordsworth's fear. Having functioned as a sign of hope and a source of fear, the Arab, as he prepares to depart, becomes the object of Wordsworth's desire: "Far stronger, now, grew the desire I felt / To cleave unto this man" (V.115–16). In the 1805 text, the fear itself "engenders" this desire:

> A wish was now engendered in my fear
> To cleave unto this man, and I begged leave
> To share his errand with him.   (1805, V.115–17)

The Arab rides on, however, frozen by the dream beyond Wordsworth's reach. The transformations of the Arab continue when in subsequent lines he becomes

> the knight
> Whose tale Cervantes tells; yet not the knight,
> But was an Arab of the desert too;
> Of these was neither, and was both at once.
>   (V.122–25)

As this "semi-Quixote," this "Arab phantom," points to the impending deluge, to "the fleet waters of a drowning world" prophesied by the apocalyptic ode, Wordsworth awakes in "terror" (V.142, 143, 137, 138).

Considerable critical attention over the years has been devoted to discovering the source of the dream. It has been traced to Descartes and his famous "three-fold dream," though other sources and agents have been suggested, most notably Coleridge, Pope, Ovid, and, of course, Cervantes.[27] I am, however, less interested in determining the source of the dream than in noting that readers of the dream have found it to be something of a shrine to the European cultural tradition. At the same time, the long and distinguished history of commentary and interpretation seems not to have remarked that the stone and the shell, symbols in the dream of the heritage of Western civilization, have passed into the hands of an "Oriental" figure, "an Arab of the Bedouin tribes."[28]

The shell-book, "of more worth" according to the Arab than the stone-book of "Euclid's Elements," is a divine object, possessing poetic "voices more than all the winds." The Arab declares the book to be "a god":

> a god, yea many gods,
> Had voices more than all the winds, with power
> To exhilarate the spirit, and to soothe,
> Through every clime, the heart of human kind.
>   (V.106–9)

The shell bears the inscription of all the voices of poetry. This is more explicit in the 1805 text, where the book is said to be composed of "A joy, a consolation, and a hope," poetic forms that correspond, respectively, to the temporal registers of present, past, and future (1805, V.109). The "loud prophetic blast of harmony" produced by the shell, however, belongs to none of those registers, nor speaks of those emotions.[29] As a prophecy, the ode would be expected to give voice to the future, linking private interior meditations and recollections to the pronouncements of public histories.

But the apocalyptic ode, carried and confirmed by the Arab stranger, bears no trace of the future or sign of redemption: it prophecies only the cancellation of prophecy, the effacement of history itself. Nor does the ode belong to any of those English poetic voices invoked throughout *The Prelude*: it is uttered instead "in an unknown tongue," which our English dreamer nonetheless understands. Within the space of the dream, ignorance of a linguistic structure in no way prevents an "understanding" that exceeds the limits of linguistic knowledge.[30] It is an understanding, however, that secures nothing but a fleeting glimpse of history's apocalyptic annihilation. In Book VIII, Wordsworth, writing of his youth, says that he sought the evidence of a historical "spirit / Diffused through time and space" that can be recovered from "the widely scattered wreck sublime / Of vanished nations" (ll. 610–11, 614–15). It is possible, in other words, to redeem "the spirit of the past" deposited in the ruins of "vanished nations"; such a method offers a model for historical knowledge.[31] No such knowledge is achieved through the song of the shell, however, which prophecies only deluge. In *Essays upon Epitaphs* Wordsworth refers to the "deluge" as "the most tremendous event in the history of the Planet," and thus its prophesied return promises only the erasure of all signs of "wreck sublime" that provide the decipherable tracks of history (*Literary Criticism*, 141). Moreover, the deluge issues not from nature but from myth; it is a deluge that exists only "as it is written," as it is inscribed in the voices of the shell. And it remains only the image of an apocalypse "evermore about to be": the prophecy goes unfulfilled, frozen in the dream at the very moment of its realization.

Though the Arab's declaration that he was "going then to bury those two books" has often been interpreted as the promise of their preservation, there is no evidence that the burial implies anything more than interment in an unmarked grave.[32] Nothing indicates that these "meditations of mankind" will find "shrines" adequate for their preservation. Once the images of the Stone and the Shell are condensed with the image of the Book, the promise of burial signifies only that they will not escape the fate destined to befall any "Poor earthly casket of immortal verse" (V.154). In the fire that consumes Don Quixote's library, even the books "which should have been preserved in everlasting archives" go up in smoke.[33] In Wordsworth's dream of the Arab, no "everlasting archive" or sheltering crypt or lettered stone appears that might preserve the spirit of these books from the deluge or give them voice beyond the grave.[34] This is burial without epitaph, an entombment without the monument and inscription that would guard such cultural remains or preserve their memory.[35]

The dream itself might be understood to perform the work of the crypt, enclosing the narrative of the Other, containing its apocalyptic prophecy, and thereby preserving the life story of the spirit. We shall have the opportunity to consider how the text preserves the poet's story and how, by refiguring the appearance of this Otherness, it binds that life story to the cultural tradition. But even within the space of the dream, the status of the Arab Other is unstable, sliding from a source of fear to the object of desire. This desire, like the prophecy itself, goes unfulfilled: "He left me: I called after him aloud; / He heeded not" (V.133–34). The Arab "hurries on" to his "enterprise" and remains the lost object of the Western dreamer's desire. The lost object is partially recovered in the dream's next stage through the condensation that merges the images of Don Quixote and the Arab: Quixote, and yet not Quixote but "an Arab of the desert too; / Of these was neither, and was both at once" (V.124–25). These celebrated lines represent an exemplary instance of the imagination's power, as Wordsworth describes it, "of consolidating numbers into unity, and dissolving and separating unity into number."[36]

The logic of Wordsworth's dream-text, the double movement of consolidation and dissolution that the poet calls the imagination, reveals how figures of the Other are preserved in the structures of European monuments of cultural self-representation, such as *The Prelude*.[37]

We discover that the subject in his pursuit of the Other is, in Lacan's words, "already pursuing more than half of himself."[38] Without noting the role of Otherness in the dream, Hartman identifies the Arab, what he calls this "desert-shape," as the direct envoy of "Imagination."[39] But if the "Oriental irruption" and the deluge it prophecies threaten like "an unfathered vapour" the narrative movement of the poem or even the history of European civilization, the poem stages a series of interpretations that, beginning during the dream itself and continuing through the epilogue to the dream, set in motion a process of identification and appropriation—a process of enshrinement—which empties the Arab figure of his Otherness.

As the narrative passes from the dream into its commentary in the epilogue, a refiguring of the dream begins and the Other recedes, becoming an inaccessible "Arab phantom" at the very point the image is endowed with "substance":

> Full often, taking from the world of sleep
> This Arab phantom, which I thus beheld,
> This semi-Quixote, I to him have given
> A substance, fancied him a living man,
> A gentle dweller in the desert, crazed
> By love and feeling, and internal thought
> Protracted among endless solitudes;
> Have shaped him wandering upon this quest!
>   (V.141–48)

As Wordsworth has "shaped him," we recognize in the "gentle dweller" "crazed / By love and feeling, and internal thought" considerably less of the now "phantom" Other than of the culturally certified figure of Cervantes's knight. By "taking from the world of sleep / This Arab phantom," the poem carries out its conversion of the radical and threatening Otherness, recasting it in the form of a familiar European narrative. In the waking hours, the memory of a future deluge has disappeared and the surfacing of the Other is rewritten, once again, as a sign of "internal thought."

Wordsworth's dream of the Arab is both preceded and followed by memories of Cervantes, a figure whose appearance should come as little surprise in a poem about the work of memory and imagination, about "internal thought" and its engagements with and withdrawals from the "o'erpressure of the times." According to Lukács, for instance, Cervantes's novel must be regarded as the first scene of this drama of interiorization, the "first great battle of interiority against the prosaic vulgarity of outward life" (*Theory of the Novel*, 104). Lukács locates in *Don Quixote* the earliest and most pronounced narrative expression of the decisive "historico-philosophical" rupture between an interior subjectivity and an exterior world. "The extensive totality of life is no longer given" in *Don Quixote*; "the immanence of meaning in life has become a problem" (56). The consequences for narrative form are considerable when "the basis of all the hero's adventures was his inner certainty and the world's inadequate attitude towards it" (110). We recognize in the decisive disjunction between self and world foregrounded by *Don Quixote* the condition of language: the discrepancy between self and world is a displacement of the discrepancy between word and thing, a discrepancy that is the condition of signification and that simultaneously generates unavoidable errors of interpretation.

J. Hillis Miller remarks that it is "no accident that Wordsworth's dreamer has been reading *Don Quixote* before he falls asleep."[40] Nor is it an accident that such a notorious misreader as Don Quixote appears in a chapter titled "Books," for it is the "famous gentleman's" "habit of reading books of chivalry" that gives rise to "the strangest idea that ever occurred to any madman in the world." Quixote's mission, which he conceives of in explicitly patriotic terms, is "to become a knight-errant and roam the world on horseback, in a suit of armor; he would go in quest of adventures, by way of putting into practice all that he read in his books" (*Don Quixote*, 27). Quixote's adventures result from his consistent failures to put his reading into action: the narrative can be said to be produced by errant translations of theory into practice.

These problems of translation should influence any reading of the novel: we recall, for instance, that the narrator purports the novel to be a translation of an Arabic manuscript, *History of Don Quixote de la Mancha by Cid Hamete Benegali, Arabic Historian*. The scene of the Arabic manuscript's discovery in the Toledo marketplace, argues Ramón Saldívar, "turns the telling of Don Quijote's adventure into a story about the narration of *Don Quijote*, and is the circumstance that first calls attention to the synchronic reading in the novel."[41] It is also the circumstance that first calls attention to the inscription of the Arab drama at the heart of the novel's story and discourse. For though the narrator asserts the authenticity of the manuscript, and though all subsequent reading is based on this text, he nonetheless acknowledges that one "legitimate" objection can be "raised against the veracity" of the manuscript: "the author was an Arab, and that nation is known for its lying propensities" (73). Suspicions regarding the veracity of the manuscript are never altogether dispelled; and they continue to shadow any reading of the novel. Consequently, *Don Quixote*, the text that has come to be regarded as the first properly European novel, presents itself as the questionable translation of an Arabic text. This problem of translation is emblematic of a fundamental narrative instability in *Don Quixote* that, as Saldívar argues, makes it impossible to fix the grounds of interpretation.[42] The interpretive instability and the representation of an internal Arab Otherness are intertwined and transferred through Wordsworth's reading of the novel to Book V of *The Prelude* and reinscribed there in an apocalyptic dream. The particular form the narrative instability takes in both texts is occasioned by the eruptions of disturbing figures of Otherness. We are only beginning to learn how to read the inscriptions of such Otherness, to understand how Otherness, as it is figured in narratives such as *The Prelude*, serves ultimately to consolidate a sense of European cultural identity.[43]

Miguel de Cervantes's *Don Quixote* was published as Spain, the first of the modern European absolutist state, struggled to consolidate its control of the Iberian peninsula. This political and cultural consolidation of the nation came to a head in 1609 when Philip III expelled from Spain all unconverted Muslims of Arab and Berber descent.[44] By 1614, the year before the publication of the second volume of *Don Quixote*, more than 300,000 *moriscos* had been expelled. The expulsion, purging the residual elements of centuries of Islamic cultural and political control over the peninsula, has long been recognized as a constitutive act of the Spanish nation and as an ideological condition for the institution of the modern European state.[45] Modern Spain, as an identifiable (if unstable) cultural, geographic and linguistic object, derives its coherence from the expulsion. In the words of historian Américo Castro, "the adjective 'Spanish' (*español*)" cannot be assigned to Iberians prior to the coming of the Moors.[46] "Prior to the Moorish invasion," writes Castro, "the inhabitants of the peninsula are not situated in the life structure that has been manifest from the year 1000 til today" (*Spanish History*, 54). It cannot therefore be said "that Christian Spain had been a given and fixed entity upon which fell the cloak of Moorish language, literature, and institutions"; rather, what Castro, following Dilthey, calls the "awareness of social community" or "national feeling" is created by the Moorish expulsion (82, 44). What distinguishes Arab from Spaniard according to Castro's Hegelian and deeply Orientalist account is the ostensible absence in the "Arab's vital interests" of a model of internal thought, of a fundamental disposition towards an interior "dwelling-place": "The direction of the Arab's vital interest impelled him to express himself in the objects exterior to him. . . . In the Spaniard, the direction of vital dynamism was from object to person, since that was the nature of the reality of his 'dwelling-place'" (252). What produces the "historical cleavage" that makes expulsion unavoidable is thus the *perceived* absence in the Muslim "world" of precisely the form of Western subjectivity evident in the cultural tradition that links *Don Quixote* to *The Prelude*.

The expulsion has long been understood as indispensable for the coherence of a Western identity, for a properly Christian and European "spirit of community." In the *Aesthetics*, for instance, Hegel regards the expulsion as the condition for the fulfillment of Romanticism's historical mission: "The romantic world had only one absolute work to complete, the spread of Christianity and the continued activity of the spirit of community. . . . The further act, related to the like end is . . . the expulsion of the Moors, the Arabs, Mohammedans in general, from Christian countries" (*Aesthetics*, 587). According to the Hegelian itinerary of the spirit, Romanticism is the consolidation of a European community predicated on the expulsion of the Oriental Other. In the more restricted and canonical periodization of Romanticism, in which Hegel's *Aesthetics* is itself a major theoretical document, such historical consideration of and justification for the violent expulsion of the Muslim Other coincides with the advent of European Orientalist discourse. The question of the relationship between Orientalism and Romanticism is raised by Raymond Schwab in his magisterial study of "the Oriental Renaissance." "Suddenly emerging in the nineteenth century as a sign of separation," Schwab asks, "was Romanticism itself anything other than an Oriental irruption of the intellect?"[47] It is my argument that any reading of the "Oriental irruption" in *The Prelude* known as the dream of the Arab must recognize that the figure of the Oriental Other is not contingent but structurally indispensable to the story of self-consolidation told by this exemplary Romantic text. Or as Schwab argues, "the relation between the Orient and Romanticism is less a local and temporal one than an essential one."[48]

Schwab's scholarship is devoted to reestablishing the extensive historical legacy of Oriental sources and images, and not to the principles of European representation that require and produce the "Orient" in the first place. It is one thing to assert that Orientalism is a recurrent feature of Romantic poetry, quite another to demonstrate that Orientalism, the production and management of a Western discourse of knowledge about the "Orient," might well be the effect of a Romanticism that secures visions of itself by looking to an "Orient" of its own making. In Hegel, for instance, Romantic art comes to find in the symbolic art of the Orient images of its own condition. As Rodolphe Gasché has argued in his reading of the *Aesthetics*, Romantic art, "at the moment of its dissolution, is characterized by a return to Oriental pre-art."[49] In order to tell Hegel's story of "the liberation of subjectivity," Romanticism gazes upon the Orient and sees there the mirror image of its own dissolution.

Which is not to say that Wordsworth adhered to or even knew of Hegel's Orientalism. To read Wordsworth alongside Hegel in this regard is to recognize a certain necessity shared by both: their philosophical and poetic productions of self and community can be written only by way of the figures of an Oriental Otherness. Nor does the Wordsworthian "dream" exhaust the possible modes of such "Oriental irruptions" in Romanticism, as the more radically politicized (if more exoticized) "Orientalisms" of Byron or Shelley attest. Wordsworth's staging of the "dream of the Arab" does allude to the historical role played by Spain in the drama of European and, more specifically, English cultural self-representation. The persistent ideological purchase of the rift between

English and Spanish national and imperial projects and the historical formation of Spain as the double site of Islamic and Western culture, a doubleness monumentalized in *Don Quixote*, are the discursive conditions of the Wordsworthian theater of the imagination.

The Romantic relation to the Orient is introduced into the heart of Wordsworth's "internal thought" through his reading of Cervantes and his dream of the Arab. Appearing in the crypt of the dream, the story of the Arab opens the dialectics of internalization to a more elaborate economy, one that implicates the narratives of global expansion, the acquisitions of empire, and the consolidation of European nation-states. We discern the lineaments of such an economy in the lines subsequent to the dream when the figure of the Arab gives way to an emphatic invocation of the tradition of English poetry. As Wordsworth recounts his sense of identification with the "maniac" of his dream, he continues to empty the figure of its Otherness and embarks on an interpretation of the dream that affirms, in the wake of his apocalyptic nightmare, the "divinity" and "immortality" of Shakespeare and Milton. "Contemplating in soberness the approach / Of an event so dire, / by signs in earth / Or heaven made manifest," Wordsworth says that he

> could share
> That maniac's fond anxiety, and go
> Upon like errand. Oftentimes at least
> Me hath such strong entrancement overcome,
> When I had held a volume in my hand,
> Poor earthly casket of immortal verse,
> Shakespeare, or Milton, labourers divine!
> (V.157–65)

These lines, which conclude the episode, reroute the dream, burying the last signs of Otherness and reasserting a cultural history that bestows upon Wordsworth his poetic authority and guarantees his place in the shrine of English literature.

Though the dream and the effects of its "terror" would appear to have receded as the poem assumes its celebratory voice, memories of the dream persist, inscribed in the form of rhapsodic memorials to the history of Western literature. Although he makes no further reference to the dream, Wordsworth later in Book V speaks with such urgency to the "memory of all books" that we can only read these lines as an epitaph for the "earthly casket" of "labourers divine":

> Yet it is just
> That here, in memory of all books which lay
> Their sure foundations in the heart of man,
> Whether by native prose, or numerous verse,
> That in the name of all inspired souls,
> From Homer the great Thunderer, from the voice
> That roars along the bed of Jewish song,
> And that more varied and elaborate,
> Those trumpet-tones of harmony that shake
> Our shores in England,—from those loftiest notes
> Down to the low and wren-like warblings,
>
>   . . .
>
> 'Tis just that in behalf of these, the works,
> And of the men that framed them, whether known,
> Or sleeping nameless in scattered graves,
> That I should here assert their rights, attest
> Their honours, and should, once and for all, pronounce
> Their benediction; speak of them as Powers
> For ever to be hallowed.   (V.197–207, 213–19)

As the lines perform their act of "benediction," they become a memorial to the shell-book of poetry that appeared in the dream of the Arab. Much of *The Prelude* is devoted to such forms of "benediction," to the preservation of the "hallowed" names of poetry. The poem itself serves to assure "Fit reverence for the glorious Dead," as the books of the poem become "Sacred catacombs, / Where mighty minds lie visibly entombed" (III.340–42). But the acts of benediction not only "affirm" the "honours" due to a library of books, they enshrine and preserve the historical narrative engraved in the cultural tradition. The narrative, what we might call Wordsworth's history of the spirit of literature, passes from Homer's Greece through the world of the Old Testament and culminates, not surprisingly, on the shores of England. We may therefore read Book V of *The Prelude*, the book of "Books," as an epitaph for the "hallowed" "Powers" of literature and, at the same time, as the enshrinement of English culture and history. The dream of the

Arab both introduces the apocalyptic vision of "Destruction to the children of the earth / By deluge" and engenders an interpretation that, forgetting the visitation of Otherness, preserves the "sacred" tradition. By forgetting the dream of the Arab and recollecting this tradition, Wordsworth can move from entombment to enshrinement and begin to dream of home, to dream of England.

"England's Dreaming!"

The proper names that belong to the shrine—Chaucer, Spenser, Shakespeare, Milton—punctuate the poem, encasing the "growth of a poet's mind" in the frame of a national literary history. At decisive moments in the poetic record of his aesthetic and ideological education, Wordsworth asserts his direct kinship with the "visionary company" of English poetry, a company he conceives of as prophetic. Through an "animating faith," Wordsworth writes in Book XIII, he holds the conviction that "Poets, even as Prophets, each with each / [are] Connected in a mighty scheme of truth" (*The Prelude*, XIII.300–302). Another name for the "mighty scheme of truth" that binds together this chain of celebrated names is the imagination: it grants the poet access to the "visionary company" and produces prophetic visions, not of apocalyptic deluge but of the history of a nation. In the reverie of Sarum Plain, which follows his declaration of kinship, Wordsworth recounts such a historical vision, the nationalist obverse to his dream of the Arab. The new vision of a "Desert," like its counterpart in Book V, is prefaced by meditations on the history of poetry and appears at a moment of isolation. In the 1805 text, the vision of the past seems to erupt from the very weight of the poet's "solitude": "by the solitude o'ercome, / I had a reverie and saw the past" (1805, XII.318–20). The past he sees, in this and later versions of the passage, is a "dim ancestral Past":

> Time with his retinue of ages fled
> Backwards, nor checked his flight until I saw
> Our dim ancestral Past in vision.
> (XIII.318–20)

As the poet gazes unchecked through time with "vision clear," he sees in this "dim ancestral Past" aboriginal figures of Englishness, a Druidian world of "monumental hillocks" and "sacrificial altars" (XIII.334, 331). He sees

> multitudes of men, and, here and there,
> A single Briton clothed in wolf-skin vest,
> With shield and stone-axe, stride across the wold.
> (XIII.321–23)

With his own two-fold charge, the "single Briton," which as Gayatri Spivak argues is both a "*subject*-representative" and the "*object* of Wordsworth's attentive reverie," lends to the poem its proper figure of identification and consolidates the dream as a mythical vision of England.[50]

Both the memory of "A single Briton" from England's "ancestral Past" and the "visionary company" of English poetry that preserves such memories are encrypted in the nationalist language of cultural heritage. The poem demands that we consider how the formation of an English poet and the enshrinement of the poetic imagination are implicated with the cultural and political fate of the nation. But as in the case of the "dream of the Arab," the enshrinements of "imagination" or "spirit" or "nation" in *The Prelude* are formed through recalcitrant and alien material. In Book VIII, for instance, Wordsworth concludes a long recollection of a sighting of London with lines that honor England's cultural and political ascension as a world power. The poet declares that he is

> moved,
> In the presence of that vast metropolis,
> The fountain of my country's destiny
> And of the destiny of earth itself.
> (VIII.746–48)

Nothing in the lines that lead to the declaration would predict such an outcome. The sequence opens with an account of the poet's approach to the "great city" in an "itinerant vehicle" when he is suddenly struck in "a moments pause" (1805, VIII.694–95, 707):

> That aught *external* to the living mind
> Should have such mighty sway, yet so it was:
> A weight of ages did at once descend
> Upon my heart—no thought embodied, no

> Distinct remembrances, but weight and power,
> Power growing with the weight.
>   (1805, VIII.701–6)

The city is registered, according to this recollection, as nothing but
"weight and power, / Power growing with the weight," as that which
we, following Kant, might call the "dynamic sublime." Retrospectively,
the "blank sense of greatness passed away," the empty but sublime moment is restaged as a spectacle. "As when a traveller hath from open
day / With torches passed into some vault of earth" (1805, VIII.711–
12), the poet transforms the "blank sense" into a scene, a "pageant."
Here what is first encountered as a "senseless mass" of "shapes, and
forms, and tendencies to shape, / That shift and vanish, change and interchange" (ll. 731, 721–22), is "beheld" after a "pause" (l. 728) as a
"picture of the world" (l. 737). The "picture" produced here belongs,
once again, to the dream of a nation, to the memory of England's "ancestral past":

> forests and lakes,
> Ships, rivers, towers, the warrior clad in mail,
> The prancing steed, the pilgrim with his staff,
> The mitered bishop and the throned king—
> A spectacle to which there is no end.
>   (1805, VIII.737–41)

The early unsettling moment of sublimity is restaged here as a Spenser-
ian "spectacle to which there is no end" and that, thus monumentalized, confirms the triumphant story of England as "destiny of earth itself": a "blank sense of greatness passed away" is filled in by the spectacle of England's majesty.[51] The episode demonstrates the means by
which, as Edward Said describes it, England is rewritten "within a
much larger circle of the world map": we can read in this poetic restaging the cultural and ideological conditions for empire.[52] It is this process
that prompts the reference in the heading above to The Sex Pistols'
"Anarchy in the U.K.": "*England's* dreaming!" Johnny Rotten's sneering
derision of England's self-delusion can also be taken, in a quieter mode
and without Rotten's contempt, to describe what happens in *The Prelude,* for it is as if England itself is dreaming its imperial dream, one

that however mystified certainly bears considerable worldly consequences.

The literary destiny of the poet to join in the "mighty scheme of truth," to become England's poet-prophet, is linked directly to a national destiny that is itself staged as the very "fountain" of world destiny. In this light, the names of Chaucer, Spenser, Shakespeare, Milton, and, now, Wordsworth, not only serve as the touchstones of the English literary tradition but become markers, even agents, of a powerful ideological narrative of "Englishness," a narrative whose cultural and political effects are far from exhausted.

If the condition of thought that we, following Hegel, call Romanticism has rendered enigmatic the relationship between self and world, Wordsworth's story of the imagination allows us to interpret the relationship as another narrative, as the circuitous passage from "internal thought" to "love of mankind," a passage that would bind subject with society. *The Prelude* tells us that such a passage from the private interior space of subjective meditation and recollection to the public space of national political and cultural history can be secured only through the enshrinement of the imagination. But the poetic activity of enshrinement, preserving the spirit of the imagination for "future restoration," cannot be separated in Wordsworth's poetry from acts of entombment, markings of the dead. If *The Prelude* records the enshrinement of imagination, and if in the traditions of literary and cultural history the poem has itself become a shrine to the imagination, we may also read the poem's disclosures of the historical entombments—of Otherness, of revolution, of sublimity—engraved in this Romantic shrine.

CHAPTER 3

SHELLEY

The Ends of Imagination, the "Triumph" of Ideology

From the "Education of Error" to an "Epistemological Break"

When Shelley turns to the imagination, it is not as "another name for absolute strength of Mind" or as a "repetition in the finite mind of the infinite I AM" but rather, in *Epipsychidion* for instance, as a "reverberated lightning" that "As from a thousand prisms and mirrors, fills / The Universe with glorious beams, and kills / Error."[1] The Wordsworthian strain in Shelley's poetry is important and well-chronicled, but one aspect of the inheritance that Shelley resists from the outset is the religiosity present in the elder poet's sense of the imagination as a reverential "enshrining." The imagination in Shelley is best understood as the agent of a radical historical "legislation." He conceives of the imagination as the source of an explosive illumination that liberates us from the imposed darkness of theological and political ideology, releases us from "false consciousness" to the *process* of historical truth-making.[2] The Shelleyan imagination thus works in the interest not of enshrining what Wordsworth would call the singular "Mighty scheme of Truth" but of legislating what Shelley in *Epipsychidion* identifies as the plurality of "many truths." The corrosive and performative power of the poetic imagination is enlisted to inform "an education of error," an education that undertakes the destruction of "error" and "the roots of error."

A Defence of Poetry makes this case for the imagination: poetry, conceived in its broadest sense, is another name for the process of demystification in social and political history as in literary culture. The imagination can conduct such an activity because poetic language and social history are inextricable for Shelley, and the connections he describes unsettle the presumed boundaries of both: much of the *Defence* is devoted to restoring an understanding of the historical effectivity of poetry. Poetic language is treated throughout the essay as a material force of worldly legislation in a history understood as the strife-ridden and discontinuous confrontation of cultural and social forces. Shelley stakes the success of his *political* defense of poetry on the articulation of language and history, an articulation produced through the transformative agency of imagination. Shelley's expansion of the concept of poetry is thus indispensable to his ambitious project in *A Defence of Poetry*. In "a general sense" poetry is for Shelley the imagination's historical legislation: poetry is, as Shelley quotes, "'the expression of the imagination'" (*Poetry and Prose*, 480), and this "expression" is a feature of all social and cultural forms. We are therefore called upon by the *Defence*, first, to learn to read the "poetry" of "architecture, painting, music, the dance, sculpture, philosophy, and we may add, the forms of civil life" (489), and, second, to disclose in the poetry of the world the signs of an imagination understood chiefly as the fundamental cultural and political force of history. For the imagination to be realized as "the great instrument of moral good" (488), it must not be conceived to be in the service of preservation or "enshrinement" but, according to Shelley, as the principal agent of social transformation. When we read the stories of cultural and political revolution or the "struggles for civil and religious liberty," we discover poetry: "All the authors of revolutions in opinion are," Shelley asserts, "necessarily poets" (485). Poetry in the general sense is "unfailingly" at work in the decisive, punctual moments of revolutionary change: "The most unfailing herald, companion, and follower of the awakening of a great people to work a beneficial change in opinion or institution, is Poetry" (508).

But importantly for Shelley's project and for the critical expectations his work continues to bear, the agency exercised by the imagination is not regarded as a subjective agency: the imagination Shelley refers to in the *Defence* and elsewhere exceeds the "circumference" of the self or the mind.[3] The acts of legislation achieved by the imagination do not, therefore, so much issue from subjects already constituted as they legislate subjectivity as a historical effect. The imagination functions as a demystifying force: it prevents Shelley's work from being reducible to empiricism, and it lends to his idealism its insistently critical edge. But like magnetism or the wind, phenomena that also fascinated Shelley, the imagination remains an "unseen Power," a force that can only be known by its effects. When we attribute to the self the source of truth or agency, according to Shelley, we replicate the metaleptic confusion of cause and effect: the subject is an effect that our theologies and philosophies habitually mistake for a cause. The imagination is a force that, like magnetism and the wind and, perhaps, like history, remains always "immanent in its effects."[4]

To Shelley, the same rhetorical principle is regarded as a historical and *historicizing* process. In the Preface to *Prometheus Unbound*, for instance, Shelley invokes the critical "spirit" that gives rise to social revolutions and great literature alike: "We owe the great writers of the golden age of our literature to that fervid awakening of the public mind which shook to dust the oldest and most oppressive form of the Christian Religion. We owe Milton to the progress and development of the same spirit" (*Poetry and Prose*, 134).[5] It is such a reckoning of historical "debts" that results in Shelley's celebrated formulation that "poets"— in the extended sense—are as much the "creations" as the creators of their age.

The demystifying and liberating aspect of Shelley's notion of the imagination is pervasive and compelling: one can in fact regard his negotiations between idealism and skepticism as the difficult forging of a political aesthetic for which the available secular and philosophical vocabularies are judged to be inadequate. Shelley's poetics represents a radical "working through" in which there are bound to be false starts and dead ends. As Jerrold Hogle characterizes it in the most sustained recent critical study of Shelley's career: "Shelley's writing fairly explodes with revolutionary potential" (*Shelley's Process*, vii). The sense of "revolutionary potential" we encounter in Shelley's poetics is the effect of his unfinished project, unfinished in part because of his untimely death, of course, but unfinished also because of the very nature of his "untimely meditations."[6] This is particularly the case for the central concept Shelley inherits from the "first generation" of Romantic discourse: the imagination must be wrenched from its discursive context, made into "a re-enlisted conceptual reserve" that "stands in for new concepts" which in Shelleyan fashion still await their "conception."[7]

This chapter does not address Shelley's version of the imagination, however, but his *break* from it. I am interested here in what happens when Shelley's radical "working through" takes him to the ends of the imagination. We are, I believe, delivered to a problem and a possibility that cannot be accounted for by the conflicting traditions of skepticism and idealism, and for which the "reverberated lightning" does not presume to destroy error. Instead, Shelley's poetry and prose come to name in the most challenging form available the *ineliminability* of ideology from representation. We are thus asked to read in a very different light the phrase "education of error": no longer as a critical consciousness learning to destroy error and the roots of error but as an "education" bound to error, issuing from error itself.

These are the new lessons and demands posed most dramatically by *The Triumph of Life*: there is no end to the delusion that has victimized all who venture the "path of life"; there is no way to avoid acting on the basis of such delusion; and there is no end, the poem tells us, to ideology. In Shelley's last poem, we are presented with a notion of ideology that can no longer be characterized as the mystification of false consciousness. If "our whole life is thus an education of error" (*Poetry and Prose*, 477), it is the "inextricable error," for instance, that we "behold" in Shelley's "On the Medusa of Leonardo da Vinci" and that makes *The Triumph of Life*—punctuated with the unanswered question "What is Life?"—into the *"triumph"* of "error."[8] What remains difficult but necessary is to grasp the late formulation as an "advance" of sorts, and *not* as an "advance" from the naive voluntarism of political commitment to the insightful but paralyzing pessimism of sheer resignation. For as compelling as Shelley's commitment to a critical enlightenment and a radical imagination can often be in the early poems and political writings, I believe that the questions of history, subjectivity, and politics, as they are confronted by Shelley's last poem, announce for Romantic discourse something fully on the order of what Louis Althusser, following Gaston Bachelard, called an "epistemological break." Much as in the rupture that Althusser describes in Marx's thinking in the 1840's, Shelley's last poem marks a break from both idealism and empiricism, a break for which the term "skepticism" is no longer sufficient, a break with the imagination itself—a *materialist* break. In this chapter I hope to demonstrate how *The Triumph of Life* announces something that breaks from Shelley himself and that breaks from poetry as such, something that still awaits, to invoke Walter Benjamin's famous phrase, to be "blasted out of the continuum of [literary] history."

"Signs of Thought's Empire over Thought"

The Triumph of Life is not a bolt from the blue. Signs of the "break," of a nonempiricist poetry that is ruptured from an idealist imagination, are legible throughout Shelley's work at least after 1816. One need only look to "Mont Blanc" to find Shelley wrestling with a sense of materiality that resists the idealization and anthropomorphism it invites: "The secret strength of things / Which governs thought." And in the *Defence* we find Shelley addressing the peculiar agency of the imagination: "Language is arbitrarily produced by the imagination" (*Poetry and Prose*, 483), an imagination that is not, as Shelley conceives it, a property of self or faculty of mind. Language is "vitally metaphorical": the rhetoricity of our "arbitrarily produced" language "marks the before unapprehended relations of things" and simultaneously introduces, as in the case of allegory, the Janus-like "double face of false and true" (482). For Shelley the "vitally metaphorical" aspect of language means that poetry derives not from the self but rather from figurations of concealing and revealing: the poetic play of curtains and veils "*makes us* the inhabitants of a world" with which we are not "familiar": "And whether it [poetry] spreads its own figured curtain, or withdraws life's dark veil from before the scene of things, it equally creates for us a being within our being. It makes us the inhabitants of a world to which the familiar world is a chaos" (505). Poetry's "defamiliarization" can thus be effected either by the sudden "withdrawal" of "life's dark veil" or by the "spreading" of "its own figured curtain." The passage asserts that in both operations the fundamental relationship between subject and world is formed through poetic language. Models of self and world are, therefore, open to the "transmutation" and "alchemy" of poetry. But given the unsettling play of light and shadows that Shelley calls poetic language, subjective control over the course of these "transmutations" is difficult to secure, particularly since poetry possesses the power to "distend, and then burst the circumference" of the "mind" (485).

We encounter an "awful doubt" in "Mont Blanc," but to make something of the doubt that Shelley registers in this great poem, to teach the "lessons" spoken by the mute voice of the mountain, Shelley needs recourse to the "ideal" force represented by the imagination. Much of the rhetorical power and risk-taking of Shelley's poetry can be understood as the attempt to overcome the gap the poet recognizes between social history and the critical spirit that engenders change. In "Ode to the West Wind," for instance, the nonsubjective and nonempirical power, the "unseen" but radical spirit, can be summoned only by the most extravagant apostrophes of the poet in his most vocative mode. Readers have long remarked the poem's excessiveness and even potential embarrassment.[9] That the poem can be made into a case study of what John Hollander calls the "poetic imperative" is, I believe, a testimony to the considerable demands made upon the poem, the demand of invoking a spirit that depends for its liberating and demystifying power on its ideality. The force that Shelley invokes there, a force registered only in its effects, is a historical and nonpersonal force that remains ideal. The imagination in Shelley always marks a nonidentity between subject and object, a nonidentity that gains its critical dimension from its capacity never to be exhausted, its capacity to open a rift in what we would now call social and aesthetic "hegemony." Such an imagination authorizes the critical utopianism most evident in *Prometheus Unbound*.

Something else happens in *The Triumph of Life*. No imagination is summoned and no imagination appears as the "reverberated lightning" that can "kill error." The mere absence of the term "imagination"

would not of itself necessarily mark a shift worthy of note. The term itself is not a common one in Shelley's poetry. But, more importantly, the
operations explicitly assigned to the imagination in work as recent as
Epipsychidion and *A Defence of Poetry* are themselves absent from the
poem.

That *The Triumph of Life* marks an advance in Shelley's skills as a
poet has long been noted by the critical tradition; but the radical epistemological and rhetorical ramifications of the break opened by the
poem have only more recently been explored, most powerfully by Paul
de Man's "deconstructive" reading of Shelley. In "Shelley Disfigured,"
de Man discloses the poem's resistance to any interpretation that might
wish to find there the progressive movement of enlightenment or the
Promethean trope of liberation. Instead, the trajectory de Man identifies in Shelley's last poem is the "trajectory from erased self-knowledge
to disfiguration."[10] What we encounter in *The Triumph of Life* are "tangles of meaning and figuration" from which the poem and its personas
do not presume to extricate themselves. We find instead the imposition of ever "new visions" that preclude the possibility of true knowledge: according to de Man, "Rousseau is not given a satisfactory answer
[to his question], for the ensuing vision is a vision of continued delusion
that includes him" (*Rhetoric*, 99). As a consequence of the pervasive
mystifying depicted in the poem, "to 'wake' is only to become aware of
one's persistent condition of slumber . . . a deeper forgetting achieved
by an act of memory which remembers one's forgetting," a "pseudo-
knowledge." From the tradition of the theories of ideology we have
explored, de Man's characterization of the poem's "vision" is that of a
perpetual and *inclusive* "false consciousness," one that by definition extends to the reader, in this case to Paul de Man. The poem would thus
be an instance of the *mise-en-abyme* structure familiar to readers of deconstruction. In de Man's sense, we are in this poem never free from
"figure" that "shapes" our understanding of the "shapes" that appear in
the poem: "It is the alignment of a signification with any principle of
linguistic articulation whatsoever, sensory or not, which constitutes the
figure" (*Rhetoric*, 114).

If, according to de Man, all worldly knowledge or self-under-
standing is blocked in—and by—*The Triumph of Life*, by the "self-

receding scenes" that are exemplary of the narrative movement of the poem, the poem's "trajectory from erased self-knowledge to disfiguration" leaves the reader with a "haunting" residue. "Whenever this self-receding scene occurs," writes de Man, "the syntax and the imagery of the poem tie themselves into a knot which arrests the process of understanding. The resistance of these passages is such that the reader soon forgets the dramatic situation and is left with only these unresolved riddles to haunt him" (*Rhetoric*, 98–99). What we are left with, as de Man renders it, may well appear surprising to many familiar with deconstruction's suspicion of truth claims made in the name of experience. For, according to de Man, Shelley's poem itself becomes an *experience*: the "text becomes the successive and cumulative experience of these tangles of meaning and figuration." The reader's "experience" is, of course, scarcely a positive one; it resists the knowledge and understanding that it demands, and it voids the categories that we would invoke to redeem it, most notably the "aesthetic." De Man tells us that the "tangles of meaning and of figuration" that plague the figures of Rousseau and Shelley and give to the poem its narrative "shape" necessarily implicate the readers of *The Triumph of Life*, who find themselves caught in the very "tangles" they are trying to interpret (106).

But "Shelley Disfigured" does more than record "tangles of figuration," though critics of de Man rarely proceed beyond that point. By de Man's own reckoning, his confrontation with Shelley's poem produced an encounter with the "questions about history and fragmentation," an encounter that left unclear the future "path of departure": "How and where one goes on from there is far from clear, but certainly no longer simply a matter of syntax and diction" (*Rhetoric*, ix).

One might go back to *A Defence of Poetry*, where Shelley's account of the relationship between imagination, poetic language, and social institutions is complicated by the appearance of the "shadows of futurity." The notion that the poet is both prophet and legislator necessarily lends the essay much of its historical charge. The poet, according to Shelley, "not only beholds intensely the present as it is, and discovers those laws according to which present things ought to be ordered, but he beholds the future in the present" (*Poetry and Prose*, 482–83). Rather than an unmediated view of the future, what the poet "beholds" in his prophetic vision is the future as it is inscribed—or, better still, *entombed*—in the laws of the present. The poet is assigned both the task of "recording" the "voice" of liberty, as Shelley declares in the ode by that name, and the task of *unearthing* its now buried spirit. Thus, in "England in 1819," what Wordsworth might have identified as appropriate *shrines*—religious, political, cultural—are described by Shelley as "graves from which a glorious Phantom may / Burst, to illumine our tempestuous day" (ll. 13–14). Though Shelley never wavers in his critique of enshrinement, his faith in the prospect of "illumination" is qualified considerably. Shelley returns to the question of the future's "illumination" by poetry in the closing sentences of the unfinished *Defence*; poets are, he declares, "mirrors of the gigantic shadows which futurity casts upon the present" (*Poetry and Prose*, 508). Shelley presents the poet's relation to the future in a curiously specular form: a reflection produced by "gigantic shadows," the image of "futurity" acts not to enlighten but to shroud the present, its structures of representation and its models of perception, in history's shadows. We are reminded that in Shelley's most famous declaration—"Poets are the unacknowledged legislators of the World"—the lack of acknowledgment is clearly extended to the poets themselves.

The shadows grow in Shelley's last work, the effects of a total eclipse of all inherited sources of illumination. However much we may insist on the inclusiveness of poetry in the "general sense" or the radical historicizing of Shelley's poetics, it is difficult not to regard *A Defence of Poetry*, Shelley's response to Thomas Love Peacock's "The Four Ages of Poetry," as an enshrinement of poetry and the imagination. But if we read *A Defence* by the light and shadow cast by *The Triumph of Life*, Shelley's earlier prose shrine to the poets, his monument of poetic prophecy and legislation becomes fragmented and "reshaped." Many of the principal names of the Western cultural tradition celebrated in the *Defence* reappear in *The Triumph of Life*, disfigured by its visions and "caught within the shadows of the tomb."[11] The poem considers in the form of a dream the practices and institutions of making and reading monuments, another name for which is "history." And the poem tells the story of the insistent revisions of the triumphal processions of European cultural history, revisions that unfold through the poet's visionary encounter and dialogue with the shape of Rousseau. The presence of Rousseau links the poem's visions to the status of Romanticism itself: by enjoining the fallen image of Rousseau—defaced origin of Romantic thought—Romanticism is simultaneously implicated as one more broken monument of the Western cultural shrine and cited as the condition and perspective of this inherently occluded revaluation.

De Man's essay on Shelley emphasizes these processes of disfiguration, though their ideological implications are not much pursued. "At the far side"—to use one of the critic's favorite expressions—of de Man's attention to figure, we encounter a confrontation with fragmentation and history that in the last sentence of "Anthropomorphism and Trope in the Lyric" he calls "*historical* modes of language power" (*Rhetoric*, 262). In Shelley's poem, de Man asserts, there is "another aspect of language that has to come into play" to perform the text's "undoing and erasure of the figure" (115). This de Man identifies as language's "positing" power: the disfigurations performed in and by the poem, "the repetitive erasures by which language performs the erasure of its own positions" (119), nonetheless leave a residue—the disfigured—that we are forced to read. "Positing," de Man says, "'glimmers' into a glimmering knowledge that acts out the aporias of signification and of performance" (119).[12] The performative dimension of language is inherently forceful, even violent, and according to de Man the poem records, enacts, and repeats the performance of violence: "the initial violence of position can only be half erased, since the erasure is accomplished by a device of language that never ceases to partake of the very violence against which it is directed" (119). These acts are not "merely" linguistic; or rather, they speak to a capacity of language or figure that, when literalized, exists not on the order of meaning but on the order of "actual events," just as does what Shelley's poem names "Life." Thus, when we encounter "disfiguration," such as that which characterizes *The Triumph of Life*, we are confronting the effects of language's historical power: we are delivered to "historical modes of language power." It is for this reason that *The Triumph of Life* cannot be reconciled to "the available props of literary history," for those historicizing devices are far removed from the kind of historico-linguistic power experienced in the poem itself.

De Man's reading of *The Triumph of Life* stresses how the poem is itself propelled by a permanent process of displacement, one that disallows the grounding of any perspective which might claim to be free from the repeated and disorienting acts of positing. Displaced from the poem in de Man's reading are Shelley's Promethean thematics: the presentation of struggle and critique as the process of demystification and the projection of a utopian dimension beyond the limits of history—at the "far goal of time." The pattern of displacement that governs *The Triumph of Life* discloses instead that "wreaths of light" are not the signs of illumination but "signs of thought's empire over thought" (l. 211), signs that demonstrate thought's monumentalization and *inevitable* subordination to political power.[13] But this understanding demands that we push at the implications of de Man's reading in order to learn how the "signs of thought's empire over thought" may be *ideological* signs, the linguistic tracks of the historical connections between the formation of thought and the exercise of power.

In *The Triumph of Life*, the positing of origins is represented as a political act, one nowhere more evident than in the poem's own beginning. *The Triumph of Life* opens by marking such an origin: the sudden "springing forth" of the sun is invested with such rhetorical *éclat* that it could be said to announce the origin or the mythic "awakening" of history itself:

> Swift as a spirit hastening to his task
>   Of glory & of good, the Sun sprang forth
> Rejoicing in his splendour, & the mask
>
> Of darkness fell from the awakened Earth.
>   (ll. 1–4)

"Awakened" by the sun and "rejoicing in his splendour," earth becomes a natural temple, celebrating the "birth / Of light" (ll. 6–7) with "smokeless altars" (l. 5), "orient incense" (l. 12), and "matin lay" (l. 8).[14] For de Man, the power of the sun in the opening lines derives from the sun's detachment "from all antecedents" (*Rhetoric*, 116) and makes the passage an allegory of language's power to posit. The sun does not, writes de Man, "appear in conjunction with or in reaction to the night and the stars, but of its own unrelated power." Through its unmotivated exercise of its power, the sun appears to inaugurate time it-self, or, in a more Heideggerian rendering, to awaken the earth to its historicity and thus to call the world into being.

But de Man's reading of the passage is challenged by the very process of displacement that he identifies as the poem's governing struc-tural principle. The poem displaces the sense that the sun appears "of its own unrelated power" when in subsequent lines we are referred to a preexisting world. The "birth / Of light" that awakens earth reveals that such positing entails the story of a prior "imposition":

> And in succession due, did Continent,
>
>   Isle, Ocean, and all things that in them wear
> The form and character of mortal mould
>   Rise as the Sun their father rose, to bear
>
>   Their portion of the toil which he of old
>   Took as his own and then imposed on them.
>   (ll. 15–20)

We find that what de Man read as an allegory of the sheer positing power of language belongs to a sequence of events that reinscribes it into a story of political domination.[15] To revise de Man's formulation: language's positing power is itself already implicated by the poem as an "imposition." No longer can we regard the figure of the sun as the source and beginning "Of glory & of good," for the sun is now the name of the father whose "fathering" means the "imposition" of "toil."[16] Inscribed in the story of imposition is a global map of territo-rial expansion: the burden of "toil" is borne "in succession due" by "Continent, / Isle, Ocean" such that the sheer movement of time as "succession" is made to resonate with the political act of imperial suc-cession.[17] But nothing escapes the process of imposition, for it extends to "*all things* that in them wear / The form and character of mortal mould" (emphasis added).[18]

These are the first "signs of thought's empire over thought," early markings of power and empire, markings that grow more legible as the poem progresses. In the early stanzas of the "vision," for instance, the poet likens the "fierce song and maniac dance" of the "raging" crowd he encounters to the frenzied "jubilee" that greets a "conqueror's advance" (ll. 110–12). For Shelley, the trajectory of such "triumphal pageants" (l. 118) invariably leads to domination: soon the conqueror has "upon the free / . . . bound a yoke, which . . . they stooped to bear" (ll. 115–16). The passage recites the opening scene of the poem, where all that "wear / The form and character of mortal mould" similarly rejoice in the sun's arrival and must similarly "bear" the imposition of his burden. The positing of an originary act is already a sign of power and tells the story of a prior imposition. As scenes such as these accumulate in the poem, they set in motion a constellation of images that simultaneously displaces and revalues any originary gesture.

It remains important to understand how the pattern of displacement disclosed by de Man belongs to a more pervasive genealogical labor undertaken by the poem: the constant "revaluation of all values" for which the allusion to Nietzsche's most radical critiques is fully warranted. This includes the disclosure of the deep complicities between the positing of origins, the institutions of value, and the inscriptions of power. Shelley's last poem not only performs the perpetual displacement of values as they are "posited" but also takes up critically the very mechanisms by which (ideological) values are instituted and enshrined. One can, in fact, identify Shelley's staging of these complicities and of the disruptions of the poem's constitutive hierarchies and oppositions as the source of many readers' confusions about the values assigned to key images in *The Triumph of Life*. Despite considerable textual evidence to the contrary, many readers have insisted, for instance, that the image of the sun remains a positive image, a "wholly beneficent" figure unquestionably endorsed by the poem.[19] But if the sun is aligned in the opening stanzas with the values "Of glory & of good," if the sun designates the force that removes the "mask of darkness," the image of the sun becomes the explicit target of a process of critical reframing and reinscription that lends the poem much of its narrative energy.

The cultural power historically invested in the image of the sun makes it a primary object of Shelley's critique; however, the same ideological potency also makes the image difficult for readers to envision as anything other than "beneficent." But through its reframings, substitutions, and displacements, *The Triumph of Life* reveals the mechanisms that give "value": the questions asked by Rousseau are those raised by the poem itself, questions that address the perception of the image of the sun as well as the ways of seeing endorsed by that image. The questions of perception and value are throughout Shelley's work questions of and for the imagination: indeed, in the *Defence* the imagination is defined as the "perception of the value" of "quantities known to the Reason" (*Poetry and Prose*, 480). But in *The Triumph of Life*, the imagination never appears. Instead, the poem's dramatic revaluation of poetic, philosophical, and political values, its historical revaluation, is undertaken through the screening of a vision, through the play of "veils" and "shades," through the mirrored and prismatic refractions of a "strange trance"—all without the aegis of the imagination.

"A Vision Was Rolled"

Most of *The Triumph of Life* is devoted to the narrative of a "vision." I contend that through its unsettling oscillations between darkness and light, waking and sleeping, blindness and lucidity, the poem's screening of the "vision" banishes the imagination and, as a consequence, leaves us with the permanence of ideology. And in the version of ideology to be gleaned from Shelley's last poem, all forms of perception and representation are structured by the unstable play of light and dark and by the irreducible "veils" of figuration woven through language. Once we recognize, for instance, that the sun itself is no longer a pure, "beneficent," and originary source of light but a powerful cultural figure inscribed in a more volatile economy of value and perception, we learn to read the historical vision that follows as the shadowy and unrelenting pageant of an ideology no longer susceptible to a demystifying imagination.

The closest we come in the Marxist tradition to Shelley's late thinking about ideology is Louis Althusser's thesis that "all ideology represents in its *necessarily* imaginary distortion . . . the imaginary relation of . . . individuals to the real relations in which they live."[20] This distortion, according to Althusser, does not occur by way of the obfuscation of truth; it is not the kind of mystification that could be rectified by correct vision, better light, or the imagination. Rather, it is a

structural feature of representation. There is no space before or after
ideology ("Ideology," 175). In other words, ideological distortion is inherent in the situation of subjectivity. "The category of the subject,"
writes Althusser, "is the constitutive category of all ideology" (171).
Insofar as subjectivity is constitutive of our models of perception, cognition, belief, or action, ideology is inescapable: it has no "outside."

The significant deconstructive readings of *The Triumph of Life* have
focused attention on many of the same issues, though without broach-
ing their implications for Shelley's treatment of ideology. J. Hillis Miller,
for instance, has demonstrated the impossibility for any element in the
text to "find a fixed place that is outside the system . . . of sun, mask;
light, shadow; sleep, waking that makes up the poem."[21] Even "the
placement of the speaker-poet is not," according to Miller, "out in
light, face to face with the sun, but within the darkness of human language. The poet, that is, is also within life" (*Linguistic Moment*, 145).
To what Miller aptly calls the "darknesses" of language and mind, we
must add the "darkness" of history that belongs in Shelley's vision to
the adumbrations of the same shadows. The New Historicism might
alert us to the symptomatic significance of Miller's omission of history
in his formulation, but I believe that more is gained by exploring how
the processes of a *necessary* distortion examined by Miller or de Man
resonate in Shelley's last poem with the theory of ideology developed
by Althusser.

The Triumph of Life explores the ideological mechanisms that produce the values that the poem in its turn undoes. The poem also tracks
the relationships of the ensuing forms of darkness, what in his poem
on Leonardo's "Medusa" Shelley calls the "unending involutions" of
history, language, and mind.[22] The poem does not, therefore, so much
represent history as it presents the mechanisms that "legislate" it, mechanisms that veil us in shadow and for which the sun is no source of enlightenment or liberation. Another name for the mechanisms that produce the interminable play of shadows is ideology. The inclusiveness
of the widening region of shadows extends to the poem's readers, who
find that any act of interpretation is invariably caught within the same
system of light and dark, with no "fixed place outside the system,"

without, in other words, the guidance of the "beneficent" light of the sun or, more decisively, of the imagination.

Chief among these value-producing mechanisms is the apparatus of the vision, and the poem goes to considerable lengths to detail its theatrics. Though the poet's own meditations during the dramatic opening stanzas are notably withheld, the poem carefully records the positioning of the poet within a darker theater that he calls "the cone of night."

> But I, whom thoughts which must remain untold
>
> > Had kept as wakeful as the stars that gem
> > The cone of night, now they were laid asleep,
> > > Stretched my faint limbs beneath the hoary stem
>
> Which an old chestnut flung athwart the steep
> > Of a green Apennine.
> > > (ll. 21–26)

The "thoughts which must remain untold" are, however, only registered more forcefully by this incomplete censorship; it is as if the thoughts had imposed a burden of their own that the poet must "stoop to bear." By introducing himself in line 21 with this disjunction, the inelegant intrusion of the "But I," the poet disavows any connection between the preceding stanzas and the vision that follows. The withheld thoughts nonetheless occupy a place and declare their investment precisely by pronouncing their absence. The logic of the passage accords with that which Freud called "repression": the withholding of a representation by means of another representation. As a consequence of these syntactical and thematic disjunctions—signs of repression—the vision that follows takes the form of another sudden imposition: "And then a Vision on my brain was rolled" (l. 40). The vision does not originate with or belong to the poet; nor can its source be traced to any previous thoughts. The vision, like history or language, is imposed on a subject that in Shelley's poem is more the effect of than the source for these forces.

A typographical cut initiates the vision, marking both the ridge between consciousness and trance and the line that separates the light of

the sun from the lights, shades, and shapes of the vision.[23] The turn
away from the sun, the turn away from the story of the sun's origin,
inaugurates the screening of the vision:

> before me fled
> The night; behind me rose the day; the Deep
> Was at my feet, & Heaven above my head . . .
>
> (ll. 26–28)

If the poem anticipates the questions of representation and ideology
that are posed by the apparatus of the cinema as well as those raised by
Marx in his account of the *camera obscura* effect of ideology, it is because those questions are already implicated by the Platonic text that
Shelley is citing and restaging here, namely the "allegory of the cave."[24]
The backward turn described in the lines is not conducted by the poet,
who remains stationary, but by the poem, which uses the temporarily
stable position of the poet to shift its own axis. The description of this
backward turn—the cinematic detailing of the lighting and the positioning of the viewer before the screen of a vision—calls attention to
the poetic mechanisms that produce and project visions. The affinity
with cinema is perhaps nowhere more evident than in the detailing of
the stanzas that immediately precede the vision. Once the spectator is
positioned, a "strange trance" follows, a lucid, waking trance that is
not itself the vision but rather the vehicle or mechanism of the vision:

> a strange trance over my fancy grew
> Which was not slumber, for the shade it spread
> Was so transparent that the scene came through
> As clear as when a veil of light is drawn
> O'er evening hills they glimmer.
>
> (ll. 29–33)

Film is of course such a "veil of light" drawn over a screen, and the
effects produced in the poem closely resemble those produced by classical cinema. The veil of light spread by the "strange trance" produces
the poet's "knowledge" of a duplicate moment: the effect is one of "es-
trangement," introducing the disorientation of "feeling" what he is in
fact doing:

> and I knew
>
> That I had felt the freshness of that dawn,
> Bathed in the same cold dew my brow & hair
> And sate as thus upon that slope of lawn
>
> Under the self same bough.   (ll. 33–37)

The knowledge gained here is presented not as a recollection—a moment of recognition based on a previous experience—but rather as the effect of a "strange trance." No longer governed by the authority of the sun, this form of knowledge is the "glimmering" aftereffect of the unstable play of light and dark, veiling and revealing, waking and dreaming.

Such is the theater of Shelley's "vision," the frame for the dream narrative that follows. In this theater the blurring of oppositions and the procession of displacements cast their shadow once again over the poem's opening and demonstrate that origins, fathers, and even the light cast by the sun are all subject to, perhaps the effects of, the operations of framing and reframing. The poem continues to turn away from its magisterial beginning, detaching itself from the sun as its source of light and proceeding through the dream-vision's labyrinth of conflicting lights and shades. The figures of light and vision supply the poem's conceptual architecture and organize the poem's narrative. Sun, stars, moon, chariot, veils: such Shelleyan images form a shifting constellation, an "ever-shifting mirror" as Shelley described it in "On the Medusa," that not only serves as tenor and vehicle of the vision but also, by establishing both the necessary conditions and perpetual unreliability of perception, poses the problem of ideology as it has been explored from Marx to Althusser.

The ideological operations at work in the poem are made still more complex by the repeated interventions, even "impositions," of new sources of light "Upon that path where flowers never grew" (l. 65) that continue to upset the relationship between the stars and the sun:

> And a cold glare, intenser than the noon
> But icy cold, obscured with   light
> The sun as he the stars.   (ll. 77–79)

Mary Shelley was confident enough that the "icy cold" "glare" of this unnatural light made seeing impossible that, in order to satisfy the scansion of line 78, she inserted the word "blinding," a choice motivated no doubt by the many instances of blindness in the poem.[25] With the introduction of a third form of light, the poem sets up a new system of value that gives yet another turn to the opening scene. We must now reread the earth's "awakening" as the displacement of light: the sun, "father" of light, removes the "mask of darkness" only by "obscuring" (and, as Mary Shelley scans it, by "blinding") the light of the stars. The coming of the "cold glare" shuffles the poem's images of light: the sun, once the source and standard of value in the poem, is resituated in the lines as the middle term between stars and the "cold glare," and is thereby reduced in this new and untethered economy to a relation of difference.

In the theater of the poet's vision, the light of the sun has been displaced to the "limits of the night," framing a picture of the chariot's arrival that is likened to the phases of the moon:

> Like the young moon
>
> When on the sunlit limits of the night
> Her white shell trembles amid crimson air
> And whilst the sleeping tempest gathers might
>
> Doth, as a herald of its coming, bear
> The ghost of her dead Mother, whose dim form
> Bends in dark ether from her infant's chair,
>
> So came a chariot on the silent storm.
> (ll. 79–86)

The elaborate staging of the simile, winding its way through three stanzas, serves only to establish the inadequacy of the lunar image.[26] The undoing of the simile makes the lines a catachresis, the figure of speech that appears through the disarticulation of "tenor" and "vehicle." The advent of the chariot, it turns out, is not at all "like the young moon." Unlike the moon, which draws and bends the light of another source, the chariot is presented as its own source of light and power: it comes "of its own rushing splendour" (l. 87). The luminous failure of the stanzas to give meaning, to link tenor and vehicle intelligibly, is the triumph of the catachresis. Their powerful effect derives not from their accuracy as phenomenal description but from the *imposition* of yet another form of light into the poem, a form of light that does not derive from any natural body but that is entirely figural: neither sun nor stars nor moon can account for the light of the chariot. Even this new and apparently autonomous and undivided source of light, the chariot, is itself guided by a "Janus-visaged Shadow" (l. 94) that in its turn becomes in the course of a few lines a "four-faced" "charioteer" with "banded eyes" (ll. 99, 103).[27] The displacements, refractions, and divisions produced by the multiplying figures of light and shade, sight and blindness create such an optical confusion that to the poet in the midst of his vision, "the Shapes which drew it [the chariot] in thick lightnings / Were lost" (ll. 96–97). The sense of sight offers so little reliable knowledge in the poem that in subsequent lines the poet abandons the attempt to see the chariot, listening instead to "The music of their ever moving wings" (l. 98) to follow the chariot's trajectory. But the chariot's arrival raises more persistent questions about the conditions of sight. For the chariot is represented by figures of light that result only in blindness: even the light that "quenches the sun" is itself blind, a source of light guided by shadows and "banded eyes."

The manner by which the poem displaces the sun as its dominant image and reinscribes it in a more complex and unstable system of figures marks an important departure from the poetic strategies Shelley exhibits in his prior work. Though the reappropriation and reinscription of poetic forms and topoi characterize much of the poet's mature poetry, the reinscription at work in *The Triumph of Life* is neither a mythical drama of Promethean struggle, a "trumpet of prophecy," nor an apostrophic address to "Liberty." In the political theater of *Prometheus Unbound*, for instance, we are compelled to understand words as historical actions: to "recall" a curse, as Prometheus does in Act I, is to make recollection a revocation and thereby to make history, to set in motion the drama of liberation. Recollection is thus for Shelley not a Wordsworthian act of enshrinement but a political act that intervenes in the present. Prometheus remembers "nature's sacred watchwords," "truth, liberty and love," names that, once uttered by the throng of nations "as with one voice," bring into the world the strife of history and the reaction of tyranny:

> Suddenly fierce confusion fell from heaven
> Among them—there was strife, deceit and fear;
> Tyrants rushed in, and did divide the spoil.
> This was the shadow of the truth I saw.
>
> (I.652–55)

Asia is unleashed by Prometheus's declaration of "love" and is "borne" in Act II "to the realm / Of Demogorgon," where she begins her own enquiries into the sources and origins of domination. Once Asia learns to interpret Demogorgon's repeated response—"He reigns"—as a demonstration that domination and subjection are grammatically inscribed, she releases the triumphant nature of "eternal love" (II.iv.29–34). In such scenes, this dramatic poem proposes that through the power of language to act, through its performative aspect, we find the power of language to speak and disclose the truth. In Shelley's Promethean theater of political speech acts, truth is not something to be recognized but that which must be liberated. As Prometheus invokes it, "the many-folded shell" of poetry, "loosening its mighty music," delivers as in Wordsworth's "dream of the Arab" "a loud prophetic blast of harmony." Unlike Wordsworth's "dream," however, Shelley's political drama not only plays but plays out, enacts, the prophetic music.

Through the force of speech acts in *Prometheus Unbound*, "veil by veil evil and error fall" (III.iii.162): the "painted veil," the "figured curtain" that we call "life" (or ideology), is "torn aside" in an act of poetic demystification that heralds full political liberty:

> The painted veil, by those who were, called life
> Which mimicked, as with colours idly spread,
> All men believed and hoped, is torn aside—
> The loathsome mask has fallen, the man remains
> Sceptreless, free, uncircumscribed—but man:
> Equal, unclassed, tribeless and nationless,
> Exempt from awe, worship, degree,—the King
> Over himself; just, gentle, wise—but man.
>
> (III.iv.190–97)

These lines, delivered by "the spirit of the hour," bring the third act to a close and pronounce the end of history in *Prometheus Unbound*: Act IV, in which the principal players of the drama have disappeared from the stage, takes place "at the far goal of time."[28] There is no dramatic action in Act IV; indeed, nothing happens in its extended chorus of utopian prospect, because the strife called history has, like "evil and error," fallen with the veil of ideology.

The Triumph of Life offers no "imagination" to lead us from tyranny to freedom or from blindness to enlightenment or from error to truth or from history to utopia: in Shelley's last poem we find ourselves confronted and made complicit with forms of domination and delusion that cannot be localized in the image of error or tyrant but that, more pervasively and intractably, belong to the ideological nature of representation itself. In *The Triumph of Life* we encounter a "veiling"—inherent in language itself and, as in *Adonais*, "blindly woven"—that cannot be "torn aside" in a triumphant moment of revelation.[29] The foreclosing of the utopian moment by the blind force of a figural language "blindly woven" makes *The Triumph of Life* an attractive text for rhetorical readings performed by critics such as de Man or Miller. The Shelley revealed here is indeed the Shelley who deconstructs his own utopian poetics, the Shelley who, as de Man says of Yeats, warns "against the danger of unwarranted hopeful solutions." The "triumph of life," or ideology, indeed *The Triumph of Life* itself, can occur only in the wake of the poetic failure of imagination.

Rousseau and the Mirrors

If the imagination disappears from *The Triumph of Life*, a new figure does appear in its place: the "strange distortion" or "grim Feature" of Rousseau or "what was once Rousseau" is reflected in the course of the poet's vision. The Dantesque appearance of Rousseau introduces significant ideological implications of its own, by virtue of the political consequences attributed to Rousseau and to his importance as a source of Romantic discourse.[30] The vision itself, illuminated by the glare of the chariot, is "the triumph of life" in *The Triumph of Life*, the grim "triumphal pageant" through which Shelley replays Western history.

In the procession, "All but the sacred few" (l. 128) belong to this "captive multitude" enslaved to the chariot of Life, struggling "To reach the car of light" (l. 168). Their efforts are, of course, in vain: drawn to the "beams that quench the sun," they are left "still / Farther & deeper in the shade" (l. 169). The poet, "struck to the heart by this sad pageantry," poses the questions that one form or another circulate throughout the poem: "And what is this? / Whose shape is that within the car? & why" (ll. 176–78). The question itself seems to have the power to conjure the figure of Rousseau, whose unemphatic answer—"Life"—only gives another turn to these questions, for "life" is but another name for the history of "sad delusion," another form of what Shelley in his essay "On Life" called the perennial "deification" of "errors" (*Poetry and Prose*, 487).

In the "path" the poet distinguishes between different types of succumbing, and all are deluded, none escapes the ideological condition. Still, there are those with "power" other than "to destroy." Such is the case of Rousseau, "one of those who have created, even / If it be but a world of agony" (ll. 294–95). Himself one of the "deluded crew" (l. 184), the blind Rousseau begins "to relate the progress of the pageant" (l. 193), to narrate and interpret the historical vision. But the poet suffers at the sight of the endless procession—"mine eyes are sick of this perpetual flow" (l. 298)—and demands that Rousseau recount the story of his own "course" and "conquest." Rousseau relates that he succumbed to the imposition of a strange trance and "found [himself] asleep / Under a mountain" (ll. 311–12). The scene of entrancement mirrors the narrator's entrancement, which has in its turn generated the very vision in which Rousseau's story appears. Like the narrator before the screening of his vision, Rousseau is seated in a cave when he is seized and dizzied by a sudden burst of light.

> And as I looked the bright omnipresence
>   Of morning through the orient cavern flowed,
> And the Sun's image radiantly intense
>
>   Burned on the waters of the well that glowed
> Like gold.   (ll. 343–47)

The scene is a mirror of the earlier scene of the narrator's vision, reversing the position of the spectator vis-à-vis the position of the sun. The narrator, in his vision, turned away from the light of the sun; Rousseau faces "the bright omnipresence / Of morning." What Rousseau sees there is not the sun itself but, through the water's own mirror effect, its "image" as it is "burned" into the well.

The labyrinth of mirrors and visions in the poem confirms Miller's deconstructive reading of the interpretive undecidability generated by the poem's mirrored and mirroring structure. Moreover—and more to my point—it demonstrates that the understanding of ideology developed by the poem involves precisely such a mirror effect. To shift from the language of poetry to the speculations of philosophy, the notion of ideology proposed by the poem prefigures Althusser's thesis that "the structure of all ideology" is "*speculary*, i.e. a mirror-structure, and *doubly* speculary: this mirror duplication is constitutive of ideology and ensures its functioning" ("Ideology," 180).[31] *The Triumph of Life* is propelled by its specularity, by a sequence of mirrors that makes the poem itself into "an ever-shifting mirror." The mirror structure binds the poet to Rousseau and to the passing vision, ensuring the poet's—and by extension, the reader's—implication in the unfolding pageant.[32]

In the midst of this labyrinth of mirrors, where the mingling of beauty and terror recalls the remarkable closing stanza of Shelley's "Medusa," appears the image of a new source of light:

> there stood
>
> Amid the sun, as he amid the blaze
>   Of his own glory, on the vibrating
> Floor of the fountain, paved with flashing rays
>
> A shape all light.   (ll. 348–52)

Though by this point in the poem we have grown accustomed to the "quenching" of the sun and the multiplying of sources of light, the lines remain difficult to interpret. What, after all, is a "shape all light"? Donald Reiman demonstrates some of the difficulties and importance of the lines for our argument: he glosses the lines as meaning "literally the glare of the light from the *Sun* (345) reflected from the *waters of the well* (346)—the Ideal creativity reflected by an earthly medium (the human imagination)" (*Poetry and Prose*, 465). I would argue, on the contrary, that "literally" the lines are meaningless; a "shape all light" is, rather, a catachresis. Here the "glory" and "omnipresence" that describe the sun are not reflected but usurped by the catachretical imposition of a nonphenomenal "shape all light." That Reiman turns to the imagination to explain the meaning of the lines is understandable, for it is precisely the place in Shelley's poetry where one would expect to find the effects of the imagination. But the recourse to the imagination does not occur here: the "new figure" that arises is just that, a "figure," and we repeat the narrator's mistake if we call it the reflection by the "imagination" of the "true Sun." We should be alerted to this by the repeated—and related—revaluations of the value of the sun: without the proper orbit of a sun by which the world is illuminated, without the presence of a "true Sun" such as the imagination, there is no literal term and all language is implicated in the condition of a catachresis. Such is the result of Derrida's reading of Aristotle's *Poetics*, and his findings describe Shelley's "deconstruction" of the meaning and reference of the sun and the imagination in *The Triumph of Life*.[33]

In the lines that follow the presentation of the "shape all light," the figure is gendered, "seen" as the figure of a woman, an enchantress we call poetry whose

> feet, no less than the sweet tune
> To which they moved, seemed as they moved, to blot
> The thoughts of him who gazed on them.
> (ll. 382–84)

The poem has thus moved from the specular structure of ideology in general to the specific workings of the "aesthetic" ideology. Here in the figure of woman and the "feet" and "sweet tune" of poetry, the "shape all light" duplicates the effect of the trance, blotting "The thoughts of him who gazed." The "sweet tune" is a lure, a tease that hides the violence of the act of obliteration that transpires. The very ground of knowledge vanishes beneath her "feet": "All that was, seemed as if it had been not" (l. 385).

The catachretical appearance in the poem of this "shape all light" recalls once again the opening episode of the earth's awakening by the sun: like the "father" "hastening to his task / Of glory & of good," she promises to end darkness and ideology by dispelling in an instant all mystification and illusion: "like day she came, / Making the night a dream" (ll. 392–93). Seduced by this shape, by this figuring of language, Rousseau looks upon her as the source of truth whose provenance is unnamed, "the realm without a name" (l. 396). Rousseau asks the shape to provide him with the true story of his condition, to "shew" how and why he has fallen into "this valley of perpetual dream":

> If, as it doth seem,
> Thou comest from the realm without a name,
>
> Into this valley of perpetual dream,
>   Shew whence I came, and where I am, and why—
> Pass not away upon the passing stream.
>   (ll. 395–99)

Her reply—"Arise and quench thy thirst"—appears to promise the fulfillment of his desire, and Rousseau, "bending at her sweet command" (l. 403), drinks from the cup she offers. The story Rousseau requests, the answers to his questions, is not forthcoming; in its place, in the tracks of his unfulfilled desire, a "new Vision" appears:

> And suddenly my brain became as sand
>
>   Where the first wave had more than half erased
> The track of deer on desert Labrador,
>   Whilst the fierce wolf from which they fled amazed
>
> Leaves his stamp visibly on the shore
>   Until the second bursts—so on my sight
> Burst a new Vision never seen before.
>   (ll. 405–11)

The sudden "burst" of a "new Vision," as de Man describes it, only "dramatizes the failure to satisfy a desire for self-knowledge" (*Rhetoric*,

99). The "answer" to Rousseau's questions is the perpetual displacement of the question itself by these nonsensible "visions." The questions raised by Rousseau and by the poem—questions of origin, of causality, of history—are "answered" only by the imposition of new visions. In *The Triumph of Life* the demands for knowledge are met with narrative visions that only demonstrate the instability of the grounds of knowledge and the delusions of those who lay claim to them. With the appearance of the "new Vision," Rousseau's "brain," sign and site of cognition, "became as sand." What does remain when the desire for knowledge is denied are forms of vision or ways of seeing that, conducted in this world of shadows and "perpetual dream," can never yield knowledge since they always turn out to be another form of blindness. All this failed seeing in poetic visions confirms the lament of Shelley's Prometheus: "There are two woes: / To speak and to behold" (*Prometheus Unbound*, I.i.647–48).

As a consequence, the opposition between spectator of and actor in the vision, an opposition that would preserve a space outside the "evershifting mirror" of the vision, an opposition Rousseau holds out to the poet as a possibility, is made untenable by the poem. The poet cannot "forbear / To join the dance" (ll. 188–89) because, as the poem makes clear, joining "the triumph of life" is not a matter of choice. By demonstrating the persistence of the "perpetual dream," *The Triumph of Life* suggests not only that the imposition of visions and the appearance of light fail to free perception from the veils and shadows of figuration, but also that "light" and "vision" are themselves figures and as such are sources of the shadows and veils they are expected to remove. One could recognize such a reading as "deconstructive," as "negative self-knowledge," and leave it at that. But the poem makes further demands: it insists that we approach this process as the "movement" (l. 383), the production of history, and it insists that we reckon with its consequences.

Imagination's Eclipse, History's Shadows

In the essay "Lyric Poetry and Society," Theodor Adorno, taking as his notion of ideology "untruth, false consciousness, a lie," asserts that "the greatness of works of art lies solely in their power to let things be heard which ideology conceals: whether intended or not, their success transcends false consciousness."[34] By that measure, *The Triumph of Life* is a failure, for it reveals or gives voice to nothing *concealed* by ideology. On the contrary, in its very failure to achieve the "greatness" described by Adorno, the poem discloses the inadequacy of the model of ideology as "false consciousness." What we "hear" in this poem is the machinery of ideology in the workings of poetic language. The "vision" that transpires in the poem may have as its source of projection the glimmering play of light and shadow, but it is "seen" through the blind or deluded eyes of Rousseau and the poet-narrator. We are granted access to the "triumph," the passing pageant of history, only through the shape of Romantic "visions." Shelley's poem demonstrates that through Romantic representations of history we see not history itself but the ideological projections of history. Insofar as our visions of history remain ideological, we continue to be caught within the framework of Romanticism, and we continue to see ourselves, to cast our own forms of seeing and blindness, in Romantic visions of history.

Shelley's poem delivers us once again to Althusser, to his "vision" of the necessity of ideology: "The great revolutionary thinkers, theoreticians and politicians, the great materialist thinkers, . . . understood that the freedom of men is not achieved by the complacency of its ideological *recognition*, but by *knowledge* of the laws of their slavery, . . . by the analysis and mastery of the abstract relations which govern them." By this token, Shelley does indeed merit the status of a "great materialist thinker," who moves in *The Triumph of Life* from the "complacency" of "ideological recognition" to a "*knowledge* of the laws" of historical and ideological "slavery." Yet Althusser's emphasis on the "*analysis* and mastery of the *abstract* relations which govern" us is precisely what has been the source of much contention within Marxist and "post-Marxist" critical theory. Indeed, for a Marxist historian such as E. P. Thompson, Althusser's attention to the "analysis" of "*abstract* relations" demonstrates nothing more than that his work *cannot* be called "materialist."[35] But one need not share Thompson's vituperative and polemical hostility to "theory" or his "commonsense" faith in the empiricism of history to feel that Althusser's work addresses the course or movement of history less capably than it does the ideological machinery that produces history, about which it has many ground-breaking things to say. If, according to Althusser, "ideology has no history," how would we read the history displayed by the poem?

To say that our visions of and inscriptions in history are irreducibly ideological is not necessarily to diminish the permanent pressure of history inscribed in Shelley's final, materialist poem. While the poem stages the subject's insertion in the specular, figural, and permanent structures of ideology, the staging is itself shot through with the historicity of the vision. In a scene that transpires in the early stages of the vision, the poet observes that the record of history is made by "drawing" "figures on its false & fragile glass" (l. 247). Though the poet longs to turn away from the writing on this mirror, to resist the visions cast by the distorting glass, he is instructed by Rousseau:

> Figures ever new
> Rise on the bubble, paint them how you may;
> We have but thrown, as those before us threw,
>
> Our shadows on it as it past away. (ll. 248–51)

In his account of the figural writing on the glass, Rousseau asserts the inevitable intertwining of the figural with the specular and our inevitable entrapment therein. Throwing our "shadows" on this "bubble" "as it past away" is, Rousseau says, unavoidable: all forms of action, knowledge, perception occur within the intrication of figurality and specularity.[36]

But while the "false & fragile glass" of the "world" may reflect *en abyme* the shadows cast upon it, the historical movement of the vision and of the poem is not arrested by this specularity: the triumph's passing never comes to a close; indeed the "triumphal" vision of human history is precisely what entices the poet and at the same time drives him to despair:

> for despair
> I half disdained mine eye's desire to fill
>
> With the spent vision of the times that were
> And scarce have ceased to be . . .
>   (ll. 231–34, ellipsis in original)

The poet's "despair" leads him to "half disdain" a "desire" (which is necessarily oriented toward the future) for a "spent vision" of "times" that both belong to the past and "scarce have ceased to be." The passage is remarkable for its orchestration of the conditions of different states of temporality—movement seems at once exhausted and inexhaustible—and is exemplary of the poem's efforts to draw the constellations of subjectivity ("despair," "disdain," "desire"), ideology ("the spent vision"), and history ("times that were / And scarce have ceased to be"). The same lines also demonstrate the difficulty of turning this constellation into an instrument of reliable historical knowledge: the desire to see history, to fill one's eyes with a historical vision, gives way to "despair" because the vision is itself "spent" or consumed by the history it reveals. Within the space of the vision, it is possible to gaze upon the passing course of the triumph—the narrative of Western history—but the nature of the seeing as much as the story surveyed remain thoroughly ideological. Though the charioteer's "eyes could pierce the sphere / Of all that is, has been, or will be done" (ll. 103–4), nothing of value is gained because these eyes remain "banded," the charioteer's ostensible access to this perspective of universal history barred by his own blindness.

Poet and reader alike are directed by the poem to witness the passing of history, but both must gaze upon the "triumph" without the benefit of sunlight and with certainty only of our shared delusion, a delusion that cannot be derived from truth. But if the poem stresses both the necessity of regarding history and the ideological nature of all historical vision, how are we to behold the history that passes before our eyes? What we can see in this historical pageant belongs exclusively to the course of Western history. The poet is called on to "behold" a parade of prominent European political, religious, philosophical, and literary personages; or more precisely, he sees along this path the grim, distorted traces "of what were once" these figures. All have been deformed by the vision, and now a "captive multitude," they are enslaved to the conqueror, "Life." "The Wise, / The great, the unforgotten" (ll. 208–9) of European history have, by the power of inversion, been "chained to the car" (l. 208) of Life. Philosophers such as Plato, Voltaire, Kant, and Aristotle came no closer to escaping the enslavement than those such as Napoleon who possessed political power. Rousseau asks the poet to behold

> those spoilers spoiled, Voltaire,
>
> Frederic, & Kant, Catherine, & Leopold,
> Chained hoary anarch, demagogue & sage
> Whose name the fresh world thinks already old—
>
> For in the battle Life & they did wage
> She remained conqueror.
>
> (ll. 235–40)

Between philosopher and monarch, "demagogue & sage," the conqueror "Life" appears to draw no distinction. There are those among the "deluded crew" whose transgressions are more severe; namely, "the sceptre bearing line" that includes Popes "Gregory & John" (ll. 286, 288), who, having "spread the plague of blood & gold abroad" (l. 287), are responsible for Rome's bloody colonialism.

But for all its attention to these figures of Western political and intellectual history, the vision does not so much record historical events or offer a new historical narrative as constitute a critical reading of the official narratives of European history. *The Triumph of Life* does not enshrine the proper names that are paraded through the vision; rather, it proposes to read that list of proper names and through this reading undo the shrine-making that goes by the name of history. Shelley's historical vision discloses the signs of power and empire inscribed in the heroic processions of official histories. We recall, for instance, that in the early scenes of the vision, the poet likens the "fierce song and maniac dance" of the "triumph" to the celebration that would greet a Roman "conqueror's advance":

> such seemed the jubilee
>   As when to greet some conqueror's advance
>
> Imperial Rome poured forth her living sea
>   From senatehouse & prison & theatre
> When Freedom left those who upon the free
>
> Had bound a yoke which soon they stooped to bear.[37]
>
> (ll. 111–16)

By yoking "senatehouse & prison & theatre," the poem links political, repressive, and cultural "state apparatuses" (Althusser) and asserts that "Imperial Rome" is constituted by their linkage; each institution celebrates the "conqueror's advance" and thereby participates directly in the abuses of power. Indeed, it becomes difficult within the context of the poem's perpetual revaluation of values to characterize these historical relationships as the opposition between legitimate authority and its contamination by empire building. Just as the poem discloses the complicity between figures of truth and delusion, the vision consistently refers us to the signs of power and empire that are harbored within the triumphal narrative of European civilization and thus demonstrates, to recall Walter Benjamin's celebrated phrase, that "there is no document of civilization which is not at the same time a document of barbarism."[38]

The signs of such joint ownership are the "signs of thought's empire over thought" (l. 211): "Mitres & helms & crowns, or wreaths of light" are the markings of ecclesiastical, political, or intellectual power.[39] These marks of power become legible the moment theological or political or philosophical thought takes shape or assumes form; or to put it another way, power is at work in the institution of thought, at each and every instance of thought's institutionalization. Such a reading is reinforced by the recognition that "the sacred few" who have eluded this disfiguration by power have, in de Man's words, "no earthly destiny whatsoever" or are, "like Christ or Socrates, . . . mere fictions in the writings of others" (*Rhetoric*, 97). Power is the necessary condition of all "earthly" thought and the source, simultaneously, of "thought's empire." Such an ornamentation of thought—"Mitres & helms & crowns, or wreaths of light"—is as inescapable as the figurality of language. The signs are the marks of thought's nonadequation to itself: intellectual thought, for example, cannot be dissociated from the acts and forms of power that institute thought, that permit thought to be communicated, reproduced, circulated, understood. According to Rousseau's reading of the procession of European history, thought cannot be rigorously distinguished from its discursive conditions: the "wreaths of light" are the signs of the discursivity of thought.

Though such knowledge is not the sort that provides the foundation for an alternative narrative or utopian vision of history, it does nonetheless reveal the apparently unavoidable discrepancy between "power & will." Upon hearing Rousseau's story of Napoleon's fall, the poet begins to "grieve" over this discrepancy:

> And much I grieved to think how power & will
> In opposition rule our mortal day—
>
> And why God made irreconcilable
> Good & the means of good.   (ll. 228–31)

If *The Triumph of Life* makes no effort to write an alternative historical narrative, a "history from below," it is because the poem addresses the ideological machinery, the "irreconcilability" between "Good & the means of good" that produces the official European narratives of history, an irreconcilability those narratives must in turn conceal.[40]

When Rousseau begins to identify the instances of this irreconcilability between "Good & the means of good" in the imperial history of Roman Catholicism, he points to the "shadows" cast by the mitres and sceptres, signs of the institution of the church:

> Gregory & John and men divine
>
> . . . rose like shadows between Man & god
> Till that eclipse, still hanging under Heaven,
> Was worshipped by the world o'er which they strode
>
> For the true Sun it quenched.   (ll. 288–92)

The lines are indispensable to any reading of the poem: for though the Roman Catholic Church is the particular institution under consideration in this episode of the vision, versions of the relationship should be applicable in principle to the other forms of thought—philosophical, political, literary—reviewed by the poem.[41] After Rousseau has "pointed to" "The Anarchs old whose force & murderous snares / Had founded many a sceptre bearing line" (ll. 285–86), the poet asserts, presumably on the basis of what he sees, that the history of the Catholic Church has imposed itself "like shadows between Man & god" and has "eclipsed" or "quenched" the "true Sun." As a consequence, the "eclipse" has itself become, through the institutional power of the church, the false object of worship. The lines suggest that the corruptions of and by power inherent to the institution block the light of truth, a light given off only by the "true Sun." But the passage complicates that idealist formulation by staging the poet's own misreading of what he sees. For the poem repeatedly undoes the possibility of a "true Sun," reinscribing the sun as one light within a procession of lights and the "true" as a figure of delusion. Displaced from the origin "Of glory & of good," the sun cannot be considered to represent a source of value and knowledge. The idealism that characterizes these lines is, in other words, the idealism of the poet-narrator but not of the poem. The poet reinstates the "true Sun" to a position denied by the poem and thus demonstrates that he shares in the delusion of the triumph, and confirms that he has "from spectator turn[ed] / Actor or victim in this wretchedness" (ll. 305–6). Situated within the darkness of the shadows, the poet must posit a "true Sun," a pure source of light and knowledge "quenched" by the "shape" of the Church. Itself a symptom of the shadows and veils of the vision, the poet's desire to see history in the lucidity and certainty of sunlight is as inescapable as it is impossible. The shadows of *The Triumph of Life* perpetually "hanging under Heaven" are shadows of the "wreaths of light," the "signs of thought's empire over thought," ideological signs: these are the shadows of a history that, dreaming of the sun, passes perpetually within the eclipse of ideology.

These passages in *The Triumph of Life* call us back to the work of mirrors and to *A Defence of Poetry*, to Shelley's declaration that poets are "mirrors of the gigantic shadows which futurity casts upon the present." As *The Triumph of Life* teaches us how to read this mirror-writing, we learn that poets are the surface upon which the shadows of history cast their ideological figures, a specular surface that reflects by the "wreaths of light" the triumph of ideology. This triumph of ideology compels us to reassess the claims attributed to Shelley, and often to Romanticism, that the imagination is a figure of transcendence, for the triumph of ideology in *The Triumph of Life* is precisely the failure of the received, and of Shelley's, idea of the imagination. It is a sign of the impoverished nature of our vocabularies of literary and cultural history that we can only characterize Shelley's poetry by the terms "idealism" or "pessimism" or "skepticism." To read for the workings of ideology in this poem is to disclose the workings of what we can only call a "materialist" poetics. By introducing the irreducibility of figurality and the effects of specularity into its marking and reading of history, by recognizing in those "wreaths of light" the signs not of thought as such but of "thought's empire over thought," and by refusing the temptation of the imagination, Shelley's poem gives "shape" to the perpetual and disfiguring force of ideology, and thus opens the way for a genuine and uncompromising "knowledge of the laws" of historical domination.

Small wonder, then, that Shelley could be regarded as "the ineffectual angel," for it seems a necessary act of containment to render the potential of such a thought "ineffectual." But if there is an angel in *The Triumph of Life*, it is much closer to the "Lost Angel of a Ruined Paradise" that we confront in *Adonais*, or perhaps closer still to Benjamin's "angel of history," which, no longer looking into the blinding light of the imagination, *and* aware that the blinding is irreparable, nonetheless turns his face toward the past, toward the wreckage that history casts at his feet. Still, there is an "unacknowledged" truth here to the rendering of the Shelleyan myth, for in Benjamin as in Shelley, the *angel* is indeed "ineffectual," *without* the "power to stay, awaken the dead and make whole what has been smashed." But the truth of the myth is also its undoing, for in Shelley as in Benjamin the truth of "messianic" impulses resides ultimately in their cancellation, announcing a materialism that spells the end of the imagination.

CHAPTER 4

∼❧

KEATS

The Materialism of Poetic Resistance

"Things" "Tease Us out of Thought"

I have taken as my epigraph to this study of the ideology of the imagination Keats's famous remark in his letter to Benjamin Bailey: "the imagination may be compared to Adam's dream—he awoke to find it truth." The remark demonstrates the degree to which the imagination had by the coming of the "second generation" of poets been successfully "instituted" and "enshrined" in Romantic discourse. Keats is both close enough to the ascent of the imagination to regard it as an event of historical significance and distant enough from it to take the imagination as the "given" of poetic discourse. Thus, Keats's poetry is written under the auspices of an imagination already instituted and enshrined, and, as I argued in the preceding chapter, an imagination decisively broken with by Shelley's last poem. In this chapter I shall consider how Keats's poetry contributes to the "break" we register in Shelley: I hope to reveal a "materialism" at work in Keats, a materialism that questions the truth claims made for the imagination and takes this "waking dream" to its breaking point.

Not so long ago, the claim of a "Keatsian materialism" would likely have appeared as little more than a willful perversion of the critical tradition. There is little doubt that without the recent good for-

tunes of "materialist" analysis, few would entertain seriously the attri-
bution of a materialism to the most aestheticized of English Romantic
poets, the poet who left instructions for an epitaph that is scarcely a
materialist manifesto: "here lies one whose name was writ in water." In
fact, the most important recent book-length study of Keats, Marjorie
Levinson's *Keats's Life of Allegory: The Origins of a Style*, is "materialist"
in its approach to the poet and his career.[1] This work powerfully and
compellingly reveals the pressures of social class that contribute to the
formation of the poetry. It is a measure of Levinson's rigorous materialism that she returns us to the cockney "origins of a style" that yield a
poem such as the one written to *Chapman's* Homer; but I believe it is
a measure of *Keats's* materialism that he makes those origins and that
education into the occasion for a radical engagement with the material
opacity of poetic language.

Keats belongs to the "epistemological break" in Romantic discourse, but not by way of the Shelleyan commitment to the radical intertwining of politics and language. We encounter in Shelley a poetry
that exerts such force on its "idealist" and "skeptical" assumptions that
in *The Triumph of Life* it achieves something else altogether, namely a
"materialist poetics." But Keats's materialism occurs in a poetry that is
at once more traditionally ethical and more immediately "material,"
not by virtue of any adherence to a historical or even mechanical materialism but by virtue of its almost obsessive attention to *things*, primarily such aesthetic things as books and marbles and urns. By way of
this attention, Keats's poetry compels "thought" to encounter the resistance of "things." This tense confrontation throws both the humanist ethics to which Keats himself subscribed and the "aestheticism" that
would serve as a refuge or compensation into a crisis of such magnitude
that the imagination is "Lost in a sort of purgatory blind," a crisis that
thus warrants the name "materialist." Keats's poetry is far indeed from
being a "flight" of the imagination.

To argue, however, for the presence of a materialism in Keats's poetry, to ascribe this achievement to the textual workings of the poems
themselves, risks reasserting the traditional privilege accorded poetic
language, a privilege closely associated with the "aesthetic ideology":
namely, that poetry has access to a truth that, if not empirical, is none-

theless the special aesthetic truth of "beauty." But the Keatsian materialism I want to explore in my readings of his poetry challenges the ideological and aesthetic identification of truth and beauty long attributed to the poet himself. This materialism is by no means the announced project of the poetry. Rather, it is hinted at in some early poems such as *Sleep and Poetry* in largely thematic expressions of uncertainty regarding the poetry's ethical and deeply humane vision. More significantly, Keats's materialism is encountered both formally and rhetorically in the odes and the *Hyperion* fragments through the corrosive action of "things" on "thought," an almost physical action that yields a poetics of resistance.

What remains to be seen is whether or not such a Keatsian materialism can be redeemed for what we would recognize as a materialist political thought (as I claimed in the case of Shelley), particularly since there are few explicitly political themes in Keats and since the tropes of redemption are themselves undone in the course of the poetry. But to answer such a question, or rather to locate the more productive place from which it can be asked, is not to assert a position outside the representations that constitute the text (the strategy of the New Historicism) but to *read* for Keats's materialism, to pursue the nature of the poet's (and the critic's) implications in those textual representations. Only at this point can we begin asking of Keats what the poet is already asking of aesthetic objects. Only then can we return to *The German Ideology*, the text Althusser cites as the inauguration of the "epistemological break" with idealism and empiricism to begin asking of Keats what Marx asks of German philosophy. Only at this point do we encounter a poetic resistance, figured as the resistance of things to thought, that deserves to be called a "materialism."

Keats's Humanism: Destructive Poetics, Redemptive Ethics

Keats never abandons his ethical project, his imperative that poetry be made the agent of "sympathy." These aspirations appear most assertively in the flat declarations of a conventional humanitarian sentiment. "The great end / Of poesy," writes Keats in *Sleep and Poetry*, is "that it should be a friend / To sooth the cares, and lift the thoughts of man."[2] Indeed, this is the "ideology," taken in the most general sense of a formal or relatively coherent program, of Keats's poetics. And it is the version of Keats we recognize from a long and respected tradition of criticism, which reaches a culmination of sorts in Helen Vendler's magisterial study of the odes, a study premised on the belief that "Keats was attempting in the odes 'a system of salvation' which had for him a religious seriousness."[3]

But Keats's assertions of a fundamentally humanitarian dimension to poetry circulate throughout the poems alongside equally persistent and increasingly acute presentations of an inherently destructive, even inhuman aspect of poetic language. This is the aspect of Keats's poetry emphasized and explored by Paul de Man. In his Introduction to the Signet edition of Keats, de Man asserts that in order to fulfill its redemptive mission, poetry "must move through the deathlike trances that abound in Keats."[4] But, as de Man goes on to suggest, the completion of the poetic trajectory through those "deathlike trances" is by no means assured. Indeed, the identification of poetic language with human redemption is explicitly challenged in *Sleep and Poetry*: "We've had / Strange thunders from the potency of song," and unless these "strange thunders" that issue directly from the source of poetry ("though of the muses born") are "mingled" with sweetness, their effect can only be likened to the apocalyptic devastation brought by a "fallen angel":

> But strength alone though of the muses born
> Is like a fallen angel: trees uptorn,
> Darkness, and worms, and shrouds, and sepulchres
> Delight it; for it feeds upon the burrs,
> And thorns of life; forgetting the great end
> Of poesy, that it should be a friend
> To sooth the cares, and lift the thoughts of man.
>
> (ll. 241–47)

An act of ethical recollection is required to reconcile these divergent aspects of poetry, a "recollection" that assigns these discontinuous poetic features to opposite poles ("birth" and "end"), and thereby manufactures the appearance of an organic narrative of maturation. But the syntax of the passage leaves no space for the subject of such recollection:

"strength alone" "forgets" "the great end / Of poesy." Poetry itself, as the syntax insists, has no ethical subject: left to its own devices, poetry can be the source of limitless destruction. Poetry must be made to remember something that exists only as its "end," and it can be redeemed only to the extent that the *poetic* account of poetry's destructive power invites a supplementary ethical interpretation.[5] What we confront in these lines from *Sleep and Poetry* is what Keats would describe in his letters as an "intensity," a negativity that, though "poetic," threatens to remain a sheerly disruptive force.[6]

The act of ethical redemption in Keats is distinguished from but intertwined with the destructive element of poetic force. Redemption thus follows the logic of "enshrinement/entombment" we witnessed in Wordsworth: the "intensity" that leads poetry to "Darkness, and worms, and shrouds, and sepulchres" must be redeemed from these tombs by an enshrining consciousness that remembers "the great end / Of poesy." The act of ethical redemption is characteristic of the work of criticism, at least as it is understood in the strain of moral criticism inherited from Matthew Arnold.[7] But "redemption" need not take the pious form of Arnold's criticism or Wordsworth's late poetry. We know well enough the temptations, evident in certain strains of post-structuralism, to recuperate the sort of poetic "disruption" we find in Keats as an anticipation of the contemporary critique of humanism.[8] But without succumbing to neoconservative caricatures of post-structuralism, it remains necessary to resist the invitations to celebrate Keats's destructive poetics, for there is nothing to indicate that such destructive "strength alone" can be enlisted in the services of a properly political critique or, for that matter, transformed into anything other than pure loss.

If it is unclear what is to be gained by poetic "strength alone," there is little doubt that Keats's emphasis on a destructive poetics entails a crisis for his own sense of the available "humanist" models of ethics and aesthetics, a crisis indicated in part by the poet's anxious insistence on the necessity of a supplementary redemptive vision. It is worth noting that Keats is writing in these lines of *Sleep and Poetry* as a *reader* of Romantic poetry; and reading for Keats always courts a forgetting of "the great end / Of poesy." Attendant to the act of genuine reading (whether one is "reading" a Romantic poem, the Elgin Marbles, or a Grecian Urn) is the risk of a destruction for which redemption cannot be assured. This is explicitly thematized in "On Sitting Down to Read *King Lear* Once Again," where nothing guarantees that the phoenix-like rebirth the poet requests will occur from the incendiary act of reading: "when I am consumed in the fire," the poet implores his "Chief Poet," "Give me new phoenix wings to fly at my desire." The "desire" named in the sonnet's closing couplet is, moreover, an ambivalent one, for "to fly *at* my desire" can be construed equally as an entrapment or as a liberation, particularly since the poem presents the experience of reading and its consequences in the form of a painful and almost compulsory repetition.

We are thus brought round again to the work of de Man, where we find the most rigorous and relentless contemporary interrogation of the operations and implications of the act of reading and the disruptive aspect of Romantic poetics. We can recognize what I have described primarily as a *thematic* confrontation between poetic destruction and redemption as an attempt to understand (and to contain) what de Man revealed to be the more fundamental and inherent *textual* incompatibility between the ethics and linguistics of poetry, an incompatibility encountered in the act of reading. We will return in this chapter to the problems and imperatives produced through de Man's practice of rhetorical reading; here it suffices to stress that the very urgency of an ethical imperative in Keats's poetry brings into relief what de Man would call the "fundamental non-human character of language." During the discussion of his Messenger Lecture on Benjamin's "The Task of the Translator" de Man asserts, "the 'inhuman' is: linguistic structures, the play of linguistic tensions, linguistic events that occur, possibilities which are inherent in language—independently of any intent or any drive or any wish or any desire we might have."[9] It is not immediately at issue whether one accepts de Man's assertion regarding the nonhuman aspect of language, or whether one prefers what de Man's interlocutor in this instance, M. H. Abrams, calls the "humanistic perspective," namely that language is the "most human of things" since it "makes its meanings" (in de Man, *Resistance*, 99). The point to be stressed is that Keats's poetry stages this very confrontation between a "non-human aspect" of poetic language ("strength alone though of the muses born") and its "humanistic" compensation ("that it [poetry] should be a friend . . . of man"): the passage can be read as an allegory of the encounter between what has come to be known as "decon-struction" and "humanism."[10] But the reader of *Sleep and Poetry* is likely to regard the contest as one decided in advance, for despite the poet's sense of human urgency, Keats's assertions of a sheer linguistic power result in a poetry whose destructive effects ("trees uptorn, / Darkness, and worms, and shrouds, and sepulchres") demand a compensatory ethical sentiment that appears as just that, compensatory, secondary, and prescriptive.

Such is the case of *The Fall of Hyperion*, where the divergence between the destructive and the redemptive aspects of poetry assumes more disturbing, more irreconcilable forms. In *The Fall of Hyperion*, poetry does not coincide with the human, and the desire to lend poetry a human face, to "humanize" poetic "saying" (II.1, 2) is registered as failure. When the poem's dreamer first encounters the goddess Moneta, the words of her "holy power" are heard from "white fragrant cur-tains" as "Language pronounc'd." Much like the "high prophetess" as she "parts her veils," poetry discloses an inhuman visage that, blind to the external world ("visionless entire" of "all external things," I.267, 268), "works a constant change": "Deathwards progressing / To no death was that visage" (I.260–61). Many readers of the poem have dem-onstrated that the perpetual "Deathwards progressing" cannot be rec-onciled with patterns of dialectical progression; nor does the temporal figure of progressing/falling allow for redemption. The lines remain poetic "strength alone," which, like the sublime language of the gods, can be registered only as "barren noise" (II.5), no friend to man. Un-til the poem is broken off, it repeats over and over the incompatibility, thematized as redemption and destruction, between the ethical longings of a human world and the "barren noise," the "blank splendor" of po-etic language.

We are confronted with a poetry whose genuine commitment to a "system of salvation" demands the poetic passage through a negation, through a potentially endless burning and falling—what Keats famously calls a "negative capability"—that in the process suspends, even "oblit-

erates" the very salvation it was to accomplish. The urgent ethical declarations in Keats's poetry and letters are legible as both symptoms of
and responses to what de Man characterized as the pervasive noncoincidence between a human domain and the material, nonhuman operations of language, a noncoincidence disclosed in the poetry itself.
The difficulty, which is by no means restricted to the interpretation of
Keats, consists in achieving a mode of reading this materialist "negative
capability" that can explore its implications while resisting restorative
gestures that would prematurely recuperate its negativity. The difficulty
may well reveal a paradox inherent in the activity of interpretation, for
even as we stress the failures of Keats's *ethical* vision, we do so by way of
an inevitable valorization of the "destructive" element. To call the situation "ideological" is not to propose a solution but to name the full
dimension of the predicament.

"Lost in a Sort of Purgatory Blind": *The German Ideology* and the Keatsian Imagination

It is precisely the assignment of the imagination to reconcile the
contradiction between the destructive impulses of poetry and the fulfillment of an ethical vision. And though Keats will invest such hopes in
the imagination, given the term's volatility in his poetry, its promise of
a reconciliation is far from guaranteed: given its oscillation between
"confinement" and transgression, we are not, in other words, likely to
wake and find it "truth." In "Dear Reynolds," for instance, Keats describes the consequences of the "imagination brought / Beyond its
proper bound, yet still confined" (ll. 78–79): is it, he asks, that such an
imagination becomes "Lost in a sort of purgatory blind," one that "cannot refer to any standard law / Of either earth or heaven?" (ll. 80–82).
We will return to these lines in more detail below; here it suffices to
note both the imagination's potential for instability and wandering and
Keats's sense of the consequences of an imagination that has lost its
way.

The precariousness of the imagination is also at issue in the famous early lines from *The Fall of Hyperion*, where it must be "saved" by
the "telling" of "Poesy":

> For Poesy alone can tell her dreams,
> With the fine spell of words alone can save
> Imagination from the sable charm
> And dumb enchantment.   (ll. 8–11)

Poetry is not simply the most fitting idiom for the imagination; it is moreover its salvation: "the fine spell of words *alone* can *save* / Imagination," can deliver the faculty from "the sable charm / And dumb enchantment." What we have described as the *problem* of ideology is evident in this hope of poetic redemption. The promise of poetry in *The Fall of Hyperion* is that it might retrieve the imagination from a "sable charm" and "dumb enchantment," from what in another register we might call ideological mystification. But the promise of poetry is threatened even as it is made since the result of a "spell," particularly such a "fine spell of words," is a trance. How are we to determine from within the "spell" cast by poetic language whether the imagination has been saved from or lost to "sable charm / And dumb enchantment"? Such a judgment is made particularly difficult because we know this charm and enchantment to be precisely the lure that is performed by much of Keats's own poetry, as readers drawn to the luxuriant language of "The Eve of St. Agnes" or to the sensuousness of "To Autumn" will testify.[11]

If the lines from *The Fall of Hyperion* presume the imagination's poetic value, they simultaneously propose an imagination that remains subject to and dependent upon a linguistic vehicle. The poetic vehicle not only casts a spell that cannot be regulated or determined in advance but manufactures states of dreaming, states not associated with epistemological certainty. At the poem's beginning the *intrication* between the spirit and the language of the imagination suspends the authority of the poet and the status of the imagination and thus acknowledges that the poem is subject to what we have described as the ideological predicament.

We are delivered in an unexpected way to that "other" text of the "break," *The German Ideology*. In the Introduction I discussed how Marx's reading of German philosophy yields a materialism. Here, we may recall that for Marx, contemporary German thought was "idealist" from its very point of departure: "not only in their answers but in their

very questions there was a mystification."[12] German philosophy symptomatically ignores or denegates the determinant relation between
"mind" or "spirit" and "matter": "the 'mind' is from the outset afflicted with the curse of being burdened with matter" (*German Ideology*,
43–44). We have seen how "the curse of being burdened with matter"
is in Wordsworth the problem of the imagination, a problem that
prompts as symptom and response the "dream of the Arab." The anxiety over "spirit's" material burden is a pervasive one for Keats, a condition that the poems return to—almost as if by compulsion—less in an
effort to resolve than to address. Keats's poetry does not of course seek
to explain how "consciousness is . . . from the very beginning a social
product, and remains so as long as men exist at all" (44). But at the
point where Keats's poetic thought begins to "jostle" against things, it
asks questions of thought that place an unrelieved pressure on the claims
of spirit's autonomy or transcendence. The poems do not, in other
words, block the recognition of the material "burden," or sever the de-
terminate linkage between "matter" and "spirit." Contrary to the
claims made for or against it, Keats's poetry at its most "advanced" does
not—returning now to Marx—ascribe to spirit an autonomous existence, or believe that accordingly "life is . . . determined by consciousness" (37).

   Though the Keatsian materialism implied through "negative capability" may seem an unlikely candidate for the convergence with a
"historical materialism," we might return to a critical strain within
Marxism that would, as Roy Bhaskar phrases it, "treat materialism more
as a *prise de position*, a practical orientation, than as a set of quasi-
descriptive theses, and more specifically as . . . a series of denials, largely
of claims of traditional philosophy—e.g. concerning the existence of
God, souls, forms, ideals, duties, the absolute, etc."[13] In the case of
Keats, such a materialist *prise de position* primarily occurs not at the level
of theme (though it often resonates thematically) but at the material
level of poetic language: these are the points of its refusals via poetic
"strength alone" of the claims of a humanist redemption, refusals that
from the perspective of the thoroughly human desire to redeem can
only be thematized as "destruction." I want to characterize this aspect
of Keats's poetry along the lines suggested by Pierre Macherey's ac-

count of a philosophy that works in a "materialist way": "If there is a 'struggle' between materialism and idealism, . . . it is not some eternal dialogue between two independent and divergent protagonists. . . . If materialism there is, then it is in the very development of idealism that it is to be sought."[14] This is Keats's "materialism": it is not a "materialist poetics" that yields "materialist knowledge" but the eruption of a materialist disposition through the faultlines of an idealist (humanist and aestheticist) poetics.

That Keats's materialism does not result in such materialist knowledge is apparent in the early lines of *The Fall of Hyperion*. While they do not of themselves disrupt the privilege Keats assigned to poetry, they attest that the living poet does not have access to a space free from ideology. The passage challenges, moreover, the possibility of liberation from ideology through demystifying gestures: the lines assert that the ideological predicament is shared by poet and critic, their difference becoming as undecidable as that between poet and fanatic. The more extensive ideological implications of this antinomy become evident in the face of Keats's insistence on poetry's ethical mission.

Keats's Materialism: Things to Thought

The provocation of Keats's materialism transpires in a poem such as "Dear Reynolds" much as it does in *The Fall of Hyperion*, through the invocation of the imagination, the faculty most likely to be associated with a Romantic idealism. Confronting the discrepancy between extravagant dreams or dream-visions and our prosaic "jostling" "in the world," addressing the divergence between "thought" and "things," the poet dares not "to philosophize," refusing to spirit away "things" for the "prize" of "high reason" (ll. 74–75). The poet does not, in other words, commit the error that Marx imputes to the German ideologues: resisting the model of philosophy, Keats presents the unsettled ideological situation as the problem named by the imagination.

The ideological staging of the imagination occurs in a poem known primarily for the themes and the passages it contributes to the "Ode to a Nightingale" and the "Ode on a Grecian Urn." Written in 1818 to Keats's friend John Hamilton Reynolds, "Dear Reynolds" opens with a chronicle of the poet's "disjointed" nocturnal dreams, "shapes, and shadows, and remembrances." These are played out as a procession of historical personages disfigured into the fantastic and grotesque images of childhood dreams:

> Dear Reynolds, as last night I lay in bed,
> There came before my eyes that wonted thread
> Of shapes, and shadows, and remembrances,
> That every other minute vex and please:
> Things all disjointed come from North and South,
> Two witch's eyes above a cherub's mouth,
> Voltaire with casque and shield and habergeon,
> And Alexander with his night-cap on—
> Old Socrates a tying his cravat;
> And Hazlitt playing with Miss Edgeworth's cat;
> And Junius Brutus pretty well so so,
> Making the best of's way towards Soho.
>   (ll. 1–12)

Though Keats records them as the text of his private visions, such scenes of sleep and dreams and visions "That every other minute vex and please" and that give passage to the imagination are conventional enough in poems of the period to be recognized as "Romantic." Keats affirms that "few are there who escape these visitings" (l. 13), Gothic "visitings" of an "Enchanted Castle": "You know it well enough, where it doth seem / A mossy place, a Merlin's Hall, a dream" (ll. 33–34). If we read Keats, we know dreams well enough to know how little the dreamer can control the migrations and transformations of the dream images:

> The doors all look as if they oped themselves,
> The windows as if latch'd by fays and elves—
> And from them comes a silver flash of light
> As from the westward of a summer's night;
> Or like a beauteous woman's large blue eyes
> Gone mad through olden songs and poesies.
>   (ll. 49–54)

If this landscape of enchantment and madness, "olden songs" and "sweet music," "vexes" "every other minute," it is because these Romantic "dreamings," knowing no natural colors or images, must "shadow our own soul's daytime / In the dark void of night" (ll. 70–71):

> O that our dreamings all of sleep or wake
> Would all their colours from the sunset take:
> From something of material sublime,
> Rather than shadow our own soul's daytime
> In the dark void of night.
>
> (ll. 67–71)

Keats laments that our "dreamings," composed as they are of shadows, cannot instead be derived "from something of material sublime." The apostrophic expression of the poet's desire is phrased as an unrealizable wish: dreamings are forever fated to "shadow our own soul's daytime / In the dark void of night." The Gothic dreams, thoughts, and visions that have unfolded in the earlier lines assert their distance from an inescapable worldliness and open the rift between mind and world that calls for the reconciliations often promised by a Romantic imagination:

> For in the world
> We jostle—but my flag is not unfurl'd
> On the admiral staff—and to philosophize
> I dare not yet!—Oh never will the prize,
> High reason, and the lore of good and ill,
> Be my award. Things cannot to the will
> Be settled, but they tease us out of thought.
>
> (ll. 71–77)

The poet refrains from philosophizing as he recognizes the obstinate irreducibility of our "jostling" "in the world." A disruptive physicality of motion is implied in the image of "jostling": "in the world / We jostle" because the materiality of the world impinges upon our trajectory through it. This elicits Keats's admission of the failure of poetry to achieve a philosophical or ethical vision: neither "high reason" nor ethical judgment are ever to be "awarded" the poet. The lines thematize the materialism of the poem; they announce the poem's *prise de position*, its refusal of a poetics of sympathy or redemption, foreclosing in a definitive fashion the anxious question, posed urgently by the poet to the goddess Mnemosyne in *The Fall of Hyperion*, whether "a poet is a sage; / A humanist, physician to all men" (I.189–90).

This should not be construed as a renunciation of philosophical speculation or ethical considerations in the name of a poetry that removes itself from the pressures of such concerns; we should read it rather as the scrupulous recognition that poetry, caught as it is in the opening between reason and the world, "dare not" "philosophize." Nor can the poet, situated in this gap, propose to teach the lessons of "good and ill." Barbara Jones Guetti has taught us to read the lines and this strain of Keats's poetry as an allegory of what de Man names "the resistance to theory."[15] In Keats's poetic epistle to Reynolds, the resistance to theory is the resistance of things to thought, a resistance generated *through* thought and not by some unthinkable immediacy of the thing itself. The "things" that "cannot to the will / Be settled" mark the material limits to thought and as a consequence "jostle" our negotiation with the world. We may feel that we are in a position to "know" the images that circulate in our waking and sleeping dreams—we may "know well enough" the "Enchanted Castle"—but this does not secure our knowledge of the "thing," of a thingliness that is not subject to will or knowable through reason. "Things" "tease us out of thought" in both senses of the verb: thought is "teased" and seduced by the allure of things, a tease that by nature cannot be satisfied; and thought is teased "physically" by things, the strands of thought separated and defined by the materiality, the resistance of things.

This is a materiality encountered in the first instance by what Heidegger in *The Origin of the Work of Art* calls the "thingly aspect of the art work."[16] The "thingly aspect," which "even the much-vaunted aesthetic experience cannot get around," is that in the art work which "joins" or articulates and, as in allegory, "manifests something other" (*Origin*, 19, 20). Materiality is the *poetic* aspect of any "work of art," poem or temple or urn, that which is not mimetic or aesthetic but "projective" (74). In other words, the thingliness of the art work is its nominative power, which does not "mean" but signifies "something other": "Language, by naming beings . . . first brings beings to word and to appearance" (73). The material "projective" and "nominative" dimension of the work of art—its poetic aspect—invites our efforts to give meaning, prompts our interpretive responses, but remains itself a nonmeaningful material residue.

If "things"—even the "overwrought" urn of Greek antiquity—resist the impulse to "aestheticize" or "moralize" or "philosophize," can the same be said for the exquisitely wrought poetic ode to the classical urn? The ode allegorizes the feverish desires of Keats's Hellenism, which is to say that it stages the desire that produced Romantic Hellenism in the first place. By its insistence on the urn's materiality as object, the ode confounds the hermeneutic activity that it must itself perform. This mute but written thing, this "silent form" and "Sylvan historian" "dost tease us out of thought / As doth eternity." Jones Guetti describes the particular allure and frustration of the "tease": "The urn 'teases us out of thought *as doth eternity*.' It offers us the appearance of a timeless, eternal 'object'—very much as the term, or signifier, 'eternity' permits us to think we are thinking our way outside time or history."[17] The poem itself, victim of the aesthetic ideology it stages and resists, has offered such an "appearance of a timeless eternal 'object.'" But like the urn, covered with figures that give the appearance of a story, the poem remains a "Cold pastoral," a signifying "thing" that refuses to yield the aesthetic or historical meaning it invites.

The poet's ode to this remnant of Greek antiquity allows us to read in "a materialist way" the Romantic Hellenism it appears to espouse.[18] The urn is the fragmented material of a pastness that can never be reconstructed, that can never be known as such. The urn "remains," but not as a living testimony to "the sheer presence of the past" or to the Gadamerian sentiment that "its world is still part of ours."[19] Rather, the world of Keats's urn is a remainder, a *still part*, a fragment for which there is no whole: the urn simply, mutely "remains" as the material insistence of the alterity and untotalizability of history. The poem's celebrated and exhaustively rehearsed closing lines appear to recuperate that strangeness of history by a restoration of the ethical vision, now proclaimed as a triumph of the aesthetic. The urn "say'st, / 'Beauty is Truth, Truth Beauty'"; such a "saying" makes it "a friend to man," but to say this is to say *to the urn* that it gives us a figure of speech, the citation of a chiasmus that by marking itself as figure simultaneously invites and resists the aesthetic interpretation it declares. "That is all / Ye know on earth, and all ye need to know": far from celebrating this aes-theticization of truth, far from the serene acceptance of the identity between truth and beauty, a reading of the urn such as the one per-formed in the poem remarks on the limits of earthly knowledge and stresses the desire, the inexhaustible need *in* knowing. We find in Keats's account of this "tease" by "things," where the course of thought is drawn to the limits posed by materiality, an inscription of the ideolog-ical instance. The Marx of *The German Ideology* would have recognized it as such, and Adorno would call it the moment of nonidentity, a "ma-terial preponderance" that cannot be philosophized or aestheticized or moralized away.[20]

"Or is it," as Keats asks in "Dear Reynolds," that the "unsettling" and "teasing" gap between thought and things, what we are calling the ideological instance, is another name for the "improper" work of the imagination:

> Or is it that imagination brought
> Beyond its proper bound, yet still confined,—
> Lost in a sort of purgatory blind,
> Cannot refer to any standard law
> Of either earth or heaven?
>
> (ll. 78–82)

Owing to the ambiguity of this "Or," we cannot know whether the trajectory of the imagination, invoked at this important moment of self-evaluation in the poem's narrative, is to be understood as another way of saying that "things tease us out of thought," *or* whether the re-sistance of things to thought, the ideological instance, is a symptom of the imagination's transgression. If the imagination within "its proper bound" holds out hope for the reconciliation of thought and things, or between "high reason" and worldly "jostling," the destination of the imagination as it is "brought" in the passage is a dead end that offers no illumination or reconciliation: as in the case of *Sleep and Poetry*, imag-ination is "lost in a lovely labyrinth" (l. 265). In such a disposition and without an identifiable source in "earth or heaven," the imagination is no longer fit to provide what Keats in a letter to Benjamin Bailey calls the "rudder" of poetry (*Letters*, 170). The imagination both exceeds "its proper bound" and remains simultaneously "confined." Unteth-

ered yet confined, transgressive yet transcendent, the imagination called
upon to account for the poet's Gothic visions is itself "Lost in a sort of
purgatory blind." The passage reproduces the uncertain direction and
ambiguous agency of the imagination: beginning as subject, the imagination is "brought" in these lines and repositioned as its object. This
syntactical displacement from grammatical subject to object is exemplary of the "blind" movement of the imagination throughout these
lines. It may be that the vexing condition described by the poet is the
effect of an imagination simultaneously "lost" and "confined," in tran-
sit without the stabilizing reference to any existing or imaginable "standard law."

If the absence of reference that condemns the imagination to a
"purgatory blind" were an exceptional circumstance incurred when
imagination strays "Beyond its proper bound," one might expect Keats
to offer a vision of a secured reference to a "standard law / Of either
earth or heaven" that would be the wonted circumstance of an imagination functioning within "its proper bound." But he does not. Nor
could one get further from the truth than by saying that the notion of
the imagination in Keats represents the spiriting away of the ideological condition. Without promising a stabilizing reconciliation between
thought and things, the imagination invoked by Keats in these lines
opens the question of the ideological connections between law, value,
and perception. The succeeding lines confirm that this lost version of
the imagination is the rule rather than the exception: "It is a flaw / In
happiness to see beyond our bourn / . . . It spoils the singing of the
nightingale" (ll. 82–83, 85). Nothing indicates that the condition of
imagination in which we "see beyond our bourn," that the condition of
self-consciousness and mourning and desire, that the "flaw in happiness" we have learned to identify as our Romantic condition as fallen,
temporal beings can be avoided. This disposition of the imagination,
where thought meets its resistance, offers no positive knowledge of self
or world, and does not, therefore, serve as "sage, humanist, or physician." Situated in the passage between thought and things, and "Lost in
a sort of purgatory blind," the imagination can disclose only a certain
"negative capability": we see in the imagination, in its blindness and
confinement and by its reflection on the material limits to thought, the
figure of ideology.[21]

The encounter with this material limit is confirmed by the subsequent stanza of the poem, which, as if to demonstrate formally the dead end reached by the imagination, must renew its address to Reynolds, though the renewal only asserts the incapacity of the poem to "speak" its "mysterious tale": "Dear Reynolds, I have a mysterious tale / And cannot speak it" (ll. 86–87).[22] Despite the disclaimer, what in fact follows Keats's admission that he has a tale he cannot speak is an account of a "mysterious tale," an apocalyptic vision that is either prompted or delivered as the poet commences to read:

> The first page I read
> Upon a lampit rock of green sea weed
> Among the breakers. . . .
>   . . .
>
> I was at home,
> And should have been most happy—but I saw
> Too far into the sea; where every maw
> The greater on the lesser feeds evermore.
>   (ll. 87–89, 92–95)

The sense of being "at home," now irrevocably in the past, is shattered by an act of seeing that exceeds its "proper bound." Having gazed "too far into the sea," the poet sees "an eternal fierce destruction":

> But I saw too distinct into the core
> Of an eternal fierce destruction,
> And so from happiness I far was gone.
>   (ll. 96–98)

The "eternal fierce destruction" that forever banishes the poet "from happiness" is a vision of the "greater" perpetually and eternally feeding upon the "lesser." The vision of power and domination, "strange thunders from the potency of song," erase the conditions for happiness, for they hold out no hope of redemption. But if the imagination in this poem undoes the ethical and aesthetic claims that Keats often made—and that we continue to make—in its name, this "negative capability" makes possible the discovery of the "overdetermined forms" of the imagination's materiality, a discovery that should resonate corrosively for the eminently ideological forms of our own aesthetic education.

CHAPTER 5

ELIOT

Sympathy, Or the Imagination of Community

"The Extension of Sympathies"

I have argued in the preceding chapters for the existence of a significant faultline in Romantic discourse, fully on the order of an "epistemological break," that is linked to the figure—and failure—of the
imagination. To describe this as an "epistemological break" in the Althusserian sense is, I believe, the most accurate and productive way of
describing what takes place in and *after* Romanticism. To call it an
"epistemological break," then, and to name Shelley and Keats, as poets
of the break, "materialist" poets, is not to assert in the Kuhnian sense
the appearance of a new poetic "paradigm." The radical break we have
described in Romantic discourse is just that, a *rupture* that remains the
condition of social and cultural discourse. "Obviously," writes Althusser
in "Lenin and Philosophy," the "epistemological break [that he attributes to Marx] is not an instantaneous event. . . . Whether or not we
accept the fact, we are still inscribed in the theoretical space marked
and opened by this break today. . . . [T]his break inaugurates a history
which will never come to an end."[1] What we find in the Romantic
poets of the "break" is not the announcement of a new poetics but—
now paraphrasing Althusser—the declaration of a rupture with the
imagination that opens the space for a new poetics.

But to those with eyes to see it, such a rupture may well appear less the condition for new cultural practices than simply a bad break, one that threatens poetry and indeed the range of social discourses that make it possible to sustain, or even to conceive of, community. I want here to pursue this path opened by the "break," to consider how a significant Victorian writer perceives and responds to the consequences of such a discursive rupture. What motivates the choice of George Eliot— beyond her stature as England's most significant novelist of the century—is my belief that Eliot's work emerges from the Romantic ideological situation and embarks on one of the most sustained and sophisticated efforts to address its ideological condition, in the wake of the imagination. George Eliot, in spite of what Althusser might rightly call her "Feuerbachian humanism," has the eyes to see the break we have been describing, although it stands before her as something to be repaired, for the possibility of community itself hangs in the balance.

The appearance of a chapter on George Eliot also brings into bold relief a crucial omission in this book: the role played by gender in the constitution and division of the imagination. In the story I have been telling, gender is indeed at work—in the feminized projections of the imagination, in the elaborate mechanics of desire, and in the feminization of Shelley and of Keats. But with George Eliot a new complication appears, for we now find ourselves at a remove from "official" or radical poetic and philosophical discourses and on the resolutely feminized terrain of the novel, a terrain in which gender is a governing feature from production through consumption, from theme and character to the modes of narrative discourse. Thus, the novels of George Eliot not only tell us the Victorian story of the imagination in Romantic discourse, the story of the "break" wrought on cultural discourse by the imagination, but also constitute a deeply gendered narrative response to this Romantic predicament.

The Victorian novels of George Eliot are thus not "after" Romanticism: they demonstrate that the ideological problems opened by the imagination remain the *internal* conditions of Victorian fiction. Moreover, the novels perform their own ideological work on their Romantic discursive conditions, ideological work that in the case of a novelist such as Eliot necessarily implicates the operations of its narrative discourse. For George Eliot, the imagination is figured as an obstacle to genuine community, which must be overcome for some imaginary social resolution to be narrated. To say that a resolution is *narrated* is not, moreover, to diminish its importance, because for Eliot narration is understood as a fully social and ethical act, a worldly performance. To read for the imagination in the novels of George Eliot is thus to attend to the point at which *formal* questions of narration confront the social and cultural issues present in the stories told: repeatedly and insistently, that ideological point is the imagination. This chapter is devoted to the figure of the imagination in two early novels by George Eliot, *Adam Bede* and *The Mill on the Floss*, works that register forcefully the formal and thematic pressures of the Romantic heritage, works that are crucial to the formation of the narrative principle of sympathy that is itself a primary achievement of Eliot's art.

"Sympathy" is what Eliot employs as the solution to the ideological predicament; it is, as I will argue below, the means by which the Romantic wound opened by the imagination is to be sutured, the break closed. "The greatest benefit we owe to the artist," writes Eliot in "The Natural History of German Life," "whether painter, poet, or novelist is the extension of our sympathies."[2] What gives Eliot's project its power and distinguishes it from other conservative Victorian responses, those of Arnold or Carlyle for instance, is her deployment of a Romantic figure, of sympathy, as the very means by which the rupture introduced by Romanticism can be overcome. We should, moreover, understand the deployment of sympathy to be the narrative principle and performative work of her novels: it makes the novels into the agents of cultural history that they have indeed become.

We have noted in earlier chapters the alliances between imagination and sympathy, terms with closely linked genealogies in British literary and philosophical texts of the eighteenth and nineteenth centuries. And a long tradition of criticism has taught us to recognize "sympathy" as an important ethical theme of Eliot's novels. The insistence of this ethics of sympathy and the close cultural affiliations between sympathy and the imagination can make the two concepts difficult to distinguish.[3] While Eliot presents both sympathy and imagination as the effects of a Romantic desire to extend consciousness, to address the "contrast between the outward and the inward," sympathy, unlike the imagination, is the medium of resolution.

The divergence between imagination and sympathy is for George Eliot a persistent one. Reviewing the successes of Elizabeth Barrett Browning's *Aurora Leigh*, Eliot asserts that only the most successful works of literary art manage to "inform" "melody, fancy and imagination—what we may call its poetic body" with a "*soul*," with the "genuine thought and feeling" Eliot will identify consistently as "sympathy."[4] Sympathy is the imaginative impulse that, transcending the egotism and renouncing the desires of self, promises to bridge the epistemological and ethical gap between self and world.[5] We find a story of this morphology in Philip Wakem's letter to Maggie near the end of *The Mill on the Floss*, a story of the "transformation" of imagination into sympathy:

> The new life I have found in caring for your joy and sorrow more than for what is directly my own, has transformed the spirit of rebellious murmuring into that willing endurance which is the birth of strong sympathy. I think nothing but such complete and intense love could have initiated me into that enlarged life which grows and grows by appropriating the life of others; for before, I was always dragged back from it by ever-present painful self-consciousness. I even think sometimes that this gift of transferred life which has come to me in loving you, may be a new power to me.[6]

This sense of a "new power" is, of course, the "gift of a transferred life" from Maggie to Philip, the lessons of a distinctly feminized sacrifice and "willing endurance" Philip learns from Maggie. But I believe that we must read Philip's letter as an emblem of the novel's own project: the sense of a "new power" that Philip describes is the gift of a life "transferred" from the Romantic "spirit of rebellious murmuring" identified with the imagination to the "birth of strong sympathy." The letter both testifies to the power of Maggie's "strong sympathy" and affirms the convergence of an aesthetic and ethical judgment. Eliot's novels are predicated on the possibility of this convergence: through it they propose to tell the stories of the "transferals" and "transformations" achieved by sympathy. These stories purport to demonstrate how sympathy might create from the conditions of Romantic self-consciousness a genuine spirit of community, a sustained and sustaining sense of "enlarged life."[7]

For George Eliot, imagination is the disfiguration of sympathy, the extension of a consciousness deflected and distorted by the "rebellious murmuring" of subjective desire and thus devoid of sympathy's ethical dimension, "ideological" in the narrow sense of "false consciousness," incapable of sympathy's "wide fellow-feeling" (*Mill on the Floss*, 435). To use Eliot's metaphors, sympathy is the binding "thread" that "weaves" —or, better perhaps for our purposes, *stitches*—the self into the ostensibly organic textures of community.

Romanticism's "Painful Collisions"

When the proper name "Romanticism" and the proper names that we associate with it make their appearances in Eliot's narrative discourse, they are presented typically either as fevered Byronic excess or sympathetic Wordsworthian morality. In *Middlemarch*, for instance, the narrator, looking back to the days before Romanticism had migrated to England, considers Romanticism itself a "movement" that no longer offers its peculiar seductions, having long been absorbed into the currency of everyday thought: "Romanticism, which has helped to fill some dull blanks with love and knowledge, had not yet penetrated the times with its leaven and entered into everybody's food; it was fermenting still as a distinguishable vigorous enthusiasm in certain long-haired German artists at Rome, and the youth of other nations who worked or idled near them were sometimes caught in the spreading movement."[8] The narrator brackets the lure of Romanticism such that its "spreading movement" does not threaten to entangle the fragile weave of the narrative: Romanticism is defined here as a "movement" that emerged too late to disturb the plot or characters of the novel and that has since been absorbed into the main currents of cultural life. But by inscribing the figure of Romanticism as the historical horizon of this story, the narrator introduces if only to defuse the extent of its entanglements. The passage is deceptive, moreover, since the seductions and dangers of the more turbulent currents or "spreading movement" of Romantic thought are by no means so summarily contained in

George Eliot's novels. Far more than an isolated literary school, Romanticism is the discursive condition of Eliot's novels, a condition that the narrator must explicitly address and resolve in the course of narrative production. What we may initially presume to be a secondary issue of literary periodization—whether or not to classify the novels of George Eliot as part of a Romantic tradition—turns out to be a formal narrative matter of considerable proportions.[9]

If Romanticism in George Eliot is no longer taken merely as the proper name of a literary "movement" but instead names the ideological condition of an internal thought in persistent conflict with the matters of the world, then "Romanticism" is at the heart of the difficulties faced by a Dorothea Brooke or a Maggie Tulliver.[10] Throughout *The Mill on the Floss*, the incommensurability between a subjective interiority and an external world is written in the rhetoric of Romanticism. At an early stage of her education, for instance, Maggie recognizes the discrepancy between the Romantic texts she reads and the "hard, real life" she must negotiate. This discrepancy takes the form of the need for something "*more*":

> Even at school she had often wished for books with *more* in them: everything she learned there seemed like the ends of long threads that snapped immediately. . . . Sometimes Maggie thought she could have been contented with absorbing fancies; if she could have had all Scott's novels and all Byron's poems!—then, perhaps, she might have found happiness enough to dull her sensibility to her actual daily life. And yet . . . [ellipsis in original] they were hardly what she wanted. . . . She wanted some explanation of this hard, real life. (251)

The names of Scott and Byron operate, predictably enough, as the convenient metonyms for the thematics of a withdrawal from the world into the "absorbing fancies" of literature. These are names that offer no key to the "explanation" or interpretation of this "hard, real life." Thus Maggie substitutes for the reveries of these romances the narrative of religious devotion she finds in Thomas à Kempis, and there she discovers what she believes to be a guide for action: "Blessed are those ears that receive the whispers of the divine voice," she reads, "and listen not to the whisperings of the world. Blessed are those ears which hearken not unto the voice which soundeth outwardly, but unto the Truth, which teacheth inwardly" (254). Maggie believes she has uncovered "a secret of life," "a sublime height to be reached without the help of outward things" (254): the soundings of this unworldly "voice" promise the "key" to happiness.

The writings of Thomas à Kempis fail to deliver this promise not because, as with Byron and Scott, they are the "absorbing fancies" of a misguided Romanticism but because Maggie remains a Romantic reader who misinterprets them. Approaching these religious texts "with all the hurry of an imagination that could never rest in the present" (255), Maggie cannot perceive "the inmost truth of the old monk's outpourings" (255). In a world divided between the stirrings of the imagination and "the voice which soundeth outwardly," the "truth" of religious devotion cannot be realized: to the very extent that these stories are alluring to this Romantic reader, their meaning remains elusive. As a consequence of this disquieted imagination, the unreconciled division persists between the worlds of internal thought and "hard, real life." "No wonder," says the narrator in a sentence that Hegel or, subsequently, Lukács would find symptomatic of Romanticism, "when there is this contrast between the outward and inward, that painful collisions come of it" (208).[11]

What the narrator calls the "contrast between the outward and the inward" is what we, after Hegel and after Lukács, have learned to call Romanticism. The "painful collisions" that come of this Romantic discrepancy between inward and outward are the results of an imagination marked always as desire. As the narrator of *Middlemarch* remarks, "we are all of us imaginative in some form or other, for images are the brood of desire" (335). The urgency, the "hurry of imagination" is the desire to reconcile the very division that gives rise to imagination in the first place. The desire generated by this imagination is, moreover, a sexual one and as such is destined to result, time and again, in the "painful collisions" that are inescapable for a character such as Maggie Tulliver, "painful collisions" that subsequently become thematized in the novel as "tragedy."

But the thematics of tragedy are not sufficient to describe what Jacqueline Rose, drawing our attention to the strains of desire in these novels, has powerfully characterized as the "spectacle of woman" in

George Eliot. Situated outside the more authorized official discourses of poetry and philosophy, Maggie's consciousness of her dislocation, her conjurings of the imagination, her desires for "something more," become the stage for the spectacle that befalls her, a spectacle that, as Rose describes it, shows "the disturbance of the feminine" to be "bound into the very form of the narrative": "George Eliot could be seen as bringing to fruition a structure of fantasy which greatly exceeds the domain of the novel, in which the man and the woman are distributed between the poles of spectacle and the tale of female sexuality becomes the ultimate story to be told because . . . she has already been made the cause of a crisis in the telling itself."[12] Once the imagination leaves the domain of those "long-haired German artists" and is installed in the likes of Maggie Tulliver, it becomes an agent of this spectacle and tells this spectacularized tale of female sexuality: once it is gendered in this way, the imagination can only be "the cause of a crisis in the telling."

Imagination compels the characters of Eliot's novels—male as well as female—to engage the world, to read, to judge, to act; and the same imagination is inseparable from the compulsions that cause these characters to misread, to misjudge, to err. "Romanticism" is thus the condition and imagination the sign of ideology understood in the restricted sense of mystification, delusion, and misinterpretation. But the consequences of the imagination, the effects of Romantic error, are marked by a deep gender division once they enter into the terms of what Nancy Armstrong calls the "sexual contract of the novel." Such is the case, for instance, in Maggie's "Great Temptation" in *The Mill on the Floss.* When in Book VI Maggie's "highly-strung, hungry nature" encounters the charms of "Mr. Stephen Guest," it has the "effect of rousing and exalting her imagination in a way that was mysterious to herself" (335). This strongly sexual "rousing and exalting," this erotics of her imagination, remains "mysterious" to Maggie, but the narrator makes it clear that Stephen Guest is not its source but a symptom:

> It was not that she thought distinctly of Mr Stephen Guest; or dwelt on the indication that he looked at her with admiration; it was rather that she felt the half-remote presence of a world of love and beauty and delight, made up of vague, mingled images from all the poetry and romance she

had ever read, or had ever woven in her dreamy reveries. Her mind
glanced back once or twice to the time when she had courted privation,
when she had thought all longing, all impatience was subdued; but that
condition seemed irrevocably gone, and she recoiled from the remembrance of it. (335–36)

With this rousing of the imagination, Maggie's Romantic and mystified
condition of "longing" and "impatience" returns and, governing her
judgments and actions, propels the narrative to its conclusion.[13] Though
the imagination is the sign of the subject's longing for a world outside
itself, it is simultaneously—for Eliot most notably in its sexual charge—
the sign of self-mystification and misjudgment: "vague, mingled images," "woven" in "dreamy reveries."

Sympathy in the novels of George Eliot is the solution to such
mystification; and sympathy assumes its most personified form with the
character of Dinah Morris, who throughout *Adam Bede* is so closely
and consistently associated with the figure of sympathy that we come to
see her not only as its agent but as its very embodiment. Early in the
novel, Dinah is called on to display and exercise sympathy: as Dinah
looks out the bedroom window that "gave her a wide view over the
fields," she begins to consider "all the dear people whom she had
learned to care for among these peaceful fields."[14] She then moves from
this synoptic view of her community to the interior "presence of a
Love and Sympathy" that transcends what is worldly available: "She
closed her eyes, that she might feel more intensely the presence of a
Love and Sympathy deeper and more tender than was breathed from
the earth and sky. That was Dinah's mode of praying in solitude. Simply to close her eyes, and to feel herself enclosed by the Divine Presence" (134). The passage is an important one in the novel, not so much
for what it contributes to the development of the story but for what it
demonstrates about the organic work to be performed by the narrative figures of sympathy. By the "presence of a Love and Sympathy,"
Dinah can fulfill her religious mission of tending to the spiritual concerns of her community; the spiritual invocation of "Love and Sympathy" makes it possible to extend "care," in this case to the wayward
Hetty Sorrel.

But in an important regard the passage is at odds with the organic rhetoric and reconciling work of sympathy in George Eliot: the sympathy invoked in the passage does not describe an activity or process that incorporates an individual self within the community; "Sympathy" is here a proper name, an allegorical presence invoked "in solitude." By allegorizing the terms of "Love and Sympathy," the novel demonstrates that the means by which the novel constructs values, a phenomenology of subjectivity invested in the form of characters, is a rhetorical effect of such personifications as "Sympathy." The successful operations of a narrative would thus be to conceal its rhetoricity, to disguise personification, to make "sympathy" appear as if it were not an allegory but a process, such as the one associated in Eliot's novels with the metaphors of "weaving." Though the narrator gives no indication that we are to read the passage as anything other than an affirmation of Dinah's feelings of "Love and Sympathy," "Divine Presence" is here registered "in solitude" as an "enclosure," and these are the very conditions that the figure of sympathy is expected to abolish in the name of a spiritual community. In "solitude," her eyes shut to the world, "enclosed" by the "Divine Presence," Dinah's "fears, her yearning anxieties for others, melted away" (*Adam Bede*, 134).

The divine visitation of "Love and Sympathy" only leads, moreover, to Dinah's serious misinterpretations of both the situation and the Scripture. As Dinah continues to consider Hetty, who sits in the adjoining bedroom, her "feeling about Hetty gathered a painful intensity":

> [H]er imagination had created a thorny thicket of sin and sorrow, in which she saw the poor thing struggling torn and bleeding, looking with tears for rescue and finding none. It was in this way that Dinah's imagination and sympathy acted and reacted habitually, each heightening the other. She felt a deep longing to go now and pour into Hetty's ear all the words of tender warning and appeal that rushed into her mind. . . . Still she hesitated; she was not quite certain of divine direction; the voice that told her to go to Hetty seemed no stronger than the other voice which said that Hetty was weary, and that going to her now in an unseasonable moment would only tend to close her heart more obstinately. Dinah was not satisfied without a more unmistakable guidance than those inward voices. (135)

Dinah looks to Scripture for this "unmistakable guidance." She opened the Book at random, and the "first words she looked at" were those of Acts 20:37—"'And they all wept sore, and fell on Paul's neck and kissed him.' That was enough for Dinah" (136). Dinah interprets these lines as the "unmistakable guidance" she seeks and she proceeds to console Hetty. The course of their exchange only demonstrates, however, that Dinah has listened to the wrong "inward voice" and has misread the Scripture: confirming Dinah's earlier misgivings, Hetty only closes "her heart more obstinately" to Dinah's display of concern and comfort. This failure of sympathy is matched in the passage by the prophetic and almost perverse accuracy of Dinah's imagination: in spite of a "heightened" sense of sympathy, only what Dinah's imagination had "created" for Hetty—"a thorny thicket of sin and sorrow," "the poor thing struggling torn and bleeding, looking with tears for rescue and finding none"—is realized in the novel. That the passage demonstrates a failure of sympathy in a character such as Dinah is disconcerting, both because her spiritual duties as a preacher depend on such sympathetic concern and because we can imagine no character in Eliot's novels who more personifies this "wide fellow-feeling." While the passage does nothing to question the authenticity of Dinah's self-renouncing sympathy, it marks dramatically the limits and failures of sympathy to establish ethical interpretation and judgment within the movement of the plot.[15]

The scene illustrates what Neil Hertz calls "a structure common in Eliot's novels, of double surrogation, in which the author's investment in her characters is split into 'good' and 'bad' versions, and the valued imaginative activity of the 'good' surrogate is purchased by the exiling of the 'bad.'"[16] The workings of such "surrogation" in this scene implicate Dinah's "valued imaginative activity," her sympathy, with the fate—the suffering and the banishment—of Hetty Sorrel. Within the logic of the narrative, Dinah imagines what Hetty suffers: the imagination "creates" what sympathy cannot prevent.

Sympathy's failure has important consequences at the level of plot, since Hetty's refusal of this sympathetic appeal—and her eventual succumbing to the seductions of Arthur Donnithorne—lead inexorably to her eventual banishment from the community of the novel.[17] Sympathy must fail at the level of the story or *récit*—the progression of events, the actions of characters—for the plot to proceed and a narrative *discourse* of sympathy to be established.[18] Since no individual character in Eliot's novels can make sympathy work, and since imagination creates in these stories "thorny thickets of sin and sorrow," the effective work of sympathy must be assigned—"transferred"—to the act of narration itself.

The Narration of Sympathy

There is no more distinctive signature of George Eliot's novels than the imposing architecture of her narrative discourse. The modernist reaction against Eliot derives in part from a distaste for her elaborate narrative superstructure composed of long-winded didactic and moralizing excursions.[19] But the narrator's often sententious speculations do more than draw attention to the moral implications of the narrative act. They also address generally the aesthetic and ethical issues of literary representation and, more particularly, the tensions between ethics and aesthetics faced by the mimetic artist.[20] We begin to perceive this narrative apparatus not as the mere outdated and expendable convention of Victorian fiction or as the unmediated vehicle of its author but as the site of significant narrative energy. As we consider the function of the narrator, a fully performative dimension of Eliot's narrative discourse, we find in the story of that fictive subject called the narrator a powerful ideological inscription of the scene of writing.

The drama of the narrator involves most directly the eliciting, the *naming*, and the *making* of what remains lacking in the events and actions of the story: a sympathy forged out of the Romantic conditions of the imagination. The sympathy that is withheld at the level of the *récit* must be supplemented by the work of the *discours*.[21] The pattern of repeated mystifications, misinterpretations, and misdeeds set in motion by the desires of imagination can only be arrested in Eliot's novels by the narrator's own "gift of transferred life," which collects the frayed and disconnected threads of sympathy displayed in the story and weaves them into the meaningful narrative of a coherent community. If imag-

ination is necessary for the production of plot—Dinah's misreadings,
Dorothea's misjudgment, Maggie's misdeed—sympathy is necessary for
the binding terms of narrative coherence and closure. As D. A. Miller
argues, the lack of sympathy is the condition of narratability in George
Eliot: "The symptoms of a missing sympathy between self and other
(indifference, fascination, fear, hostility) are part of a single, highly narratable syndrome."[22] The story of imagination *needs* the narration of
sympathy. Considered from the perspective of the narrative discourse,
imagination is necessary for the ideological mystifications that in turn
provide the occasion for the invocation of an ethically grounded narrator. "Sympathy" proves to be a difficult principle to narrate within
the conventions of the realist novel, for it is expected to exist in its genuine form only as a process, and thus its immanence is abolished, its
organic weaving undone once it presents itself allegorically.[23]

The narrator of *Adam Bede* names this principle during the famous
narrative interruption of Book XVII, "In Which the Story Pauses a
Little."[24] The title and tone of the chapter recall Fielding's frequent narrative asides, but unlike the narrator of *Tom Jones*, George Eliot's commentary directly addresses the problems posed by the production of
narrative realism, alluding both to the resistances of readers who want
more "idealized" fictions and to the resistances of the "real" to fictional
representation.[25] Since the mirror used by the narrative "is doubtless
defective," the narrator admits that "the outlines will sometimes be dis-
turbed, the reflection faint or confused" (*Adam Bede*, 151). It will always
prove to be "a very hard thing," in other words, for the narrator not
to succumb to the "rousing" or "hurry" of an idealizing imagination
that wants to "paint" an "angel . . . with a floating violet robe, and a
face paled by the celestial light" (153).

For the fictional project to maintain its fragile specular relationship to the "truth," the narrative must not bind itself to the "divine
beauty of form"; rather, it should dedicate itself to the "secret of deep
human sympathy": "All honour and reverence to the divine beauty of
form! Let us cultivate it to the utmost in men, women, and children—
in our gardens and in our houses. But let us love that other beauty too,
which lies in no secret of proportion, but in the secret of deep human
sympathy" (153). While the novel is predicated on the suspension of

sympathy, while the "narratability" of the story requires such suspension, the narrator and narrative discourse of the novel must appear to hold fidelity to an *ethics* of sympathy that is bound to no aesthetic of beauty. To make such a narrative work, to weave together the various strands of the story, "it is more needful," asserts Eliot's narrator, "that I should have a fibre of sympathy connecting me with that vulgar citizen who weighs out my sugar in a vilely-assorted cravat and waistcoat, than with the handsomest rascal in red scarf and green feathers" (153). Though the passage asserts that an ethics of sympathy must serve as a principle of representation, how this "fibre of sympathy" is to make its narrative connections becomes difficult to determine.[26] The "secret of deep human sympathy," named during this hiatus "In Which the Story Pauses a Little," must be in effect from the outset in the narrative discourse. This complicates considerably the task of the narrator, compromising the demands for strict verisimilitude. It remains unclear, moreover, whether sympathy can be made to square with other functions of narrative discourse. The narrator of *Adam Bede* examines the incompatibility between the essentially reductive tendency of explanation and an enlarging sympathy: "I tell it as he told it, not attempting to reduce it to its natural elements: in our eagerness to explain impressions, we often lose our hold of the sympathy that comprehends them" (44). Here and throughout Eliot's novels, the narrator takes pains to restate the commitment to the "great benefit" of the discovery and elaboration—the "extension"—of sympathy.

The project, then, for Eliot's narrator in *Adam Bede* or *The Mill on the Floss* or *Middlemarch* is to secure a sympathetic idiom for the narrative discourse: this idiom is expected to bestow upon the recalcitrant materials of the story "the gift of transferred life" and to affirm through narrative the "wide fellow-feeling" of sympathy. In *The Mill on the Floss*, for instance, the narrator records the search for narrative forms or generic models appropriate to its prosaic subject, to lives "irradiated by no sublime principles" (239). These lives belong to the past, however, to a rural England prior to the post–Reform Bill world of the narrator. Though the historical gap separates the narrator from the story, it also establishes the conditions for a narrative rememoration that, in a voice conjuring Wordsworth, would enshrine the past. The novel opens with a wistful pastoral sketch of the river Floss: "It seems to me like a living companion while I wander along the bank and listen to its low placid voice, as to the voice of one who is deaf and loving. I remember those large dipping willows. I remember the stone bridge" (7). Such affective form of remembrance works not only to establish narrative authority but further, by effacing the gap of temporality, to find the past resurrected in the present moment of narration. The narrator's recollections are underwritten by frequent references to a pastoral literary tradition that appears to provide a language and a convention for the representation of this rural story and that plays on the ideological split between town and country.

But the story itself admits too many connections and makes too many narrative demands to sustain its pastoral models. "In order to see Mr. and Mrs. Glegg at home," the narrator tells us near the end of Book I, "we must enter the town of St. Ogg's—that venerable town with the red-fluted roofs and the broad warehouse gables, where the black ships unload themselves of their burthens from the far north, and carry away, in exchange, the precious inland products, the well-crushed cheese and the soft fleeces, which my refined readers have doubtless become acquainted with through the medium of the best classic pastorals" (103). With the appearance of this new commerce "from the far north" we find the tokens of a new social formation unsuited to the "medium" of the pastoral. By the conclusion of Book II, when Mr. Tulliver has lost the mill because of the economic forces that he cannot comprehend, the pastoral has clearly exhausted its narrative currency. Tom and Maggie have "entered the thorny wilderness, and the golden gates of their childhood had for ever closed behind them" (171).[27] The gates have closed on the language and images of a pastoral mode that can no longer renew the sympathetic links between past and present. As the passages devoted to the narrator's nostalgic remembrances disappear, another narrative vehicle for sympathy must be found.

That the narrator of *The Mill on the Floss* appears to adopt and discard a variety of literary models during the novel's unfolding dramatizes the need to establish a mode of narration compatible with, and even productive of, sympathy. At moments the novel resembles a classic *Bildungsroman*, at others a pilgrim's progress, and when the narrator invokes the history of St. Ogg the novel appears to be the mythic reenactment of legend.[28] This itinerary is further complicated when the locus of the story shifts from the river and hedgerows of Dorlcotte Mill to the drawing room of Lucy Deane, and Maggie finds herself in the "bright aerial world" of Lucy Deane's "fairy tale." None of these models or conventions is ultimately satisfactory, none can sustain the novel's movement or manage the breadth and, to use the language of Barbara Hardy, the "particularity" of its realism. Faced, for instance, with the description and evaluation of the character of Mr. Wakem, the narrator raises the familiar problem that continually shadows the production of this discourse of realism: "But it is really impossible to decide this question by a glance at his [Mr. Wakem's] person: the lines and lights of the human countenance are like other symbols—not always easy to read without a key" (219). The passage echoes Maggie's illusory belief that she has discovered in Thomas à Kempis the "key" to her happiness. The desire for the "key" to interpretation is often explicitly thematized in George Eliot's novels as evidence of mystification.

Though we tend to associate this search for the master "key" with Eliot's most painfully deluded characters, such as Casaubon in *Middlemarch*, the effort to find a key to the narration of these stories is a feature of the narrative discourse as well as of the characters. The narrator of *Daniel Deronda* announces explicitly the futility, even "stupidity," of all attempts to "describe" character: "Attempts at description are stupid: who can all at once describe a human being. . . . We recognize the alphabet; we are not sure of the language."[29] Passages that thematize a narrative inability as an incapacity of language recur throughout George Eliot's fictions. But though they point to a genuine crisis regarding representation, regarding the shared social language that would give individual "character" definition and significance, it is a crisis that can—and must—be addressed through the narrative discourse itself. For through this crisis of representation, only the *presumption* of knowledge is the *necessary* sign of mystification. Eliot's narrators' declarations of inability ask to be interpreted as more genuine efforts at interpretation: they function to induce the "sympathy" they must represent.[30]

At moments in *The Mill on the Floss* it appears as if the narrator has discovered in the European literary tradition the "key" to the explanation and narration of the novel's characters. The narrator suggests that we read Tom Tulliver, for example, according to an "epic" model of character: "A character at unity with itself—that performs what it intends, subdues every counteracting impulse, and has no visions beyond the distinctly possible" (271). This Schillerian model of the "naive" character cannot, of course, accommodate Maggie Tulliver's "life-struggles," which "had lain almost entirely within her own soul, one shadowy army fighting another, and the slain shadows for ever rising again" (269). We recognize in this image of Maggie's internal shadow armies a traditional and exemplary account of what Lukács would call the "romanticism of disillusionment." The irreconcilable division between Maggie and Tom is registered therefore as more than a difference of character—as a sign of the incompatibility of narrative modes. The novel's ambiguous conclusion only draws more attention to this narrative irreconcilability: the biblical epitaph inscribed on the tomb of Maggie and Tom—"In their death they were not divided"— declares that it is only death that brings an end to narrative division and desire and that thus restores community as a narrative postscript or aftereffect.

The Romantic motif of the "epic" and the "novel," of the "naive" and the "sentimental" appears in the opening sentences of Eliot's "Prelude" to *Middlemarch*, a "Prelude" that stresses the historicity of literary forms and the social-cultural organization of "meaning" by which these forms are to be interpreted. The historical unavailability of the "epic," for instance, makes individual actions—even those "motivated" by a like suffering or "depth of soul"—mean something else; and their "proper" meaning can only be restored by the narration of a sympathy through which a realism can be constructed. But as George Levine argues, by the time of *Middlemarch*, "[definite substantial reality] had become microscopically attenuated, or so densely implicated in process and relationship that it seemed at times indistinguishable from the ideal."[31] As such, it would constitute a genuine failure, the succumbing to an imagination "bred in the mists of feeling" and hence nothing but delusion.

Raymond Williams has written eloquently on this aspect of Eliot's fiction, posing the feature of narrative division as an epistemological question: how is the nineteenth-century novel to "know" the "community" it presumes to represent? This problem of knowledge in the novel is, writes Williams, an "acute" one, for to address "an evident failure of continuity between the necessary language of the novelist and the recorded language of many of the characters," a new form of narrative connection must be found between the story and its discourse.[32] The gap between the narration and the narrated is not, of course, a feature exclusive to Eliot's novels but is rather a discontinuity inherent in novelistic representation. Given the pressing demands Eliot makes on the conventions of novelizing, however, a formal narrative division assumes an explicitly ethical significance. The division inscribed in narrative discourse is a condition of the form of novel that George Eliot inherits, a division between the "moral" demands and postures of the narrator and the social world to be narrated: "It is a contradiction in the form of the novel, as George Eliot received and developed it, that the moral emphasis on conduct—and therefore the technical strategy of unified narrative and analytic tones—must be at odds with any society—the 'knowable community' of the novel—in which moral bearings have been extended to substantial and conflicting social relationships" (*Country and City*, 168–69). In other words, the inherent disconnection between story and discourse takes the form in Eliot's novels of an ideological contradiction between ethics and aesthetics. What appear to be formal disturbances or technical incongruities, such as the disconnections of story and discourse in *The Mill on the Floss*, are the symptoms of this deeper ideological contradiction. Sympathy is the name of the narrative effort to overcome the ideological contradiction, to coordinate ethics and aesthetics, to make "wide fellow-feeling" the principle of narrative discourse, but the totalizing narrative perspective that should make visible the deep connections of a community only reveals at all levels of the novel persistent formal discontinuities and social divisions. "The problem of the knowable community," writes Raymond Williams of *The Mill on the Floss*, "is then, in a new way, a problem of language" (*Country and City*, 171).

What George Eliot leaves us with, however, is not community as such but, in Williams's words, "a paradox of language and community": this "paradox" is inscribed in the rhetoric of the narrative itself between the possibilities of a genuine community and the aesthetic perspective of the narrator. It is precisely this paradox that makes Eliot both so compelling and, ultimately, so disappointing for Williams's own conception of culture and community. On the one hand, Eliot records the strained and fragile links between available narrative modes of "knowing" and the community to be "known." But on the other hand, the very marks of this strain demonstrate Eliot's failures in representation, failures registered most dramatically in the depictions of subaltern characters. Eliot's "recognition of conflict, of the existence of classes, of divisions and contrasts of feeling and speaking" is, as Williams describes it, produced at the expense of any "unity of the idiom" (*Country and City*, 169). But Williams's judgment is not merely a formalist one: if Eliot's novels grapple with the problem of community, they do so only to preserve it "ideally in the past" (180).

Williams's reading of Eliot's narrative project is as acute as any we have. His analysis of the *class* "disturbance" and "the unease" that haunt Eliot's novels and culminate in the "divided construction" of the later work (174) demonstrates the nature and the stakes of the tensions between the aesthetics and ethics of narrative. But I want to argue that what Williams correctly recognizes as Eliot's failure to reconcile the ethical with the aesthetic points to the persistence of an ideological contradiction that for Eliot can be tamed if not overcome. If for George Eliot community is not there to be known, it remains something that can be made by the novel itself, by its capacity to teach.

The Teaching of Community

So much of Eliot's narrative energy is devoted to scenes of instruction, so many principal characters are teachers of some sort, that it will be of little surprise to find the author, in a letter to Frederic Harrison, devote herself to an aesthetics of teaching. The stories are so bound up with the narrative work of teaching that the tragic outcomes of *The Mill on the Floss*, *Adam Bede*, and *Middlemarch* inevitably derive at

least in part from failures to teach well or to heed good teaching. In
the machinations of the plot, teaching for George Eliot is narratable
primarily as failure.[33]

Beyond the thematized aesthetics of teaching, George Eliot conceives her narrative project itself as constituting an aesthetic education.
In her 1856 review of the third volume of *Modern Painters*, George Eliot
praises Ruskin's "teaching" of "realism": "The truth of infinite value
that he teaches is *realism*, the doctrine that all truth and beauty are to be
attained by a humble and faithful study of nature, and not by substi-
tuting vague forms, bred by imagination on the mists of feeling, in
place of definite, substantial reality."[34] We may read this account of
Ruskin's teaching as the model for George Eliot's own conception of
the novel: a realism that distinguishes itself from the "mists of feeling"
and "vague forms" bred by the imagination. The passage suggests the
significance not only of realism but of teaching, of teaching as the public role of the Victorian intellectual. In "Leaves for a Notebook" Eliot
writes, "a man or woman who publishes writings inevitably assumes
the office of teacher or influencer of the public mind" (*Essays*, 279).
The explicit insistence on what we would call the ideological function
of the intellectual and of culture informs Eliot's notion of the fundamental duties of "Authorship": to "enlarge the area of moral sentiment" (282). In the letter to Harrison, Eliot asserts: "aesthetic teaching
is the highest of all teaching because it deals with life in its highest
complexity."[35]

It is also true for Eliot that the articulation of aesthetics and teaching is always precarious, for if the teaching "ceases to be purely aesthetic—if it lapses anywhere from the picture to the diagram—it becomes the most offensive of all teaching" (*Letters*, 318). When teaching
is "purely aesthetic," however, and fully sustained at the level of the
"picture," it is the most effective of all teaching, for it can, as she writes,
"'flash' conviction on the world by means of aroused sympathy" (318).
A "purely aesthetic teaching" is, in a word, the most highly developed
and persuasive *ideological* activity, capable of securing in a "flash" of insight, "by means of aroused sympathy," nothing less than the "convic-
tions" of the reader. The insistent presence of teaching in the novels
thematizes what Eliot perceives to be the primary function of aesthetic

representation. Eliot's novels propose to teach "purely" by way of an aesthetics of sympathy, their ideological effectivity secured precisely by their aesthetic disavowal of any ideology, just as their gendering of sympathy is secured by their attempt to disavow gender at the level of narrative discourse.[36]

Among other lessons, these novels propose to teach that the "rousing" of imagination, unlike the "aroused sympathy," leads characters and readers alike to confuse "idealizing" fictions with "hard, real life." It is a form of mystification that we also call "ideology." For the characters of Eliot's novels this lesson is always a hard one to learn, because the imagination, as a subjective desire that courts misdoing and misreading, proves to be a difficult force to translate without resistance into the more binding social relationship of sympathy. A successful translation of imagination into sympathy is possible only after imagination has done its work and created a narratable condition of mystification and desire, once it has, in other words, manufactured "false consciousness." Maggie's overnight conversion in the penultimate book of *The Mill on the Floss* from a character misguided by imagination into a character guided by sympathy offers an exemplary lesson. The source of Maggie's "Great Temptation" during her trip downriver with Stephen Guest is, I have argued, not so much Stephen as the force of a desiring imagination that, as the conventional image of the river suggests, generates currents of its own that are difficult to resist. And though Maggie's relationship with Stephen is not consummated, she must commit what her community can only perceive as an "irrevocable trespass" (*Mill on the Floss*, 408–9) before the conversion into sympathy is realized.

The conversion is sealed by Maggie's refusal of Stephen's marriage proposal, a refusal that in the name of moral duty assumes the weight of a narrative law. When Stephen invokes the rhetoric of Romanticism to assert that the "natural law" drawing them together "surmounts every other; we can't help what it clashes with" (417), Maggie appeals to a judgment, produced through sympathy, that finds its basis in the binding weight of the past: "It is not so, Stephen—I'm quite sure that is wrong. . . . [I]f we judged in that way, there would be a warrant for all treachery and cruelty—we should justify breaking the most sacred ties that can ever be formed on earth. If the past is not to bind us, where can

duty lie? We should have no law but the inclination of the moment. . . .
I see—I feel their trouble now: it is as if it were branded on my mind"
(417, 419). The "natural law" of desire and imagination "warrants" only
"treachery and cruelty" and poses a threat to "the most sacred ties that
can ever be formed on earth." The nature of these "most sacred ties" remains unspecified, but *as* "ties," they are "sacred," the bonds of the "sacred" that link all judgment and action to "duty" and "law." The language of the "sacred" and of "duty" and of "law" demonstrates that
the ideological grounds of "community" rest in the balance.

Maggie's painful renunciation of desire and acquisition of sympathy transform her trip downriver into a parable that the narrative in-
scribes as law. But the lesson Maggie *teaches*, with the full authorization
of a narrator who is conspicuously silent during the scene, and the lesson she *learns* turn out to be very different matters. During the course
of Maggie's rejection of Stephen's entreaties, imagination and desire
are displaced by a sympathy that finally asserts a narrative force. But in
narrative terms, this act of renunciation and this appearance of sympathy arrive too late: Maggie's actions can only be interpreted by her
community as a moral transgression, as the acquiescence to the "Romantic" "natural law" she has renounced, and consequently as "treacherous and cruel." Nancy Armstrong has demonstrated how "this Victorian version of the double bind condemns a woman for having de-
monic power if she swims and celebrates her innocence if she drowns"
(*Desire and Domestic Fiction*, 55). The narrator's silences here are as crucial as they are conspicuous: the novel must reenact this "Victorian version of the double bind" and punish Maggie in order for sympathy,
which drowns along with Maggie, to be resurrected at the "gender-
less" level of narration. Thus, Maggie's act of sympathetic renunciation only assures her own banishment from the community, though
we recognize that the judgment passed upon Maggie by the town of St.
Ogg is a judgment of the town itself: by its failure to recognize sympathy, St. Ogg cancels its status as community.[37] Indeed, the production of
sympathy in *The Mill on the Floss* only demonstrates the absence of what
Raymond Williams calls a "knowable community" precisely because
the forms of narrative knowledge learned through sympathy teach us
only of this absence.[38]

George Eliot's "aesthetic teaching" does not presume to know community; it is not the teaching of what is already known. Rather, Eliot's pedagogy of the novel aims to fashion sympathy: its task is to produce through narrative effect and affect, through the formal conventions of the Victorian novel, a sympathy that in its turn will establish the conditions for community.[39] By the binding work of this narrative sympathy, connections are made that would weave the (reading) self into the collective unfolding of the narrative community. This aesthetics of sympathy is therefore an ideological process in the broadest sense, for community can only be realized through a sympathy that is, in turn, realized as the narrative conversion or "transferal" of the (mystifying) imagination. In brief, Eliot's "aesthetic teaching" would teach "community" into existence. We never see in Eliot a fully coherent community governed by the principle of sympathy, by "wide fellow-feeling," since such a community can only be the effect of an aesthetics of sympathy that, as we read, is in the process of unfolding and extending its connections.

"Community" in George Eliot, to use the fortuitous title of an important recent volume of essays on the topic, is *always* and by definition "at loose ends": it always and by definition stands in need of the suturing that does not so much restore as make it.[40] But in order for community to be made effectively—which is to say aesthetically—the process must always *appear* as the restoration of a community currently lost or rent, the recovery of the original weave. Nothing in Eliot speaks to this more succinctly than Mordecai's declaration in *Daniel Deronda*, "community was felt before it was called good" (594). The declaration is another instance of the "present causes of past effects" that, as Cynthia Chase has taught us, propel the double movement of that novel.[41] Mordecai is mistaken, from the novel's perspective, not because of the value he attributes to community but because he has confused cause with effect: community is "called good" before it is "felt" and *because* it has not been "felt." George Eliot's "aesthetic teaching" reveals this metalepsis to be the rhetorical confusion of cause and effect yet perpetuates it nevertheless, precisely because it remains the only way community can be taught *aesthetically*. Eliot's novels are dedicated to the naming and evaluating of a community that must itself be made by the narrative performance, the "aesthetics" of this naming and evaluating.

The rhetoric of community in George Eliot—marked and sustained by the organic language of "unity," "centre," "wholeness," "connection," "coherence"—clearly belongs to an aesthetic ideology that remains a principal legacy of the discourse of Romanticism. It is, moreover, a rhetoric that goes both ways politically, sustaining conservative and progressive social movements at the same time. Aesthetic form lends to the rhetoric of community much of its ideological potency: by the intrication and even articulation of aesthetics and ideology, we can speak of the making of a "community effect." Novels teach us, in part, that the making of any English "community" is itself a complex and perpetually unfinished ideological project, a project to which the novels of George Eliot specifically contribute. But I want to stress that this is not a post-structuralist or post-Marxist discovery: George Eliot *knows* full well that community is always, to use Benedict Anderson's term, "imagined"; she *knows* full well that community is always "at loose ends," that the weaving of the novel will not restore a presence but must instead suture over an absence called community. To put this another way, if we find in Jean-Luc Nancy or in Ernesto Laclau and Chantal Mouffe compelling meditations on the discursive machinery that produces "imagined" and "inoperative" communities, such an analysis—even "demystification"—is already at work in the novels of George Eliot. But at the very same time these lessons are to be taught by sympathy itself, an "aesthetic teaching" that would restore through the very act of narration the "mystified" *feeling* of a community that might then be called good.[42]

Since Eliot's narrative teaching must make its own community, since it is the project of this sympathetic narrative teaching to cultivate from the discontinuous threads of society an organic sense of coherence and connectedness, community must be perpetually reestablished, not only in each story but also, as Raymond Williams puts it, in "almost each sentence she must write." To perform the cultural "reformation" of the national community and to perform the perpetual aesthetic and ideological activity that constructs as well as "extends the community of the novel," the principle of sympathy itself must assume the status of a narrative law. But we have seen that sympathy cannot be extricated from an imagination that threatens always to disfigure sympathy's teaching. The "broadening of consciousness," the extension of sympathetic "fellow-feeling," can cultivate the sense of community and perform the social mission of reform and reconciliation only by the denegation of an imagination that must be represented in terms of desire and transgression. This imagination continues to inhabit the narrative project as a "natural law," as the perpetual margin of "Romantic" error. If sympathy is the name for the narrative articulation of aesthetics and ideology, an articulation that teaches community, imagination is the pervasive threat of their disarticulation, the sign of a desire that, if realized in actions, would "break the most sacred ties" and breach the limits of this narratable community.

That George Eliot's novels produce an imagination capable of being written only as subversive, that they take this Romantic trope as the very condition of their own narrative possibility, is persuasive testimony to their considerable, and conservative, ideological and aesthetic power. For even as they fail to heal the break they know and reveal, these novels tell us that much is made by that failure: if not a community, then a model of "aesthetic teaching" that continues to be the most effective means of concealing the break that it can neither prevent nor cure.

"SOMETHING'S MISSING"
A Gap of Hope

I take the title of my epilogue from a discussion between Ernst Bloch and Theodor Adorno regarding the "contradictions of utopian longing."[1] In the course of their discussion, Bloch invokes a sentence from Bertolt Brecht's *Mahagonny* to name the critical role utopian longing plays for social thought: "Something's missing." For Bloch, utopian longing is not at odds with a genuine materialism, for the utopian introduces an absence or lack into our representations of the social. "The decisive incentive toward utopia" speaks of the "something" that is always "missing" from present as well as from *past* society, the "something" that is nowhere to be found, and the "something" that demands change and elicits hope.

Missing from my own readings of the imagination in English Romantic discourse is adequate attention to the utopian dimension. I have attempted in the preceding chapters to address the intricacy of imagination and ideology in Romanticism, to demonstrate how the question of ideology in its epistemological as well as social implications is bound up with the proceedings and performances of the imagination in English Romantic poetry and prose. And I have argued that by reading the work of the imagination we can discern a deep faultline in the discourse, one that announces what is best called a "materialist break" and that prompts powerful conservative responses in cultural politics.

The understanding of ideology developed in the preceding pages reveals it as taking two primary forms: it is a first-order confusion or mystification, but it is also the more significant, more extensive, and indeed inescapable burdening of spirit by matter, a condition registered and represented most often in Romantic texts by thought's relation to language. One consequence wrought by the ideological condition is the antagonism that makes itself felt from Coleridge and Wordsworth through George Eliot and beyond. But I have argued that Shelley's late speculations on the permanence of ideology and Keats's rhetorical and thematized resistance of things to thought offers us a poetry written "in a materialist way" (Macherey), a poetry that begins a materialist reflection on the problem of ideology. I have wanted to stress that the utopian dimension of the imagination in Shelley, which is most evident in *Prometheus Unbound*, is "broken" with by Shelley's last poem, canceled by the negativity of *The Triumph of Life*. Thus, from the point of view of the materialist break I am proposing, from the recognition of an intractable ideological condition, the "utopian" is bound to look like simple mystification, "ideological" in the most conventional sense of the term: a longing to elude the burden of materiality and the contradictions it manufactures.

Paul Ricoeur's *Lectures on Ideology and Utopia* attempts to recast the relationship between imagination, ideology, and utopia. For Ricoeur, utopia is more than an instance of ideological thought: utopia and ideology form a polarity that hinges around the notion of the imagination: "the very conjunction of these two opposite sides or complementary functions typifies what could be called social and cultural *imagination*."[2] For Ricoeur utopia is to be understood as the positive capacity to imagine what is literally and empirically "nowhere." Utopia is thus the imagination acting in its most positive mode, "the ability to conceive of an empty place from which to look at ourselves" (*Lectures*, 15). "May we not say then," asks Ricoeur, "that imagination itself—through its utopian function—has a *constitutive* role in helping us *rethink* the nature of our social life?" (16). Ricoeur's lectures offer a comprehensive attempt to link theories of ideology and of utopia through the concept or faculty of the imagination. But, if my reading of Romantic discourse has been persuasive, are we entitled to restore the imagination to the status of a positive faculty?

I believe the question cannot be answered in the affirmative, but I would insist that this does not mean that the legacy of Romanticism's investment in the imagination is beyond redemption. I want to approach the utopian element and its absence from my discussion from a rather different understanding of the same knot of figures: namely, imagination, ideology, and utopia. For Ricoeur the imagination must be understood as a *positive* capacity of consciousness, one that enables us to imagine a different future. But I want to return to the Keats and Shelley of the "break." I have argued in my readings of these poets that imagination is figured most productively in Romantic discourse through its self-negation, an outcome achieved by way of a revised sense of the imagination as a radically "negative capability": Romanticism is redeemed not by the success of the imagination—which names the spurious identity of spirit and matter, self and society—but by its failure in a poetry that delivers us to a rupture with idealism and empiricism. The poetic failure of the imagination, like a sort of photographic negative, leaves an image of the "nontotalizability" of the social.

The imagination in its most productive aspect would thus perpetually appear as the sign that "something's missing." The same lack that prevents the coherence of the present ensures that the temporary convergence of forces that offer themselves as the "real" world cannot exhaust its possibilities. The imagination is therefore the gap that names the failure to figure the social totality. As a utopian possibility, imagination will always end in failure; but this should not be the cause of hopelessness. Rather, the repeated failure of the imagination as a utopian function ensures the production of open spaces that we may read not as images of the future—not as illuminations—but, with Shelley, as the "shadows cast by futurity."

Though I initiated these final reflections with reference to the utopian dimension in Western Marxism, I believe it is precisely this strain in Romanticism—imagination's failed utopianism—that delivers us to what Gayatri Spivak has described as "the most radical challenge of deconstruction": namely, the "notion of thought being a blank part of the text given over to a future that is not just a future present but always a future anterior."[3] The faultline that we have identified in Romantic discourse issues just such a challenge: the "end" of the imagination is a failure that leaves room for hope, what Spivak calls "the blank certitude of the future anterior," what Bloch and Adorno name the perpetual opening of a "something that's missing." It is here, through the articulations of Marxism and deconstruction and in the space opened by imagination's failure, that a materialism is to be made.

REFERENCE MATTER

Notes

Introduction

1. See in particular James Engell, *The Creative Imagination* (Cambridge, Mass.: Harvard University Press, 1981). Further references to this work will be included in the text. Engell's compendious work of intellectual history examines "the growth of an idea" from eighteenth-century aesthetic theory through its full "flowering" in German and English Romanticism. Engell's study is a model of scrupulous research and scholarship, a study to which anyone who examines the concept of the imagination owes a considerable debt. My primary differences with Engell concern the narrative of his exposition, its implicit model of historical change. Though Engell is attentive to the potential divisions in the *concept* of the imagination—divisions that are, however, most often reconciled in this unifying narrative—he is much less attentive to *textual* divisions, to the fissures and contradictions residing in the texts that give us the imagination. For Engell, the imagination may speak in several languages, but it speaks, ultimately, with one mind. Engell assumes that the poetry and criticism of English Romanticism represents a "great practical application" of and "ready trust" in the imagination. I will argue that though English Romanticism made a significant social as well as philosophical and poetic investment in the imagination, that investment is by no means uniform or consistent. Moreover, the appearance of the imagination in the texts of English Romanticism can, as we shall see, scarcely be referred to as the "practical application" of a concept already specified and "refined," for it is by the very instance of its critical and, crucially, *poetic* performance that the imagination discloses its fun-

damental divisions. In his treatment of the development of the concept, Engell assumes an organicist model of intellectual history that, being governed by the "Romantic" metaphors of "growth" and "flowering," never makes contact with a notion of social or political or institutional history. The notion that the imagination could come into its own without reference to politics or society is particularly curious for a concept that harbors the dreams of reconciling subject and object or pure and practical reason. Given his model of intellectual history, in other words, Engell cannot see the imagination as a problem of ideology.

2. John B. Thompson, *Studies in the Theory of Ideology* (Berkeley: University of California Press, 1984), 25. Subsequent references will be included in the text.

3. I will draw extensively in this introductory exposition from the following work of Louis Althusser: *"Lenin and Philosophy" and Other Essays*, trans. Ben Brewster (New York: Monthly Review Press, 1971); *For Marx*, trans. Ben Brewster (London: Verso, 1979); *Philosophy and the Spontaneous Philosophy of the Scientists*, trans. Ben Brewster et al. (London: Verso, 1990); and Louis Althusser and Etienne Balibar, *Reading Capital*, trans. Ben Brewster (London: New Left Books, 1970). Subsequent references to all these works will be included in the text.

Other recent treatments of ideology of particular pertinence to my study include: Etienne Balibar, "The Vacillation of Ideology," trans. Andrew Ross and Constance Penley, in *Marxism and the Interpretation of Culture*, ed. Cary Nelson and Lawrence Grossberg (Urbana: University of Illinois Press, 1988), 159–210; Claude Lefort, *The Political Forms of Modern Democracy*, ed. John B. Thompson (Cambridge, Mass.: MIT Press, 1986); Claude Lefort, *Democracy and Political Theory* (Minneapolis: University of Minnesota Press, 1988); Slavoj Žižek, *The Sublime Object of Ideology* (London: Verso, 1989); Slavoj Žižek, *For They Know Not What They Do: Enjoyment as a Political Factor* (London: Verso, 1991); Ernesto Laclau and Chantal Mouffe, *Hegemony and Socialist Strategy* (London: Verso, 1985); and Ernesto Laclau, *New Reflections on the Revolution of Our Time*, trans. Jon Barnes et al. (London: Verso, 1990).

Some authoritative surveys of the history of the concept of ideology from Destutt de Tracy to the present include George Lichtheim, *"The Concept of Ideology" and Other Essays* (New York: Random House, 1967); Raymond Williams, *Marxism and Literature* (Oxford: Oxford University Press, 1977), 55–71; Jorge Larrain, *The Concept of Ideology* (London: Hutchinson, 1979); John B. Thompson, *Studies in the Theory of Ideology*; Stuart Hall, "The Problem of Ideology—Marxism Without Guarantees," *Journal of Communication Inquiry*, 10, no. 2 (Summer 1986): 28–43; and Terry Eagleton, *Ideology: An Introduction* (London: Verso, 1991).

4. Immanuel Kant, *The Critique of Judgment*, trans. J. H. Bernard (New York: Hafner Press, 1951), 3–15. Subsequent references will be included in the text. Discussions of *The Critique of Judgment* that consider the place and function of the imagination in Kant include Ernst Cassirer, *Kant's Life and Thought*, trans. James Haden (New Haven, Conn.: Yale University Press, 1981); Donald Crawford, *Kant's Aesthetic Theory* (Madison: University of Wisconsin Press, 1974); Crawford, "Kant's Theory of Creative Imagination," in *Essays in Kant's Aesthetics*, ed. Ted Cohen and Paul Guyer (Chicago: University of Chicago Press, 1982), 151–78; Paul Guyer, *Kant and the Claims of Taste* (Cambridge, Mass.: Harvard University Press, 1979); Eva Schaper, *Studies in Kant's Aesthetics* (Edinburgh: Edinburgh University Press, 1979); Engell, *Creative Imagination*, 118–39; and Hans-Georg Gadamer, *Truth and Method*, trans. Garrett Barden and John Cumming (New York: Seabury Press, 1975), 39–90.

5. Lyotard stresses the destabilizing effects of the Kantian "as if" in Jean-François Lyotard and Jean-Loup Thebaud, *Just Gaming*, trans. Wlad Godzich (Minneapolis: University of Minnesota Press, 1985), 77–78.

6. Perhaps the most succinct account of the significance of the Kantian sublime for the theorization of the "postmodern" is Jean-François Lyotard, *The Postmodern Condition*, trans. Geoff Bennington and Brian Massumi (Minneapolis: University of Minnesota Press, 1984), 77–79. See also Jean-François Lyotard, *The Differend: Phrases in Dispute*, trans. Georges Van Den Abbeele (Minneapolis: University of Minnesota Press, 1988), 161–71.

7. For a brief but lucid treatment of the "discordant" role of the imagination in the Kantian sublime, see Gilles Deleuze, *Kant's Critical Philosophy*, trans. Hugh Tomlinson and Barbara Hammerjam (Minneapolis: University of Minnesota Press, 1984), 50–52. On the role of the sublime in Romanticism, see Thomas Weiskel, *The Romantic Sublime* (Baltimore: Johns Hopkins University Press, 1976).

8. On the "deconstructive" effects of the sublime, see in particular Neil Hertz, "A Reading of Longinus" and "The Notion of Blockage in the Literature of the Sublime," in his *The End of the Line* (New York: Columbia University Press, 1985), 1–20, 40–60; and Paul de Man, "Phenomenality and Materiality in Kant," in *Hermeneutics: Questions and Prospects*, ed. Gary Shapiro and Alan Sica (Amherst: University of Massachusetts Press, 1984), 121–44. Subsequent references to de Man's essay will be included in the text. For an important recent account of the ideological implications of the "Kantian Imaginary," see Terry Eagleton, *The Ideology of the Aesthetic* (London: Basil Blackwell, 1990), 70–101. For a useful collection on the relationship between deconstruction and the sublime, see *The Textual Sublime: Deconstruction and Its Differences*, ed. Hugh Silverman and Gary E. Aylesworth (Albany: State University of New York Press, 1990). And see Frances Ferguson's fine volume on the Romantic

sublime and its legacies, *Solitude and the Sublime: Romanticism and the Aesthetics of Individuation* (New York: Routledge, 1992).

9. Walter Benjamin, "The Task of the Translator," in *Illuminations*, ed. Hannah Arendt, trans. Harry Zohn (New York: Schocken Books, 1969), 69–82. De Man's 1983 Messenger Lecture on "The Task of the Translator" is included in his *The Resistance to Theory* (Minneapolis: University of Minnesota Press, 1986), 73–105. Further references to Benjamin's essay and to de Man's volume will be included in the text.

10. On Schiller's interpretation of Kant, see Dieter Henrich, "Beauty and Freedom: Schiller's Struggle with Kant's Aesthetics," in *Essays in Kant's Aesthetics*, ed. Cohen and Guyer, 237–57; Jurgen Habermas, *The Philosophical Discourse of Modernity*, trans. Frederick Lawrence (Cambridge, Mass.: MIT Press, 1987), 45–50; and Paul de Man, "Kant and Schiller," in *Aesthetic Ideology*, ed. Andrzej Warminski (Minneapolis: University of Minnesota Press, forthcoming).

11. William Wordsworth, *The Prelude* (1850 text), ed. Ernest de Selincourt (Oxford: Oxford University Press, 1904), Book VI, ll. 592–93.

12. On linguistic translation as an act of "transformation," see Jacques Derrida, *Positions*, trans. Alan Bass (Chicago: University of Chicago Press, 1981), 20. For Derrida's reading of Benjamin's "The Task of the Translator," see Jacques Derrida, "Des Tours de Babel," trans. Joseph F. Graham, in Derrida's *Difference in Translation*, ed. Graham (Ithaca, N.Y.: Cornell University Press, 1985), 165–208.

13. On the implications of the figure of "catachresis" for Western models of signification and systems of meaning, see Jacques Derrida, "The White Mythology," in his *Margins of Philosophy*, trans. Alan Bass (Chicago: University of Chicago Press, 1982), 207–71.

14. Georg Wilhelm Friedrich Hegel, *Faith and Knowledge*, trans. W. Cerf and H. J. Harris (Albany: State University of New York Press, 1977), 73. For a discussion of this passage in the context of the problem of "reflection" in Hegel, see Rodolphe Gasché, *The Tain of the Mirror* (Cambridge, Mass.: Harvard University Press, 1986), 23–34.

15. "In a Materialist Way" is the title of an important essay by Pierre Macherey, student and colleague of Althusser. The essay, translated by Lorna Scott Fox, was written for the volume *Philosophy in France Today*, ed. Alan Montefiore (Cambridge, Eng.: Cambridge University Press, 1983), 136–54.

16. Karl Marx and Friedrich Engels, *The German Ideology*, trans. Clemens Dutt, in Marx's *Collected Works*, vol. 5 (New York: International Publishers, 1976). Subsequent references are to this edition and will be included in text.

17. Stephen Heath, "On Screen, in Frame: Film and Ideology," in *Questions of Cinema* (Indianapolis: Indiana University Press, 1981), 2.

18. See Balibar, "Vacillation," 162. Subsequent references to this essay will be included in the text. The problem of ideology posed in *The German Ideology* is developed and complicated by the discussion in the first volume of *Capital* of "the mysterious character of the commodity form" by which the "definite social relation between men themselves assumes . . . for them, the fantastic form of a relation between things" (Karl Marx, *Capital: Volume One*, trans. Ben Fowkes (New York: Vintage Books, 1977), 164–65). In "Vacillation," Balibar discusses the substitution of fetish for ideology: "[T]o think both *the real and the imaginary within ideology*. This is precisely what Marx tries to do in his analysis of fetishism" (168).

19. Jerome J. McGann, *The Romantic Ideology* (Chicago: University of Chicago Press, 1981), 1. Subsequent references to this book will be included in the text.

20. The passage is quoted in Jon Klancher's insightful critical essay on the historicist turn in Romantic studies, "English Romanticism and Cultural Production," in *The New Historicism*, ed. H. Aram Veeser (New York: Routledge, 1989), 77. See also Cynthia Chase's fine and lucid account of recent developments in Romantic studies in *Romanticism*, ed. Cynthia Chase (London: Longman, 1993), 1–42.

21. Jerome J. McGann, *Towards a Literature of Knowledge* (Chicago: University of Chicago Press, 1989), 131. Further references to this book will be included in the text. See also Jerome J. McGann, *The Textual Condition* (Princeton, N.J.: Princeton University Press, 1991), 3–16.

22. References to Keats's poetry are taken from *John Keats: Complete Poems*, ed. Jack Stillinger (Cambridge, Mass.: Harvard University Press, 1978), and are cited by line numbers.

23. This is how one might interpret Keats's prophetic remark—"I think I shall be among the English poets after my death"—against the grain of the aesthetic ideology it appears to embrace, however anxiously: like the English poets that have gone and died before him—like Milton and Spenser and Shakespeare—Keats will be dead and buried. On the inevitable intrication between the "archive of the 'real' and the archive of 'fiction,'" see "'This Strange Institution Called Literature': An Interview with Jacques Derrida," in *Acts of Literature*, ed. Derek Attridge (New York: Routledge, 1992), 24.

24. However brief its moment in the critical sun may prove to be, the New Historicism has had the effect of casting light on the material of history; and it is the significant stress placed on the material of history that distinguishes *New* Historicism from the traditional historicisms of its predecessors. In the most compelling work of the historically oriented Romantic critics (Marjorie Levinson, Alan Liu, Alan Bewell), the return to history offers an engagement with a materiality (of "detail" or "example" if not of language) that complicates the

complementarity of "text" and "context" and that thus opens critical attention to the "textuality" of what has been traditionally relegated to a stable and
explanatory "context."

Some significant and influential studies of Romanticism to have been written within a "New Historicist" perspective include Marilyn Butler, *Romantics,
Rebels and Reactionaries: English Literature and Its Background 1760–1830* (Oxford:
Oxford University Press, 1982); James K. Chandler, *Wordsworth's Second Nature*
(Chicago: University of Chicago Press, 1984); Alan Liu, *Wordsworth: The Sense
of History* (Stanford, Calif.: Stanford University Press, 1989); Alan Bewell, *Wordsworth and the Enlightenment* (New Haven, Conn.: Yale University Press, 1989);
and Marjorie Levinson, *Keats's Life of Allegory* (Oxford: Basil Blackwell, 1988).

25. Marjorie Levinson, "Introduction," *Rethinking Historicism* (Oxford: Basil
Blackwell, 1989), 10.

26. This is the place to note the omission of Foucault from this study. While
I find the influence of Foucault to be indispensable for the explorations of the
institutional operations and effects of culture, I would argue that the invocation
of Foucault in recent literary and cultural studies most often takes two symptomatic forms: as the "historicizing" antidote to deconstructive analysis, and
as the "solution" to the problem of ideology and thus as the supersession of
Marxism. Small wonder, then, that Foucault has served so prominently as the
theoretical framework for much of the New Historicism.

One prominent exception to this use of Foucault is Nancy Armstrong's
provocative and radically revisionist exploration of the rise of the novel, an exploration that, while calling upon Foucault's groundbreaking work on sexuality, never loses sight of the ideological dimensions of literary discourse. See her
Desire and Domestic Fiction: A Political History of the Novel (Oxford: Oxford University Press, 1987).

27. Carolyn Porter, "Are We Being Historical Yet?" in *The States of "Theory": History, Art, and Critical Discourse*, ed. David Carroll (New York: Columbia University Press, 1990), 30. Subsequent references to this essay will be included in the text.

28. Adorno, as quoted and translated by Fredric Jameson in his *Late Marxism: Adorno, or, The Persistence of the Dialectic* (London: Verso, 1990), 187.

29. The reasons for the decline in Althusser's influence are complex and, as
he would describe it, overdetermined. But it is doubtless due at least in part
to his refusal to retreat from Marxism. Althusser's opponents exacerbated the
decline by their grotesque manipulation of his terrible personal struggle with
manic depression and the tragic killing of his wife. It can also be argued that Althusser's importance (or that of Macherey or Balibar) for literary and cultural
studies in the U.S. was never as considerable as it was in the U.K. and that in the
heady days of the heavy traffic of French thought it was readily displaced by

contending post-structuralist approaches, most notably by the impact of Derrida and Foucault. Moreover, in the U.S. there is no real equivalent to the political, intellectual, and cultural influence of the French Communist Party, and thus Althusser's compelling and decades-long struggles within the Party tend to have less purchase in the North American context. The forthcoming English translation and publication of his political writings, however important for our understanding of Althusser's work, is thus unlikely to affect his position in this country. On the course of his career and his impact on political and intellectual work in France, see Gregory Elliot's invaluable study, *Althusser: The Detour of Theory* (London: Verso, 1987).

Some valuable discussions of Althusser's work include Fredric Jameson, *The Political Unconscious* (Ithaca, N.Y.: Cornell University Press, 1981), 1–79; James H. Kavanagh, "'Marks of Weakness': Ideology, Science and Textual Criticism," *Praxis*, 5 (1981): 23–38; James H. Kavanagh, "Marxism's Althusser: Toward a Politics of Literary Theory," *Diacritics*, 12, no. 2 (Spring 1982): 25–33; Paul Hirst, *On Law and Ideology* (Atlantic Highlands, N.J.: Humanities Press, 1979), 1–95; Rosalind Coward and John Ellis, *Language and Materialism* (London: Routledge and Kegan Paul, 1977), 61–92; Paul Ricoeur, *Lectures on Ideology and Utopia*, ed. George H. Taylor (New York: Columbia University Press, 1986), 103–58; Michael Sprinker, *Imaginary Relations: Aesthetics and Ideology in the Theory of Historical Materialism* (London: Verso, 1987), 177–206, 267–96; and Paul Smith, *Discerning the Subject* (Minneapolis: University of Minnesota Press, 1988), 11–29. Finally, see the fine and important volume of essays, *The Althusserian Legacy*, ed. E. Ann Kaplan and Michael Sprinker (London: Verso, 1993).

30. On the deconstructive logic of the "supplement," see in particular Jacques Derrida's reading of Rousseau, ". . . That Dangerous Supplement . . . ," in his *Of Grammatology*, trans. Gayatri Chakravorty Spivak (Baltimore: Johns Hopkins University Press, 1976), 141–64.

31. Michael Sprinker's remarks on de Man are thus very much to the point: "De Man never ceased to meditate on the concepts of history, politics, and ideology which are at the centre of Marxist theory" (*Imaginary Relations*, 240). One of the most important attempts to press at the question of ideology and aesthetics in de Man is Cynthia Chase's essay "Translating Romanticism: Literary Theory as the Criticism of Aesthetics in the Work of Paul de Man," *Textual Practice*, 4, no. 3 (Winter 1990): 349–75.

The ideological stakes of de Man's work have taken a very different turn with the disclosure of Paul de Man's wartime journalism. This is not the place to explore that vexed issue, which has often been transparently manipulated—even crudely yoked to the Heidegger "scandal"—in order to discredit not only de Man but Derrida and all those who have been influenced or engaged by their work. The most useful document through which to approach the question is the collection *Responses: On Paul de Man's Wartime Journalism,* ed. Werner Hamacher, Neil Hertz, and Thomas Keenan (Lincoln: University of Nebraska Press, 1988). See in particular Cynthia Chase, "Trappings of an Education," 44–79; Jacques Derrida, "Like the Sound of the Sea Deep Within a Shell: Paul de Man's War," 127–64; Werner Hamacher, "Journals, Politics," 438–67; Ian Balfour, "'Difficult Reading': De Man's Itineraries," 6–20; and Thomas Keenan, "Documents: Public Criticisms," 468–77. For one of the most polemical and, from my perspective, deeply misguided "responses" to the "de Man affair," see David M. Hirsch, *The Deconstruction of Literature: Criticism After Auschwitz* (Hanover, N.H.: University Press of New England, 1991), esp. 97–117; 255–68.

32. De Man pursues—or, better perhaps, *encounters*—the workings and implications of this pattern most extensively in his reading of *The Triumph of Life.* See Paul de Man, "Shelley Disfigured," in his *The Rhetoric of Romanticism* (New York: Columbia University Press, 1984), 93–123. Subsequent references to this essay will be included in the text.

33. Rodolphe Gasché, "Indifference to Philosophy: De Man on Kant, Hegel, and Nietzsche," in *Reading de Man Reading,* ed. Lindsay Waters and Wlad Godzich (Minneapolis: University of Minnesota Press, 1989), 278. This is an important volume on the work and legacy of de Man; in addition to Gasché's piece, see in particular the essays by Jacques Derrida, Deborah Esch, Neil Hertz, Carol Jacobs, Peggy Kamuf, Werner Hamacher, and Timothy Bahti. I believe the most provocative and valuable assessment of de Man's work from a Marxist perspective to be Fredric Jameson's "Deconstruction as Nominalism," in *Postmodernism, or The Cultural Logic of Late Capitalism* (Durham, N.C.: Duke University Press, 1991), 217–59.

34. See Timothy Bahti, "The Lessons of Remembering and Forgetting," in Waters and Godzich, *Reading de Man Reading,* 244–58.

35. De Man, "Kant and Schiller." On Schiller and the politics of aesthetics and the aesthetic state, see also Fredric Jameson, *Marxism and Form* (Princeton, N.J.: Princeton University Press, 1971), 83–116; John Brenkman, *Culture and Domination* (Ithaca, N.Y.: Cornell University Press, 1988), 59–101; and Eagleton, *Ideology of the Aesthetic,* 103–19.

36. On the institution as the instituting idea and the relationship between "instituting" and "institution," see Samuel Weber, *Institution and Interpretation* (Minneapolis: University of Minnesota Press, 1987); and in the same volume see Wlad Godzich's Afterword, 153–64, which focuses and elaborates on this relationship with reference to the problem of the social. For an excellent treatment of the "Social Constitution of Subjectivity," see Brenkman, *Culture and Domination,* 141–83.

37. Terry Eagleton, *Criticism and Ideology* (London: Verso, 1976), 102.

38. Terry Eagleton, Foreword to Daniel Cottom, *Social Figures: George Eliot, Social History, and Literary Representation* (Minneapolis: University of Minnesota Press), xii.

39. Gramsci's notion of "hegemony" is central to his theory of the consolidation of ideological power in the bourgeois state. See in particular Antonio Gramsci, *Selections from the Prison Notebooks*, trans. Quintin Hoare and Geoffrey Nowell Smith (New York: International Publishers, 1971). Gramsci's treatments of the concept of hegemony, which are as unsystematic as Marx's elaborations of ideology, have been deeply influential for contemporary Marxist thinking about the relationships of culture, ideology, and politics. See, for instance, Chantal Mouffe, "Hegemony and Ideology in Gramsci," in her *Gramsci and Marxist Theory* (London: Routledge and Kegan Paul, 1979), 168–204; and Christine Buci-Glucksmann, *Gramsci and the State*, trans. David Fernbach (London: Lawrence and Wisehart, 1980).

40. Benedict Anderson, *Imagined Communities: Reflections on the Origin and Spread of Nationalism* (London: Verso, 1983).

41. There have been important recent studies of the ideological significance of English literature for the discipline of literary studies and for the humanities in general. See in particular Edward Said, *The Text, the World, and the Critic* (Cambridge, Mass.: Harvard University Press, 1983); Paul Bové, *Intellectuals in Power: A Genealogy of Critical Humanism* (New York: Columbia University Press, 1986); Jonathan Arac, *Critical Genealogies: Historical Situations for Postmodern Literary Studies* (New York: Columbia University Press, 1986); Gayatri Chakravorty Spivak, *In Other Worlds: Essays in Cultural Politics* (London: Methuen, 1987); Gayatri Chakravorty Spivak, *Outside in the Teaching Machine* (London: Routledge, 1993); and Bruce Robbins, *Secular Vocations: Intellectuals, Professionalism, Culture* (London: Verso, 1993).

42. The place of the university and the intellectual within the problematic of cultural value and its ideological function within the contemporary world order has been the object of much of the recent work of Gayatri Chakravorty Spivak. See in particular "Scattered Speculations on the Question of Culture Studies," in her *Outside the Teaching Machine*, 255–84; and see Jacques Derrida, "The Principle of Reason: The University in the Eyes of Its Pupils," *Diacritics*, 13, no. 3 (Fall 1983): 3–20.

43. Theodor Adorno, *Negative Dialectics*, trans. E. B. Ashton (New York: Seabury, 1979), 165–66; the quoted material appears on p. 165.

Chapter 1

1. Samuel Taylor Coleridge, *Biographia Literaria*, ed. James Engell and W. Jackson Bate (Princeton, N.J.: Princeton University Press, 1983), 1: 304. Sub-

sequent references to this edition, by volume and page number, will be included in the text.

2. We might note in this context that Coleridge had by 1801 translated Schiller's *Wallenstein*. There is, of course, a long tradition of criticism that has minimized the significance of the German connection. See, for instance, Stephen Prickett: "Coleridge's concept of 'Imagination' cannot be satisfactorily explained in terms of its origins in German philosophy—still less as a confusion of those ideas; it is a response to a particular need to affirm the value in human experience which was threatened by the prevailing climate of mechanistic thought in England." Notable is Prickett's desire to rid Coleridge of this German debt, and to find in the English critic something of value (indeed, value itself) that the Germans lack: Coleridge "is relevant to us today in a way that they are not." Stephen Prickett, *Coleridge and Wordsworth: The Poetry of Growth* (Cambridge, Eng.: Cambridge University Press, 1970), 29, 28. Subsequent references to this work will be included in the text. In his book *Immanuel Kant in England, 1793–1838* (Princeton, N.J.: Princeton University Press, 1931), René Wellek finds that however much Coleridge dedicated himself to this Kantian project, "his fundamental weakness" to pursue philosophical speculation prevents the fulfillment of this project. For an excellent account of Coleridge's German debts and England's "image of Germany" during this period, see David Simpson's fine recent book *Romanticism, Nationalism, and the Revolt Against Theory* (Chicago: University of Chicago Press, 1993), esp. 84–103.

3. For the ways in which this differs from the "materialist method" proposed by the New Historicism, see above in the Introduction. For two attempts to treat the Coleridgean imagination as a political as well as critical concept, see Stuart Peterfreund, "Coleridge and the Politics of Critical Vision," *Studies in English Literature*, 21, no. 4 (Autumn 1981): 585–604; and F. R. Storch, "The Politics of the Imagination," *Studies in Romanticism (SiR)*, 21, no. 5 (Fall 1982): 448–64. Although neither of the following works focuses explicitly on the concept of the imagination as the conduit of politics and philosophy, see Raymond Williams, *Culture and Society: 1789–1950* (Cambridge, Eng.: Cambridge University Press, 1958); and Marilyn Butler, *Romantics, Rebels and Reactionaries* (Oxford: Oxford University Press, 1982). Both Williams and Butler develop important discussions of the relationship between the cultural projects of figures such as Coleridge and political developments in early nineteenth-century England.

4. I take my understanding of the imagination in Coleridge as an act of "instituting" from Samuel Weber's *Institution and Interpretation* (Minneapolis: University of Minnesota Press, 1987). Weber's model of institution is succinctly formalized by Wlad Godzich in his Afterword to *Institution and Interpretation*: "[A]n institution is first and foremost a guiding idea, the idea of some deter-

mined goal to be reached for the common weal; it is this goal that is sought according to prescribed behavior and by the application of set procedures. The idea itself is adopted by a group of individuals who become its public possessors and implementers" (156). The imagination is, as I will argue, just such a "guiding idea" which Coleridge would "institute" through the "public possessors and implementers" he calls the "national clerisy."

5. Terry Eagleton, *The Ideology of the Aesthetic* (London: Basil Blackwell, 1990), 102.

6. Friedrich Schiller, *Letters on the Aesthetic Education of Man*, trans. Reginald Snell (London: Routledge and Kegan Paul, 1954), 26. For a discussion of Hegel's relationship to the French Revolution, see Joachim Ritter, *Hegel and the French Revolution*, trans. Richard Dien Winfield (Cambridge, Mass.: MIT Press, 1982).

7. For an interpretation that asserts that Coleridge's substitution of a German for a French Revolution does not necessarily constitute a turn to the right, see Elizabeth Sewell, "Coleridge on Revolution," *SiR*, 11, no. 4 (Fall 1972): 342–59.

8. John Stuart Mill, *Mill on Bentham and Coleridge*, intro. F. R. Leavis (Cambridge, Eng.: Cambridge University Press, 1950), 91. Subsequent references to Mill's essay will be included in the text.

9. In Chapter Seventeen, for instance, when elaborating his objections to the "levelling" effects of Wordsworth's images of the "rustic," Coleridge posits the imagination as the source of "the best part of human language" (*Biographia*, 2: 54).

10. The functions and implications of this distinction have been developed most fully in the work of Gérard Genette, Tzvetan Todorov, and Roland Barthes. For a useful survey of structuralist narrative theory, see Seymour Chatman, *Story and Discourse: Narrative Structure in Fiction and Film* (Ithaca, N.Y.: Cornell University Press, 1978). On the role of this narrative division in autobiographical discourse, see Jean Starobinski, "The Style of Autobiography," in *Autobiography: Essays Theoretical and Critical*, ed. James Olney (Princeton, N.J.: Princeton University Press, 1980), 73–83. Perhaps the most significant recent discussion of the generic problems of autobiography and of the problems of reading and subjectivity posed by autobiographical narration is Paul de Man, "Autobiography as De-facement," in his *The Rhetoric of Romanticism* (New York: Columbia University Press, 1984), 67–82. For a provocative treatment of the ideological function of autobiographical discourse, see Paul Smith, "Autobiography," in his *Discerning the Subject* (Minneapolis: University of Minnesota Press, 1988), 101–17. Two classic studies of autobiography are Roy Pascal, *Design and Truth in Autobiography* (Cambridge, Mass.: Harvard University Press, 1960); and Karl Weintraub, "Autobiography and Historical Consciousness,"

Critical Inquiry, 1, no. 4 (June 1975): 821–48. For a discussion of the *Biographia* in the tradition of the literary autobiography, see C. M. Wallace, "The Function of Autobiography in *Biographia Literaria*," *Wordsworth Circle*, 12, no. 4 (Autumn 1981): 216–25. Jerome Christensen, in his *Coleridge's Blessed Machine of Language* (Ithaca, N.Y.: Cornell University Press, 1981), argues that as an autobiography, the *Biographia Literaria* is "crucially deficient"; rather, according to Christensen, this "Literary Life is propaedeutic toward one" (119).

11. Important treatments of the "borrowings" or "plagiarisms" and their relationship to Coleridge's self-representation include Norman Fruman, *The Damaged Archangel* (New York: Braziller, 1971); Thomas McFarland, *Coleridge and the Pantheist Tradition* (Oxford: Oxford University Press, 1969); and more recently Jerome Christensen, "The Marginal Method of the *Biographia Literaria*" in his *Coleridge's Blessed Machine*, 96–117.

12. The most notable exception is the long section of volume 2 called "Satyrane's Letters," which chronicle Coleridge's journey to Germany.

13. On the structural dimension of Coleridge's autobiography, see Christensen, *Coleridge's Blessed Machine*, 170–71.

14. In his notes for the 1818–19 *Lectures on Shakespeare*, Coleridge writes: "tho' the imagination may supercede perception, yet it must be granted an imperfection (tho' even here how easily do we not tolerate it?) to place the two in broad contradiction to each other." In Samuel Taylor Coleridge, *Lectures 1808–1819: On Literature*, ed. R. A. Foakes (Princeton, N.J.: Princeton University Press, 1987), 2: 317. Subsequent references to the *Lectures* will be included in the text.

15. Arden Reed, *Romantic Weather: The Climates of Coleridge and Baudelaire* (Hanover, N.H.: University Press of New England, 1983), 187.

16. See Coleridge, *Lectures*, 2: 208.

17. As Wimsatt and Brooks note, "the relative dignity of the terms" was "well established" by the end of eighteenth century (William K. Wimsatt and Cleanth Brooks, *Literary Criticism: A Short History* (Chicago: University of Chicago Press, 1957), 385. On the strict or essential distinction between the primary and secondary imagination, see Reed, *Romantic Weather*, esp. 186–98; and Christensen, *Coleridge's Blessed Machine*, 167–75.

18. Thomas McFarland, "The Origin and Significance of Coleridge's Theory of the Secondary Imagination," in his *Originality and Imagination* (Baltimore: Johns Hopkins University Press, 1985), 106.

19. See, for example, Prickett: "It is the union of perceiver and perceived that Coleridge means by the 'Imagination'" (*Coleridge and Wordsworth*, 37).

20. In her reading of Chapter Thirteen by the light of Lacanian psychoanalytic theory, Spivak connects the problem of the interruption to the claims made in the name of the imagination: "The greatest instrument of narrative

refraction in these chapters, the *obturateur*, if you like, is, of course, the letter that stops publication of the original Thirteen. The gesture is about as far as possible from 'the eternal act of creation in the infinite I am.' . . . It is a written message to oneself represented as being an external interruption" (Gayatri Chakravorty Spivak, "The Letter as Cutting Edge," her *In Other Worlds: Essays in Cultural Politics* [London: Methuen, 1987], 4–5). My own reading is indebted to Spivak's, particularly insofar as she asserts that this "*obturateur*" is also "the ruse that makes possible the establishment of the *Law* of the imagination." The interruption enables the presentation of the Law, which is an ideological as well as psychoanalytic operation. See also Jerome Christensen, "The Mind at Ocean: The Impropriety of Coleridge's Literary Life," in *Romanticism and Language*, ed. Arden Reed (Ithaca, N.Y.: Cornell University Press, 1985), 144–67. Christensen's essay is a lucid discussion of many of the questions that interest me here; most importantly perhaps, Christensen stresses the rhetorical and thematic significance of the "interruption" in the *Biographia*.

21. Or it may justify abandoning Coleridge altogether, corroborating F. R. Leavis's assertion that Coleridge lacked a "disciplined mind." See his introduction to *Mill*, 9.

22. See David Simpson, *Irony and Authority in Romantic Poetry* (Totowa, N.J.: Rowman and Littlefield, 1979): "this constitutes a parody of the Deductive method; what it records is the movement of mind (thought)" (95–96).

23. Samuel Taylor Coleridge, *Poetical Works*, ed. E. H. Coleridge (Oxford: Oxford University Press, 1912), 429–31. Subsequent references to Coleridge's poetry are to this edition. "Limbo" can be read as the poetic record of the failure of the imagination: we are left in this late poem with "a strange place, this Limbo!—not a Place" (l. 11), the disturbing "unmeaning" (l. 17) left in the wake of imagination's collapse: "the mere horror of blank Naught-at-all" (l. 33).

24. On this topos as a prominent image of Romantic discourse, see Thomas McFarland, *Romanticism and the Forms of Ruin: Wordsworth, Coleridge, and Modalities of Fragmentation* (Princeton, N.J.: Princeton University Press, 1981).

25. See Jerome Christensen: "The interruption of the man of the letter in the logic of the imagination limns the repressed always returning in the imagination, for what the myth of the imagination represses is literally the letter" (*Coleridge's Blessed Machine*, 173). What Christensen calls the "myth" of the imagination in this passage is the *ideology* of the imagination and, by extension, an ideology of subjectivity.

26. Coleridge refers to this "surreptitious act of imagination" in the second "Thesis": "Equally inconceivable is a cycle of equal truths without a common and central principle. . . . That the absurdity does not so immediately strike us, that it does not seem unimaginable, is owing to a surreptitious act of the

imaginations which, instinctively and without noticing the same, . . . fills out the intervening spaces and contemplates the cycle (of B, C, D, E, F, etc.) as a continuous circle (A) giving to all collectively the unity of their common orbit" (*Biographia*, 1: 267).

27. See also Tilottama Rajan's useful interpretation of the poem, *Dark Interpreter* (Ithaca, N.Y.: Cornell University Press, 1980), 243–47.

28. Though we are likely to regard Coleridge's qualification in line 18 of an "English home" as merely incidental nationalist sentiment, the effects of the "vain repetition!" lend the line more far-reaching implications, depriving an "English home" of empirical substance or "embodiment." The social, political, and historical consequences of this "vain repetition"—that "home" and thought "are one"—are, as we shall discuss below, the concern of Coleridge's *On the Constitution of Church and State.*

29. As Jerome Christensen notes in his discussion of this passage, only Coleridge's "standard [is] properly permanent and universal" (*Coleridge's Blessed Machine*, 143).

30. The woodman, writes Arden Reed in his brilliant interpretation of the poem, "is a Piranesian figure caught in a labyrinth—the 'sheep-track's maze' . . . —an impression reinforced linguistically by the convoluted syntax of the passage" (*Romantic Weather*, 97).

31. Mill suggests this as a significant pattern in Coleridge's thought: "With Coleridge, the very fact that any doctrine had been believed by thoughtful men, and received by whole nations or generations of mankind, was part of the problem to be solved, was one of the phenomena to be accounted for" (*Mill*, 100). And see Robert O. Preyer, "Coleridge's Historical Thought," in *Coleridge: A Collection of Critical Essays*, ed. Kathleen Coburn (Englewood Cliffs, N.J.: Prentice-Hall, 1967), 152–60; and Stephen Prickett, "Coleridge and the Idea of the Clerisy," in *Reading Coleridge: Approaches and Applications*, ed. Walter B. Crawford (Ithaca, N.Y.: Cornell University Press, 1979), 252–73.

32. Samuel Taylor Coleridge, *On the Constitution of the Church and State*, ed. John Colmer (Princeton, N.J.: Princeton University Press, 1976), 12. Subsequent references to this edition will be included in the text.

33. Perry Anderson, "Origins of the Present Crisis," *New Left Review*, 23 (Jan.–Feb. 1964): 30. Subsequent references to this essay will be included in the text. Anderson's review of English history outlines nothing less than a dramatic counternarrative to a long tradition of British historiography. But despite his detailed attention to questions of politics and ideology, implicit in Anderson's argument is the conception that history is propelled by a single mechanism, that the unfolding of history is governed solely by a primary, "fundamental, antagonistic contradiction." Political theorist Nicos Poulantzas makes this objection to Anderson's essay and suggests that Anderson takes as

the silent framework for his reading "a Hegelian 'functionalist' type of totality" and situates this "totality in an 'idealist' domain of class-consciousness." What Anderson describes as the "welding" of aristocracy with bourgeoisie in a unified social bloc Poulantzas characterizes as the "overlapping of several modes of production," which results in a "contradictory unity" in the ruling bloc. That there is no "fundamental, antagonistic contradiction" between aristocracy (or, more precisely, landed capital) and bourgeoisie does not necessarily mean that "secondary contradictions" are annulled or that aristocracy and bourgeoisie are synthesized in a "fused" power bloc (Nicos Poulantzas, "Marxist Political Theory in Great Britain," *New Left Review*, 43 [Jan.–Feb. 1967]: 62). Coleridge's own position is inscribed between the model set out by Anderson and the critique developed by Poulantzas: Coleridge is struggling to address and reconcile these ideological or secondary contradictions. These issues are pursued by Philip Corrigan and Derek Sayer, who argue in *The Great Arch* (London: Basil Blackwell, 1986) that English state formation should be understood as nothing less than a "cultural revolution."

34. There was, of course, something more at work here than an ideological crisis: there were profound economic changes under way during these decisive decades of industrialization, when the demand for urban labor precipitated a new rift between city and country, between a dynamic industrial and an ensconced agrarian capital. The crisis was not, moreover, restricted to the dominant power bloc or to English borders: the crisis of the nation was simultaneously a crisis of the proletariat and of colonialism. Cheap labor from Ireland, which was "annexed" under the so-called "Union of 1800," constituted almost half of the English working class during this period and was particularly crucial to the industry most responsible for England's economic "take-off" in the early nineteenth century: the English textile industry, through the cheap materials extracted from the colonies and primarily from India, dominated the world market. See E. P. Thompson, *The Making of the English Working Class* (New York: Vintage, 1963), 429–43.

35. On the ideological utility and remaking of the "past," see Eric Hobsbawm and Terence Ranger, eds., *The Invention of Tradition* (Cambridge, Eng.: Cambridge University Press, 1983); Patrick Wright, *On Living in an Old Country* (London: Verso, 1985); and Richard Johnson et al., eds., *Making History* (Minneapolis: University of Minnesota Press, 1982).

36. Nor, it goes without saying, to the working class, which remains outside the purview of Coleridge's account. Coleridge proposed but never composed his Lay Sermon to the working class. As Edward Thompson and others have demonstrated, the Reform Bill of 1832 did little for the working class, designed as it was to address those "secondary contradictions" (Thompson, *English Working Class*, 915).

37. See Prickett, "Coleridge and the Idea of the Clerisy," 252–73. And for an excellent treatment of this crisis of the English university and Coleridge's role in it, see Robert Young, "The Idea of a Chrestomathic University," in *Logomachia: The Conflict of the Faculties*, ed. Richard Rand (Lincoln: University of Nebraska Press, 1992), 97–126.

38. Tom Nairn, *The Break-Up of Britain* (London: Verso, 1977), 33.

39. Ibid., 33–34.

40. This is much the same conclusion reached by Corrigan and Sayer in their recent revisionist social-cultural history of English state formation: "The state as fiction, as illusory unity—the author of its own representations, the stage-director of all political theatre, investing every belief with moral signification—is formed in the struggle to make this violent 'awful adjustment' happen again and again" (*Great Arch*, 118).

41. Benedict Anderson, *Imagined Communities: Reflections on the Origin and Spread of Nationalism* (London: Verso, 1983).

42. On the relationship between narrative, history, and national community, see the work of Paul Ricoeur and in particular the essay "Narrative Time," *Critical Inquiry*, 7, no. 1 (Autumn 1980): 165–86.

43. For a reading of *On the Constitution of Church and State* that sees this project of "reconciliation" as supervised by the "sacred principles" of a Church-governed state, see John Colmer, "Coleridge and Politics," in *Writers and Their Backgrounds: S. T. Coleridge*, ed. R. L. Brett (London: Macmillan, 1971), 244–70.

44. Louis Althusser, *Philosophie et philosophie spontanée des savants* (Paris: Maspero, 1974), 40; as quoted by Christine Buci-Glucksmann in *Gramsci and the State*, trans. David Fernbach (London: Lawrence and Wisehart, 1980), 66.

45. Prickett, "Coleridge and the Idea of the Clerisy," 264. That F. R. Leavis in his introduction to the 1950 edition of John Stuart Mill's essays should conclude with a discussion of Coleridge's and Mill's significance for the principles of liberal education points to the contemporary currency of these ideological issues.

46. For some very suggestive remarks regarding the links between "genius" and the political and theological status of the nation, see Christensen, *Coleridge's Blessed Machine*, 139–41.

47. Samuel Taylor Coleridge, *The Statesman's Manual*, in his *Lay Sermons*, ed. R. J. White (Princeton, N.J.: Princeton University Press, 1972), 29. Subsequent references to this work will be included in the text.

48. Jacques-Alain Miller introduced the term into psychoanalytic discourse with his essay by that name, first published in 1966 in *Cahiers pour l'analyse* and published in translation as "Suture," in *Screen*, 18, no. 4 (Winter 1977/78): 24–34. For an excellent account of Miller's development of the term and of its

role in cinema studies as well as its potential significance for a theory of ideology, see Stephen Heath's rigorous exposition, "On Suture," in *Questions of Cinema* (Bloomington: Indiana University Press, 1981), 76–112. Subsequent references to Heath's essay will be included in the text. My use of the term "suture" as an ideological process derives in part from Ernesto Laclau's suggestive if sketchy discussion of the term in "The Impossibility of Society," *Canadian Journal of Political and Social Theory*, 7, nos. 1–2 (Winter/Spring 1983): 21–24.

49. Jonathan Arac, "Coleridge and New Criticism Reconsidered: Repetition and Exclusion," in his *Critical Genealogies: Historical Situations for Postmodern Literary Studies* (New York: Columbia University Press, 1986), 94–95. In *Writing and Society* (London: Verso, n.d.), Raymond Williams isolates passages by Coleridge and T. S. Eliot, a century apart, to display the ideological and cultural as well as stylistic affinity shared by these poet-critics (68).

Chapter 2

1. William Wordsworth, *The Prelude*, Book XII, ll. 277–87. All quotations from this work are from the critical edition established by Jonathan Wordsworth, M. H. Abrams, and Stephen Gill, *The Prelude: 1799, 1805, 1850* (New York: W. W. Norton, 1979). Because I am interested here in the variability of the imagination and the revisionary quality of enshrinement, I will make reference to each version of the poem. Unless otherwise specified, subsequent references are to the 1850 version, and are indicated in the text by book and line numbers.

2. When *Webster's Dictionary* gives the range of usages of the term "imagination," it turns to Roy Pascal: "Imagination is something akin to what it was in Wordsworth, a means of deepest insight and sympathy." On the relationship between the notions of sympathy and the imagination, see James Engell, *The Creative Imagination* (Cambridge, Mass.: Harvard University Press, 1981), 143–60. On the more specific textual relationship between "love" and the imagination in Wordsworth, see Engell, 275–76.

3. Engell, *Creative Imagination*, 143. On the relationship between imagination and community, see Michael H. Friedman, *The Making of a Tory Humanist: William Wordsworth and the Idea of Community* (New York: Columbia University Press, 1979). For a study that examines the poetic forms of "love" in Wordsworth's poetry and life, see John Beer, *Wordsworth and the Human Heart* (New York: Columbia University Press, 1978).

4. Paul de Man, "Sign and Symbol in Hegel's *Aesthetics*," *Critical Inquiry*, 8, no. 4 (Summer 1982): 763. Subsequent references to this essay will be included in the text.

5. Jacques Derrida, *Memoires: For Paul de Man*, trans. Cecile Lindsay, Jona-

than Culler, and Eduardo Cadava (New York: Columbia University Press, 1986), 70. The most lucid example of an interpretation of English Romanticism that both adheres to and develops the canonical model of internalization remains M. H. Abram's *Natural Supernaturalism* (New York: W. W. Norton, 1971). See esp. 235–37, where Abrams considers the autobiographical plot structure of *Erinnerung* in Hegel's *Phenomenology of Spirit* and Wordsworth's *The Prelude*.

6. G. W. F. Hegel, *Vorlesungen über die Aesthetik*, trans. T. M. Knox as *Aesthetics: Lectures on Fine Art* (London: Oxford University Press, 1975), 517. Subsequent references are to the Knox translation and will be included in the text.

7. In his *Prospectus to The Recluse*, Wordsworth describes the fear and awe that result "when we look / Into our Minds, into the Mind of Men, / My haunt, and the main region of my song" ll. 25–40.

8. In his narrative of World-History, Hegel describes the move from Orient to Occident in much the same language: "Among the Greeks we feel ourselves immediately at home, for we are in the region of Spirit." G. W. F. Hegel, *The Philosophy of History*, trans. J. Sibree (New York: P. F. Collier and Son, 1902), 300.

9. Derrida develops a reading of these passages on Egypt that links the questions of monumentality and interiorization to the Hegelian concept of the imagination through the images of the tomb and the crypt. See Jacques Derrida, "The Pit and the Pyramid," in his *Margins of Philosophy*, trans. Alan Bass (Chicago: University of Chicago Press, 1982), 82–87.

10. Responding to an earlier version of this chapter presented at the MLA special session "Scenes of Encounter: Hegel and the Discourses of English Romanticism," New York, Dec. 1986, Paul H. Fry noted the difficulty of ascribing Easternness or Westernness to the sublimity of Hebrew culture, what Fry calls "this crucial development in the emergence of what was indeed to become Western subjectivity." I am arguing that within the Hegelian narrative of the spirit, i.e., from within the perspective of nineteenth-century German philosophical speculation, the Hebrew world marks the break between East and West. As it is presented in Hegel, the sublime moment in Hebrew culture establishes the Orient as Orient, as a world distinct from the proper (Occidental) home of the spirit. Thus, the Hebrew world is the origin simultaneously for both East and West. I am indebted here to Rodolphe Gasché's, "Hegel's Orient or the End of Romanticism," in *History and Mimesis: Occasional Paper III: By Members of the Program in Literature and Philosophy*, ed. Irving J. Massey and Sung-Won Lee (Buffalo: State University of New York at Buffalo, 1983), 17–29.

11. Georg Lukács, *Die Theorie des Romans*, trans. Anna Bostock as *The Theory of the Novel* (Cambridge, Mass.: MIT Press, 1971), 113. Subsequent references to the translated edition will be included in the text.

12. William Wordsworth, "Preface of 1815," in his *Wordsworth's Literary Criticism*, ed. W. J. B. Owen (London: Routledge and Kegan Paul, 1974), 180. Subsequent references to Wordsworth's prose are to this collection and will be included in the text. For a critical edition of Wordsworth's prose, see *The Prose Works of William Wordsworth*, ed. W. J. B. Owen and Jane Worthington Smyser (Oxford: Clarendon Press, 1974).

13. The most important recent treatment of the problem of history in Wordsworth is Alan Liu's *Wordsworth: The Sense of History* (Stanford, Calif.: Stanford University Press, 1989). See, in particular, the introduction, "The History of 'Imagination.'" Liu's book is a comprehensive investigation of the poetic strategies through which Wordsworth works "to carve the 'self' out of its history." My considerable differences with Liu's influential interpretation will become evident; in brief, I disagree with Liu's claim that for Wordsworth "the theory of denial [of history] is imagination" (4–5). As I see it, the poetics of enshrining makes the imagination into the vehicle by which "self" and history are linked.

14. Each of the following studies includes a significant or provocative discussion of the workings of the imagination in *The Prelude*: Paul de Man, "Time and History in Wordsworth," *Diacritics*, 17, no. 4 (Winter 1989): 4–17; Paul de Man, "Wordsworth and Hölderlin," in his *The Rhetoric of Romanticism* (New York: Columbia University Press, 1984); Geoffrey Hartman, *Wordsworth's Poetry 1787–1814* (New Haven, Conn.: Yale University Press, 1964); Geoffrey Hartman, *The Unmediated Vision* (New York: Harcourt, Brace and World, 1966); Geoffrey Hartman, "Words, Wish, Worth: Wordsworth," in *Deconstruction and Criticism*, ed. Harold Bloom (New York: Continuum, 1979); Frank McConnell, *The Confessional Imagination* (Baltimore: Johns Hopkins University Press, 1974); Gayatri Chakravorty Spivak, "Sex and History in *The Prelude*," in her *In Other Worlds: Essays in Cultural Politics* (London: Methuen, 1987); David Simpson, *Wordsworth and the Figurings of the Real* (London: Macmillan, 1982); Abrams, *Natural Supernaturalism*; Stephen Prickett, *Coleridge and Wordsworth: The Poetry of Growth* (Cambridge, Eng.: Cambridge University Press, 1970); Frances Ferguson, *Wordsworth: Language as Counter-Spirit* (New Haven, Conn.: Yale University Press, 1977); J. Hillis Miller, "Wordsworth," in his *The Linguistic Moment* (Princeton, N.J.: Princeton University Press, 1985); Engell, *Creative Imagination*; and James K. Chandler, *Wordsworth's Second Nature* (Chicago: Chicago University Press, 1984).

15. De Man's readings of this passage are indispensable for any study of Wordsworth. See in particular "Time and History in Wordsworth"; and see *Rhetoric*, 15–16, 57–59. Harold Bloom's early discussion of the passage is instructive for his efforts to contain the threatening aspects of these lines, to return the imagination to the authority of the subject. When in *The Visionary Com-*

pany (Ithaca, N.Y.: Cornell University Press, 1971), Bloom asserts that this is the imagination before it is "recollected in tranquility," he ignores that the imagination is invoked here in the present, during the course of composition. Bloom's assertion "in the Imagination's strength to achieve transcendence is the abode and harbor of human greatness" is more indicative of an entrenched tradition of Wordsworth and Romantic criticism than it is representative of Bloom's later work. See also Liu's provocative reading—and rewriting—of this passage as a crucial instance of Wordsworth's confrontation with and denial of history, in *Wordsworth*, 33–35.

16. See Ferguson, *Wordsworth*, for a compelling and sustained account of the poetic operations of the eruptions of "language as counter-spirit." See also Liu's interpretation of "the self-engendering of the 'I'" in Book VI of *The Prelude*: "The description of the 1790 tour in Book 6, read in its own context, is a sustained effort to deny history by asserting nature as the separating mark constitutive of the egotistical self" (*Wordsworth*, 13). Imagination, as Liu writes, "at once mimics and effaces Napoleon in an effort . . . to purge tyranny by *containing* tyranny within itself" (24). Liu sees in the eruption of the imagination in Book VI, not only the "figure of history" but the very course of empirical historical events. Liu's book is distinguished by its attempt to make a way through the text in order to discover the very "bones" of history. As such, it participates in the New Historicist dream—an impossible dream, from my perspective—of escaping the text's own self-representations.

17. For a reading of these lines that develops the "deconstructive" implications of the "trace" and attends to the problem of sexuality inscribed here, see Spivak, "Sex and History in *The Prelude*."

18. See Paul de Man, "Autobiography as De-facement," in his *Rhetoric*, 67–82.

19. On this Miltonic inscription in *The Prelude*, see Robert Young, "'For Thou Wert There': History, Erasure and Superscription in *The Prelude*," in *Glyph Textual Studies 1: Demarcating the Disciplines*, ed. Samuel Weber (Minneapolis: University of Minnesota Press, 1986), 112.

20. For a reading of these lines as emblematic of Wordsworth's "epitaphic mode," see Ferguson, *Wordsworth*, 155. Two important discussions of this crucial passage are Thomas Weiskel, *The Romantic Sublime* (Baltimore: Johns Hopkins University Press, 1976), 143; and Neil Hertz, *The End of the Line* (New York: Columbia University Press, 1985), 233–35. See also Karen Mills-Courts's treatment of Wordsworth's epitaphic mode in her *Poetry as Epitaph: Representation and Poetic Language* (Baton Rouge: Louisiana State University Press, 1990), 165–202.

21. On the thanatography that is always inscribed on the limits of autobiography, see Louis Marin, "Montaigne's Tomb, or Autobiographical Discourse,"

Oxford Literary Review, 4, no. 3 (1981): 43–58; and John Freccero, "Autobiography and Narrative," in *Reconstructing Individualism: Autonomy, Individuality, and the Self in Western Thought*, ed. Thomas C. Heller, Morton Sosna, and David E. Wellbery (Stanford, Calif.: Stanford University Press, 1986), 16–29.

22. *The Excursion*, Book III, ll. 804–5, in *Wordsworth: Poetic Works*, ed. Thomas Hutchinson, rev. Ernest de Selincourt (Oxford: Oxford University Press, 1936), 623. Subsequent references to this edition, by book and line number, will be included in the text.

23. The image of the "flood" is not uncommon in *The Prelude*, and is on occasion linked closely to the powers of the imagination. See, for instance, VI.461–65, and, in particular, VI.609–16. For a discussion of the images of the flood and the deluge as *The Prelude*'s icons of the French Revolution, see Ronald Paulson, "Wordsworth's *Prelude*," in his *The Representations of Revolution* (New Haven, Conn.: Yale University Press, 1983), 254–55.

24. The problem posed by the deluge is not only that it is produced by "rivers of blood" but that it effaces the converging "currents" and "streams" of imagination and subject and ultimately submerges the tracks of history.

25. See Spivak, "Sex and History in *The Prelude*": "Wordsworth coped with the experience of the French Revolution by transforming it into an iconic text that he could write and read" (46).

26. Hartman, *Wordsworth's Poetry 1787–1814*, 229.

27. Each of the following works includes a significant discussion of the "dream of the Arab": Thomas De Quincey, "The Lake Poets: William Wordsworth," in his *Collected Writings*, ed. David Masson, vol. 2 (London: A. & C. Black, 1896), 268–69; W. H. Auden, *The Enchafed Flood* (New York: Vintage, 1950); Jane Worthington Smyser, "Wordsworth's Dream of Poetry and Sciences," *PMLA*, 71, no. 1 (Mar. 1956): 269–75; Hartman, *Wordsworth's Poetry 1787–1814*, 226–31; Evelyn Shakir, "Books, Death, and Immortality: A Study of Book V of *The Prelude*," *Studies in Romanticism*, 8, no. 3 (Spring 1969): 156–67; Harold Bloom, *The Visionary Company*, rev. and enl. ed. (Ithaca, N.Y.: Cornell University Press, 1971), 150–51; Richard J. Onorato, *The Character of the Poet: Wordsworth in "The Prelude"* (Princeton, N.J.: Princeton University Press, 1971), 369–75; Timothy Bahti, "Figures of Interpretation, the Interpretation of Figures: A Reading of Wordsworth's 'Dream of the Arab,'" *Studies in Romanticism*, 18, no. 4 (Winter 1979): 601–27; Michael Ragussis, "Wordsworth: The Arab Dream: The Language Behind Nature and Art," in his *The Subterfuge of Art: Language and the Romantic Tradition* (Baltimore: Johns Hopkins University Press, 1978), 17–34; J. Hillis Miller, "Wordsworth," in his *Linguistic Moment* (Princeton, N.J.: Princeton University Press, 1985), 59–113; and Andrzej Warminski, "Missed Crossings: Wordsworth's Apocalypses," *MLN*, 99, no. 5 (Dec. 1984): 983–1006.

28. My thinking about the dream is deeply indebted to Miller, Bahti, and Warminski for their insistently rhetorical analyses of the dream. I want here to pursue the implications of their readings, to see whether at some decisive point in the course of a rhetorical reading we can discern the figures of an otherness that introduce some unavoidable questions of history and politics. The engagement of these questions should not mean the abandonment of the practice of reading for the illusion of the empirical: it should rather mean a turning or refocusing of this reading to consider the ideological operations of aesthetic concepts such as the imagination.

29. A properly prophetic strain is not, to be sure, absent in this poet who consistently links himself to his predecessor "poet-prophet," Milton. See Geoffrey Hartman, "The Poetics of Prophecy," in *High Romantic Argument*, ed. Lawrence Lipking (Ithaca, N.Y.: Cornell University Press, 1981), 15–40.

30. This "understanding" thus represents in the form of a dream a version of what Gayatri Chakravorty Spivak calls the "sanctioned ignorance" in Western considerations of its others. See her "Imperialism and Sexual Difference," *Oxford Literary Review*, 8, no. 1/2 (1986): 125–40.

31. For a reading of *The Prelude* that deciphers these "deposits" of history in the "spots of time," see Young, "For Thou Wert There."

32. See for example Hartman, *Wordsworth's Poetry 1787–1814*, 229.

33. Miguel de Cervantes, *Don Quijote de la Mancha*, trans. Samuel Putnam (New York: The Modern Library, 1949), 59. Subsequent references to the novel are to page numbers of this edition and will be included in the text. Miller cites this episode in his discussion of the dream; see *Linguistic Moment*, 92–93.

34. Such a burial constitutes an interesting citation of Prospero's burial of his European books of magic and mystery in *The Tempest*. We remember that invocations of Shakespeare are the dream's boundaries; indeed it would seem as if the memories of Shakespeare and Milton themselves were at stake in the dream.

35. A much better fate befalls Señor Don Quixote, who, as Cervantes explains in the Prologue, "shall remain buried in the archives of La Mancha until Heaven shall provide him with someone to deck him out with all the ornaments that he lacks" (*Don Quixote*, 12). Wordsworth writes of the custom of burial in *Essays upon Epitaphs*: "Almost all Nations have wished that certain signs should point out the places where their dead are interred. . . . This custom proceeded obviously from a two-fold desire; first, to guard the remains of the deceased from irreverent approach or from savage violation: and, secondly, to preserve their memory" (*Literary Criticism*, 121).

36. Wordsworth, "Preface of 1815," 183. In *Linguistic Moment*, Miller interprets the dream of the Arab as the "affirmation" of the imagination's "dominion" (90–91).

37. On the figures of the Arab and the "Wordsworth-persona in the dream" as "two aspects of the Wordsworth-poet," see Bahti, "Figures of Interpretation," 617. The signs of this otherness are visible in a passage from *Paradise Lost* cited by Wordsworth as a paradigmatic instance of "the full strength of the imagination":

> As when far off at sea a fleet descried
> *Hangs* in the clouds, by equinoctial winds
> Close sailing from Bengala, or the isles
> Of Ternate or Tidore, whence merchants bring
> Their spicy drugs; they in the trading flood
> Through the wide Ethiopian to the Cape
> Ply, stemming nightly toward the Pole: so seemed
> Far off the flying Fiend.   (II.636–45)

As quoted by Wordsworth in "Preface of 1815," 180. For de Man, Wordsworth's insistent attention to the word "hangs" in both the poetry and the prose is crucial for our understanding of the Wordsworthian poetic imagination. See "Time and History in Wordsworth" and "Wordsworth and Hölderlin."

38. Jacques Lacan, *The Four Fundamental Concepts of Psychoanalysis*, trans. Alan Sheridan (New York: W. W. Norton, 1978), 188.

39. Hartman, *Wordsworth's Poetry 1787–1814*, 229–30.

40. Miller, *Linguistic Moment*, 91.

41. Ramón Saldívar, "In Quest of Authority: Cervantes, *Don Quijote*, and the Grammar of Proper Language," in his *Figural Language in the Novel* (Princeton, N.J.: Princeton University Press, 1984), 57.

42. See ibid., 64.

43. This project of reading has been initiated in the body of critical work that has come to be known as colonial discourse theory. Crossing disciplinary boundaries, colonial discourse theory has raised significant new questions regarding the role played by colonial and neocolonial otherness in the dominant and regulative cultural narratives of the West. It has demonstrated that the history of the encounter between Europe and its Others is constitutive for the formation of Western structures of knowledge and meaning. The imbrications between East and West not only produce the stories of Europe's exploitation and domination of its colonial Other but also demonstrate that the Other is profoundly implicated in those cultural and social forms of representation that continue to govern our thinking. Principal studies of colonial discourse theory include: Edward Said, *Orientalism* (New York: Vintage Books, 1978); Spivak, *In Other Worlds*; Gayatri Chakravorty Spivak, *Outside in the Teaching Machine* (London: Routledge, 1993); Michael Taussig, *Shamanism, Colonialism, and the Wild Man: A Study in Terror and Healing* (Chicago: University of Chicago Press,

1987); Peter Hulme, *Colonial Encounters: Europe and the Native Caribbean 1492–1797* (London: Methuen, 1986); Homi K. Bhaba, "Signs Taken for Wonders," *Critical Inquiry*, 12, no. 1 (Autumn 1985): 144–65; Homi K. Bhaba, "Of Mimicry and Man: The Ambivalence of Colonial Discourse," *October*, 28 (Spring 1984): 125–33; Abdul R. JanMohamed, *Manichean Aesthetics: The Politics of Literature in Colonial Africa* (Amherst: University of Massachusetts Press, 1983); and Jennifer Sharpe, *Allegories of Empire* (Minneapolis: University of Minnesota Press, 1992).

44. See Anwar G. Chejne, *Islam and the West: The Moriscos* (Albany: State University Press of New York, 1983). For an excellent reading of the figure of the Moor in Spanish literature, see Israel Burshatin, "The Moor in the Text: Metaphor, Emblem, and Silence," *Critical Inquiry*, 12, no. 1 (Autumn 1985): 98–118.

45. On the "inordinate" significance of the formation of the Spanish nation-state for European models of statehood, see Perry Anderson, *Lineages of the Absolutist State* (London: New Left Books, 1974), 60–84.

46. Américo Castro, *The Structure of Spanish History*, trans. Edmund King (Princeton, N.J.: Princeton University Press, 1954), 46. Subsequent references to this book will be included in the text. Castro's notions of "vital function" and "life structure," governing principles for his model of national history, are themselves symptomatic of the idealist and organicist rhetoric embedded in the "imagined community" of the nation. Though it is itself a symptom of this "Romanticism," Castro's work is noteworthy for its scrupulous attention to the place of Moorish history on the Iberian peninsula while struggling nonetheless to find in Iberian history some unifying principle of national coherence.

47. Raymond Schwab, *The Oriental Renaissance: Europe's Rediscovery of India and the East, 1680–1880*, trans. Gene Patterson-Black and Victor Reinking (New York: Columbia University Press, 1984), 482.

48. Ibid.

49. Gasché, "Hegel's Orient or the End of Romanticism," 25.

50. Spivak, "Sex and History in *The Prelude*," 68.

51. This "restaging" of the sublime into "spectacle" parallels what Neil Hertz calls the writing beyond "the end of the line"; see especially his compelling Afterword to *End of the Line*, 217–39.

52. Edward Said, "Jane Austen and Empire," in *Raymond Williams: Critical Perspectives*, ed. Terry Eagleton (Boston: Northeastern University Press, 1989), 153.

Chapter 3

1. *Shelley's Poetry and Prose*, ed. Donald H. Rieman and Sharon B. Powers (New York: W. W. Norton, 1977), ll. 166–70. Subsequent quotations of Shelley's nondramatic poetry and prose works will be from this edition and will be cited in the text by line number (for the poetry) or page number (for the prose).

2. This is the thesis of Jerrold Hogle's recent study, *Shelley's Process: Radical Transference and the Development of His Major Works* (Oxford: Oxford University Press, 1988), vii. Subsequent references to this book will be included in the text. Hogle's argument is as compelling as it is complex, and his reading of Shelley's career is the most significant since Earl Wasserman's *Shelley: A Critical Reading* (Baltimore: Johns Hopkins University Press, 1971). Hogle identifies "radical transference" as the philosophical and stylistic process that animates Shelley's poetry, the "Spirit" that produces his critical "unveilings" as well as the sense of formal evanescence. My differences with Hogle, which I will elucidate below, revolve primarily around his reading of *The Triumph of Life*.

3. Spivak's "speculations on reading Marx after reading Derrida" deliver her to Shelley's "notion of imagination" as a "plausible, though still idealist, model of deferred practice": "Writing specifically of the production of relative surplus-value and division of labour by means of technology—'a cultivation of the mechanical arts in a degree disproportioned to the presence of the creative faculty' leading to 'the abuse of all invention for *abridging and combining labour*, to the exasperation of inequality' rather than 'lighten[ing] . . . the curse imposed on Adam'—Shelley suggests that 'we want the creative faculty to *imagine* what we know; we want the generous impulse to *act* that which we *imagine*.' Although the 'we' here is clearly elite, the Imagination is nonetheless that principle of alterity housed in the Self which is directly opposed to 'the principle of Self, which money is the *visible* incarnation' [*Poetry and Prose*, 502–3]." Gayatri Chakravorty Spivak, "Speculations on Reading Marx: After Reading Derrida," in *Post-Structuralism and the Question of History*, ed. D. Attridge, G. Bennington, and R. Young (Cambridge, Eng.: Cambridge University Press, 1987), 61.

4. The formulation belongs to Althusser, who poses it in a different context to describe the determination exerted by structure. See Louis Althusser and Etienne Balibar, *Reading Capital*, trans. Ben Brewster (London: New Left Books, 1970), 189. To move from Marxist to "deconstructive" discourse, de Man's reading of Rilke addresses the phenomenon of an "absent cause" in rhetorical terms: "a power that is given the name of 'God.' . . . Like iron filings under the power of a magnet, the verbal mass turns towards a single object that causes the eclosion of an abundant poetic discourse." Paul de Man, *Allegories of Reading* (New Haven, Conn.: Yale University Press, 1979), 28.

5. Shelley, *Poetry and Prose*, 134. Further references to *Prometheus Unbound* will be to the *Poetry and Prose* edition and will be cited in the text by act, scene, and line numbers.

6. The reference is to Nietzsche's collection of essays published in 1893. See Friedrich Nietzsche, *Untimely Meditations*, trans. R. J. Hollingdale (Cambridge, Eng.: Cambridge University Press, 1983). The reference speaks to some deeper affinities between Shelley and Nietzsche, particularly regarding their conceptions of the "uses and disadvantages of history" and the work of a "genealogy"—the critical "revaluation of all values"—that I believe to be evident in the late work of the poet much as it is throughout the career of the philosopher.

7. Louis Althusser, *For Marx*, trans. Ben Brewster (London: Verso, 1977), 36.

8. This sense of the "education of error" is, as the passage from the essay "On Life" already suggests, inherent in the process of signification: "[A]lmost all familiar objects are signs, standing not for themselves but for others in their capacity of suggesting one thought which shall lead to a train of thoughts. Our whole life is thus an education of error" (*Poetry and Prose*, 477). According to the Shelley of "On Life," though philosophy "destroys error and the roots of error," it leaves a "vacancy" that prevents the mind from escaping the "misuse of words and signs" (ibid., 477).

9. See, for instance, the references to the poem by Jonathan Culler, "Apostrophe," in his *The Pursuit of Signs* (Ithaca, N.Y.: Cornell University Press, 1981), 135–54; John Hollander, "Poetic Imperatives," in his *Melodious Guile* (New Haven, Conn.: Yale University Press, 1988), 64–84; and Garrett Stewart, "Graphonic Tension in English Poetry" in his *Reading Voices* (Berkeley: University of California Press, 1990), 145–91.

10. Paul de Man, "Shelley Disfigured," in his *The Rhetoric of Romanticism* (New York: Columbia University Press, 1984), 100. Subsequent references to the book will be included in the text. The most important reading of "Shelley Disfigured" is Neil Hertz's "Lurid Figures," in *Reading de Man Reading*, ed. Lindsay Waters and Wlad Godzich (Minneapolis: University of Minnesota Press, 1989), 82–104. Hertz proposes a phrase that, while describing the process by which de Man will "conjur" a subject through its ostensible but "undecidable" effects, also aptly characterizes the "source" of Shelleyan imagination: "the pathos of uncertain agency" (86). In the case of the *Defence of Poetry*, it is both *path* and pathos, for the "uncertain agency" that produces the affects of pathos is legible only in the tracks left by "the path of its departure."

11. Important reference points in the history of the poem's discussion include W. B. Yeats, "The Philosophy of Shelley's Poetry," in his *Essays and Introductions* (London: Macmillan, 1961), 93–94; A. C. Bradley. "Notes on Shel-

ley's 'Triumph of Life,'" *MLR*, 9 (Oct. 1914): 441–56; Harold Bloom, *Shelley's Mythmaking* (New Haven, Conn.: Yale University Press, 1959); Donald Reiman, *Shelley's "The Triumph of Life": A Critical Study* (Urbana: University of Illinois Press, 1965); Edward Duffy, *Rousseau in England* (Berkeley: University of California Press, 1979), 106–52; Angela Leighton, *Shelley and the Sublime* (Cambridge, Eng.: Cambridge University Press, 1984), 150–75; and Hogle, *Shelley's Process*, 319–43.

12. This "positing" is—as Deborah Esch aptly formulates it in her compelling reading of de Man's Shelley—how the poet conceived of poetic "legislation": "Shelleyan legislation . . . is readable above all as an institution of and in language, as an exercise of positional 'power.'" "A Defense of Rhetoric / The Triumph of Reading: De Man, Shelley, and *The Rhetoric of Romanticism*," in Waters and Godzich, *Reading de Man Reading*, 71.

13. For discussions of Shelley's politics, see Kenneth Neil Cameron's two-volume biography, *The Young Shelley: Genesis of a Radical* (New York: Macmillan, 1951) and *Shelley: The Golden Years* (Cambridge, Mass.: Harvard University Press, 1974); Carl Woodring, *Politics in English Romantic Poetry* (Cambridge, Mass.: Harvard University Press, 1970), 230–330; Michael Henry Scrivener, *Radical Shelley* (Princeton, N.J.: Princeton University Press, 1982); P. M. S. Dawson, *The Unacknowledged Legislator: Shelley and Politics* (Oxford: Clarendon Press, 1980); David Punter, "Shelley: Poetry and Politics," in *Romanticism and Ideology: Studies in English Writing 1765–1830*, ed. David Aers et al. (London: Routledge and Kegan Paul, 1981), 155–72; and Manfred Wojcik, "In Defence of Shelley," in *Shelley: Modern Judgements*, ed. R. B. Woodings (London: Macmillan, 1969), 272–85.

14. The power of the opening lines has often been noted; Harold Bloom, for instance, speaks of the "precision, speed, and directness" of the passage (Bloom, *Shelley's Mythmaking*, 223). Bloom's reading of the poem and of its critical tradition remains one of the most important and helpful interpretive guides to this difficult text. Bloom is perhaps the first critic to have challenged the tradition of interpretation established by F. Melian Stawell, A. C. Bradley, and Carlos Baker, a tradition that gives the poem a curiously upbeat reading. As Bloom points out, Stawell even goes so far as to "write a happy ending" for the poem "which saw the conqueror conquered" (267). In Bloom's more sober reading, *The Triumph* is "a myth-unmaking poem" (220), in which "the myth, and the myth's maker are fully conscious of the myth's necessary defeat" (275). That the "myth and the myth's maker" are "fully conscious" of this defeat is, however, certainly cast into doubt by a poem that instead seems to call into question the possibility of a full and undivided consciousness.

15. As Bloom points out, Yeats was the first to elaborate on the political allegory at work in these lines. Bloom cites Yeats's assertion in "The Philosophy

of Shelley's Poetry" that, in *The Triumph*, "the sun's power is the being and source of all tyrannies" (Bloom, *Shelley's Mythmaking*, 270).

16. The imposition of this burden is not countered by the language of rebellion or resistance, as it is by Prometheus, for instance, in the opening speech of *Prometheus Unbound* (I.1–73). In "The Secrets of an Elder Day: Shelley After 'Hellas,'" Jerome J. McGann sees in this "toil" the lineage of Paul, Prometheus, and Christ. The essay is in *Shelley: Modern Judgements*, ed. R. B. Woodings (London: Macmillan, 1969), 253–71.

17. Paul Virilio describes an early-nineteenth century English cartoon depicting "Bonaparte and Pitt cutting chunks out of an enormous globe-shaped pudding with their sabers, the Frenchman taking the continents while the Englishman claims the sea. This is another way of parceling out the universe." *Speed and Politics: An Essay in Dromology*, trans. Mark Polizzotti (New York: Semiotext(e), 1986), 37.

18. Shelley's critique of the sun and the values attributed to it is visible elsewhere, most notably perhaps in his "Song of Apollo," where the image of the sun as the false holder of power is defeated in the "Song of Pan"—another Shelleyan reversal of the classical ascriptions, which is of a piece with his Nietzschean "revaluation of all values."

19. Carlos Baker, in *Shelley's Major Poetry: The Fabric of a Vision* (Princeton, N.J.: Princeton University Press, 1948), for example, sees the sun as a "wholly beneficent" figure, one whose "supernal" rays are never vanquished (266, 269). And, as Bloom points out, neither Stawell nor Bradley "ever recognized the ambiguity of the sun as symbol in the poem" (Bloom, *Shelley's Mythmaking*, 226). The resistance to the "ambiguity" of the image of the sun is symptomatic of a tradition of criticism that regards the poem as "hopeful" and "life affirming."

20. Louis Althusser, "Ideology and Ideological State Apparatuses (Notes Toward an Investigation)," in his *"Lenin and Philosophy" and Other Essays*, trans. Ben Brewster (New York: Monthly Review Press, 1971), 165. Subsequent references to this essay will be included in the text.

21. J. Hillis Miller, *The Linguistic Moment* (Princeton, N.J.: Princeton University Press, 1985), 144. Subsequent references to this work will be included in the text.

22. My thinking about Shelley's "Medusa," about his career, and, in particular, about his attention to the "unending involutions" of language and mind owes a great debt to Carol Jacobs's fine essay, "On Looking at Shelley's Medusa," included in her volume *Uncontainable Romanticism* (Baltimore: Johns Hopkins University Press, 1989) 3–18.

23. As Reiman comments regarding the presence of this break in the manuscript, "Shelley's suspension points indicate important breaks or divisions of

thought in the poem; below 40 are two short, heavy horizontal lines with scribbling between them" (Reiman, *Shelley's "The Triumph of Life,"* 139).

24. On Shelley's "Platonism," see James A. Notopoulos, *The Platonism of Shelley: A Study of Platonism and the Poetic Mind* (Durham, N.C.: Duke University Press, 1949). Other, more skeptical accounts of Shelley's relationship to Plato and Platonism include C. E. Pulos, *The Deep Truth: A Study of Shelley's Skepticism* (Lincoln: University of Nebraska Press, 1954); Wasserman, *Shelley*; and Miller, *Linguistic Moment*, 114–79. These studies have demonstrated that Shelley, to quote Herman Rapaport in his fine essay on the "stagings" in "Mont Blanc," "came to Plato with a skeptical frame of mind." "Staging: 'Mont Blanc,'" in *Displacements: After Derrida*, ed. Mark Krupnick (Bloomington: Indiana University Press, 1983), 59.

25. See Reiman, *Shelley's "The Triumph of Life,"* 143.

26. The passage is evidence of what Hogle characterizes as "Shelley's opening-out of *terza rima* in the poem": "his more frequent use of enjambment, verbs, disruptive rhythms, and sentence patterns that cross from stanza to stanza, breaking the attempted self-containment of each in Dante and Petrarch . . . can now be noticed more and revealed as an insistence of deferral of figure to figure in defiance of older attempts to make verbal triads betoken centered trinities" (*Shelley's Process*, 337).

27. Harold Bloom's detailed reading of the "chariot" passage is, once again, quite helpful. Perhaps it can be taken as an index of the difficulty of these stanzas that he fails to heed his own admonition: "As soon as you have identified the abstraction you believe the chariot of life and its occupants to be," Bloom writes, "then just that soon you have stopped reading Shelley's poem. . . . They are forms seen in a poet's vision, and what they mean is not something in addition to what they are" (*Shelley's Mythmaking*, 243). But Bloom makes just such an identification, asserting that the "chariot, its unseen team, and its charioteer all derive from the fourfold tradition of Ezekiel's vision of cherubim" (245). Kenneth Neil Cameron is one of the few critics to give the poem a strong historical interpretation. Cameron sees the four sets of the charioteer's eyes as the vision of history, connecting past and future to the present. See his *Shelley: Golden Years*.

28. Earl Wasserman's still unsurpassed reading of *Prometheus Unbound* is predicated on its utopian impulses. On the disappearance of time, see in particular, *Shelley*, 366.

29. For Hogle, *The Triumph of Life* is not so much a break with the past as a radicalization of the transference always evident. Stressing his differences with Miller's reading of the poem, Hogle maintains that the fragmentation and disfigurations of the poem can "be seen and then used as a renewal and extension of hope rather than its limit, denial, or death" (*Shelley's Process*, 337). Far

from spelling the end to the promise held out by the imagination, Hogle asserts, "the imagination, too, can happily come to see its function not as the worship [i.e., 'enshrinement'] of its own objectified power but as the release, realization, and extension of such renewals in 'vitally metaphorical' reveilings of existence as currently perceived" (337). Hogle's argument for the "extension of hope" is thus symptomatically dependent upon the continuing presence of the imagination, which is precisely what I claim to be "denied" rather than extended by the poem.

In Tilottama Rajan's fine treatment of Shelley's poetics, the abandonment of revelation marks the break from "idealism" to "skepticism." See "Visionary and Questionary: Idealism and Skepticism in Shelley's Poetry," in her *Dark Interpreter* (Ithaca, N.Y.: Cornell University Press, 1980), 58–96.

30. For an extended treatment of the figure of Rousseau in *The Triumph of Life* and of Rousseau's role in English Romanticism, see Duffy, *Rousseau in England*; and see Leighton, *Shelley and the Sublime*.

31. Althusser's understanding of the specularity of the ideological process, of the "interpellation" of subjects, is drawn from Lacan's theorizing of the "mirror phase" in the formation of subjectivity. See Jacques Lacan, "The Mirror Stage," in his *Ecrits*, trans. Alan Sheridan (New York: W. W. Norton, 1977), 1–7. Some authoritative discussions on the "mirror phase" and on Lacan's work generally are Anika Lemaire, *Jacques Lacan*, trans. David Macey (London: Routledge and Kegan Paul, 1977); Shoshana Felman, *Jacques Lacan and the Adventure of Insight* (Cambridge, Mass.: Harvard University Press, 1987); and Stephen Heath, *Questions of Cinema* (Bloomington: Indiana University Press, 1981). For discussions of Althusser's controversial use of Freud and Lacan, see Rosalind Coward and John Ellis, *Language and Materialism* (London: Routledge and Kegan Paul, 1977), and Paul Smith, *Discerning the Subject* (Minneapolis: University of Minnesota Press, 1988). For an important consideration of the relationship between Lacanian psychoanalysis and Marxism, see Fredric Jameson, "Imaginary and Symbolic in Lacan: Marxism, Psychoanalytic Criticism, and the Problem of the Subject," *Yale French Studies*, 55/56 (1977): 338–95.

32. See Miller, *Linguistic Moment*, 126–27.

33. In "White Mythology," Derrida argues that Western structures of perception and cognition are organized around the figure of the sun: "the sun is the unique, irreplaceable, natural referent, around which everything must turn, toward which everything must turn. . . . The very opposition of appearing and disappearing, the entire lexicon of the *phainesthai*, of *aletheia*, etc., of day and night, of the visible and the invisible, of the present and the absent—all this is possible only under the sun." In Jacques Derrida, *Margins of Philosophy*, trans. Alan Bass (Chicago: University of Chicago Press, 1982), 251.

34. Theodor Adorno, "Lyric Poetry and Society," trans. Bruce Mayo, *Telos*, 20 (Spring 1974): 56–71.

35. E. P. Thompson's tirade against Althusser and his influence over a strain of British Marxist and post-Marxist thought is chronicled in the long title-essay to his collection, *The Poverty of Theory* (New York: Monthly Review Press, 1978), 1–211.

36. Though Miller's reading of the passage introduces the issue of ideology, he implicitly defines it as sets of ideas that are freely and consciously chosen and discarded. This makes ideology into a second-order phenomenon, distinct from what Miller calls "the linguistic moment." In "Representation and Ideology in *The Triumph of Life*," *Studies in English Literature*, 17, no. 4 (Autumn 1978): 639–57, David Quint offers the most provocative and relevant discussion of these issues to date. However, Quint's argument maintains the opposition between what he calls "ideological representation" and the "free imagination," the very opposition that I contend the poem undoes. The remains of *The Triumph of Life* have erased the "free" or liberating imagination that is a feature of Shelley's earlier work.

37. Cf. Shelley, *Adonais*, ll. 424–39.

38. Walter Benjamin, "Theses on the Philosophy of History," in his *Illuminations*, trans. Harry Zohn (New York: Schocken Books, 1969), 256.

39. See Reiman, *Shelley's "The Triumph of Life,"* 43–44.

40. What Michel Foucault says of Nietzsche's genealogical analysis could in this context be extended to the historical knowledge produced by *The Triumph of Life*: "In a sense, only a single drama is ever staged . . . , the endlessly repeated play of dominations. The domination of certain men over others leads to the differentiation of values." "Nietzsche, Genealogy, History," in Michel Foucault, *Language, Counter-Memory, Practice*, trans. Donald Bouchard (Ithaca, N.Y.: Cornell University Press, 1979), 150.

41. As Shelley argues in his essay "On Life," religion is the answer most often produced by "all recorded generations of mankind" to the question, "What is the cause of life?" (*Poetry and Prose*, 478).

Chapter 4

1. Marjorie Levinson, *Keats's Life of Allegory: The Origins of a Style* (London: Basil Blackwell, 1988).

2. *John Keats: Complete Poems*, ed. Jack Stillinger (Cambridge, Mass.: Harvard University Press, 1978), ll. 245–47. All references to Keats's poetry are from this edition and will be cited by line numbers in the text.

3. Helen Vendler, *The Odes of John Keats* (Cambridge, Mass.: Harvard Uni-

versity Press, 1983), 7. Perhaps the most symptomatic recent declaration of Keats's humanism is to be found in Hermione de Almeida's "Intellectual Keats": "In an age of warring and self-destructive ideologies when it is considered unfashionable to speak of serving humanity, . . . and ridiculous to wish to be a philosopher and a humanist when meaning has been dismantled, deconstructed and banished from earth, Keats has nevertheless survived by doing all these things. He has kept his humanizing place among the greatest English poets." Introduction to *Critical Essays on John Keats*, ed. Hermione de Almeida (Boston: G. K. Hall, 1990), 8.

4. Paul de Man, "Introduction to the Poetry of John Keats," in Paul de Man, *Critical Writings, 1953–1978*, ed. Lindsay Waters (Minneapolis: University of Minnesota Press, 1989), 187.

5. Keats's invocation of a necessary ethical response could thus be understood to conform to the "supplementary logic" developed by Jacques Derrida in his reading of Rousseau; see " . . . That Dangerous Supplement . . . ," in his *Of Grammatology*, trans. Gayatri Chakravorty Spivak (Baltimore: Johns Hopkins University Press, 1976), 141–64.

6. *The Letters of John Keats*, ed. Hyder Edwards Rollins (Cambridge, Mass.: Harvard University Press, 1958), 1: 192. Subsequent references to the letters are to this edition and will be included in the text. We will have occasion to return to this interpretation of "Negative Capability," that capability "of being in uncertainties, Mysteries, doubts, without any irritable reaching after fact & reason" (1: 193).

7. On the Arnoldian strain of "moral" criticism, see Paul de Man, "Wordsworth and the Victorians," in his *The Rhetoric of Romanticism* (New York: Columbia University Press, 1984), 83–92.

8. For a critical analysis of the purchase of the model of "redemption" on our interpretations and conceptions of culture, see Leo Bersani, *The Culture of Redemption* (Cambridge, Mass.: Harvard University Press, 1990).

9. Paul de Man, *The Resistance to Theory* (Minneapolis: University of Minnesota Press, 1986), 96. Subsequent references to this work will be included in the text.

10. The repeated engagements (and many missed encounters) between deconstruction and humanism have produced a considerable body of discussion. M. H. Abrams has elaborated his "humanistic perspective" on the questions posed by deconstruction in an extensive series of essays and discussions collected in *Doing Things with Texts*, ed. Michael Fischer (New York: W. W. Norton, 1989), 236–363. The stakes and the temperature of the debate were raised considerably with the disclosure of Paul de Man's wartime journalism. See the references in Introduction n. 31, above.

11. At the outset of her fine essay on the "Ode to a Nightingale," Cynthia

Chase has very neatly formulated this dilemma in Keats: "The difficulty of interpreting Keats's poetry is closely bound up with its loveliness, its power to gratify our wish for beauty. This is a power to provoke nearly unanimous value judgments together with widely disparate accounts of their occasion." *Decomposing Figures: Rhetorical Readings in the Romantic Tradition* (Ithaca, N.Y.: Cornell University Press, 1986), 65.

12. Karl Marx and Friedrich Engels, *The German Ideology*, trans. Clemens Dutt, in Karl Marx, *Collected Works*, vol. 5 (New York: International Publishers, 1976), 29. Subsequent references to this edition will be included in the text.

13. Roy Bhaskar, "Materialism," in *A Dictionary of Marxist Thought*, ed. Tom Bottomore et al. (Cambridge, Mass.: Harvard University Press, 1983), 328.

14. Pierre Macherey, "In a Materialist Way," in *Philosophy in France Today*, ed. Alan Montefiore (Cambridge, Eng.: Cambridge University Press, 1983), 142.

15. Barbara Jones Guetti, "Resisting the Aesthetic," *Diacritics*, 17, no. 1 (Spring 1987): 33–51. Guetti's essay, which mentions these lines in the course of her reading of the "Ode on a Grecian Urn" with *The Communist Manifesto*, is an excellent discussion of the role of the aesthetic in what de Man called the "resistance to theory." On the aspect of resistance and the materiality of language in de Man, see also Wlad Godzich's lucid Foreword to de Man's *Resistance to Theory*, ix–xviii. For an extensive and serious interpretation of "Dear Reynolds," see Stuart M. Sperry, *Keats the Poet* (Princeton, N.J.: Princeton University Press, 1973), 117–31.

16. Martin Heidegger, *The Origin of the Work of Art*, trans. Albert Hofstadter (New York: Harper & Row, 1971), 19. Subsequent references to this essay will be included in the text.

17. Jones Guetti, "Resisting the Aesthetic," 40.

18. The sources and contexts of Keats's sometimes idiosyncratic, sometimes conventional Hellenism are well established. See, for instance, Robert M. Ryan, "The Politics of Greek Religion," in de Almeida, *Critical Essays on Keats*, 261–79; Alan J. Bewell, "The Classical Implications of Keats's Classicist Aesthetics," *Studies in Romanticism*, 25 (Summer 1986): 220–29; Marilyn Butler, *Romantics, Rebels and Reactionaries* (New York: Oxford University Press, 1982), 113–37; Martin Aske, *Keats and Hellenism* (Cambridge, Eng.: Cambridge University Press, 1985); and Levinson, *Keats's Life of Allegory*. We have a keen sense of the class determinations and political resonances of Keats's often anxious fascination with "Grecian manner" and Grecian things. But to read this Hellenism "in a materialist way" is not merely to stress, as does Levinson, that Keats's sonnet to "*Chapman's* Homer" testifies to the poet's lack of Greek; the sonnet ironizes the "adventure" it narrates and emphasizes the linguistic medi-

ation by which the "discovery" is achieved, a "discovery" that is ironically rendered impossible by the sort of classical education that would make the "original" *appear* accessible.

19. Hans-Georg Gadamer, *Truth and Method*, trans. Garrett Burden and John Cumming (New York: Crossroad, 1975), 144–46. See also Hans-Georg Gadamer, "Aesthetics and Hermeneutics" in his *Philosophical Hermeneutics*, trans. David E. Linge (Berkeley: University of California Press, 1976), 95–104.

20. Theodor Adorno, *Negative Dialectics*, trans. E. B. Ashton (New York: Seabury, 1979), esp. 183–86.

21. Geoffrey Hartman, in his influential essay on "To Autumn," proposes a very different notion of "ideology" and its presentation in literary texts. See "Poem and Ideology: A Study of Keats's 'To Autumn,'" in Geoffrey Hartman, *The Fate of Reading* (Chicago: University of Chicago Press, 1975), 124–46.

22. Once we have begun to think of "Dear Reynolds" as addressing the problem of ideology, these lines resonate with Pierre Macherey's account of the relationship between literature and ideology. For Macherey, ideology is precisely that which "the text that cannot say." See his *A Theory of Literature Production*, trans. Geoffrey Wall (London: Routledge and Kegan Paul, 1978).

Chapter 5

1. Louis Althusser, *"Lenin and Philosophy" and Other Essays*, trans. Ben Brewster (New York: Monthly Review Press, 1971), 39–40.

2. *Essays of George Eliot*, ed. George Pinney (New York: Columbia University Press, 1963), 270. Subsequent references to this work will be included in the text.

3. See, for instance, Barbara Hardy, *Particularities: Readings in George Eliot* (Athens, Ohio: Ohio University Press, 1982), 193–94, for an account of this "sympathy" in an important passage in *The Mill on the Floss*. My reading of the narrative operations of the "imagination" in George Eliot is at odds with Hardy's discussion of the same subject in *Particularities*, 181–204; I would argue that even as lucid a reader of realistic fiction as Hardy conflates sympathy and imagination. For a discussion of the intellectual framework of "sympathy" in the context of Eliot's early fiction, see Thomas A. Noble, "The Doctrine of Sympathy," in his *George Eliot's "Scenes of Clerical Life"* (New Haven, Conn.: Yale University Press, 1965), 55–92.

4. George Eliot, "Belles Lettres," *Westminster Review*, 66 (1856): 307.

5. In "Recognizing Casaubon," Neil Hertz identifies "two kinds of imagination" in George Eliot, a "moral" and a "narcissistic" imagination. "The differences," Hertz argues, "between these two kinds of imagination . . . may not, under scrutiny, be all that clear. Both activities, whatever their outward effects,

would seem to originate within the same enclosure. . . . George Eliot is here engaging the same problem that led Romantic theorists like Coleridge to insist on a sharp and essential difference between the mental activities they named Imagination and Fancy." In Neil Hertz, *The End of the Line* (New York: Columbia University Press, 1985), 84–85. Much of what I say in this chapter is prompted by the connections Hertz establishes between Coleridge and Eliot. But I would argue that the analogy Hertz develops in this otherwise compelling essay between Coleridge's definition of "Fancy" and Eliot's "narcissistic imagination" cannot be sustained: "Fancy" for Coleridge is a faculty of "association" and is not "narcissistic" in this sense. Moreover, what Hertz calls "narcissistic" imagination is a much more active faculty or process than what Coleridge calls "Fancy." However we refer to the imagination in Eliot, we are certainly called upon to see it as the name of the consistently vexed relationship between self and world.

6. George Eliot, *The Mill on the Floss*, ed. Gordon S. Haight (Boston: Houghton Mifflin, 1961); subsequent references to this edition will be included in the text. Some of the principal and provocative studies of the novel include: Jerome Thale, *The Novels of George Eliot* (New York: Columbia University Press, 1959); U. C. Knoepflmacher, *George Eliot's Early Novels: The Limits of Realism* (Berkeley: University of California Press, 1968); Jeanette King, *Tragedy in the Victorian Novel* (Cambridge, Eng.: Cambridge University Press, 1978), 70–96; and Mary Jacobus, "Men of Maxims and *The Mill on the Floss*," in her *Reading Woman: Essays in Feminist Criticism* (New York: Columbia University Press, 1986), 62–79.

7. In his important study of the "social figures" of George Eliot's work, Daniel Cottom argues persuasively that the term "sympathy" also "represents the negotiation between private and public worlds." See his *Social Figures: George Eliot, Social History, and Literary Representation* (Minneapolis: University of Minnesota Press, 1987), 187.

8. George Eliot, *Middlemarch*, ed. Gordon S. Haight (Boston: Houghton Mifflin Company, 1956), 140. Subsequent references to this edition will be included in the text. From the massive and rich tradition of criticism, I have found the following studies of *Middlemarch* particularly helpful: Hardy, *Particularities*; Thale, *Novels of George Eliot*; J. Hillis Miller, "Optic and Semiotic in *Middlemarch*," in *The Worlds of Victorian Fiction*, ed. Jerome H. Buckley (Cambridge, Mass.: Harvard University Press, 1975), 125–45; George Levine, *The Realistic Imagination: English Fiction from Frankenstein to Lady Chatterley* (Chicago: University of Chicago Press, 1981), 291–316; Gillian Beer, *Darwin's Plots* (London: Routledge and Kegan Paul, 1983), 149–80; D. A. Miller, *Narrative and Its Discontents* (Princeton, N.J.: Princeton University Press, 1981), 107–94; Hertz, "Recognizing Casaubon," 75–96; and Franco Moretti, *The Way of the World*

(London: Verso, 1987), 214–28. For an introduction to George Eliot's relationship to Romanticism, see K. M. Newton, *George Eliot: Romantic Humanist* (London: Macmillan, 1981).

9. For an important study that explicitly links the problems of literary periodization to pervasive formal problems of representation, see Henry Sussman, *The Hegelian Aftermath* (Baltimore: Johns Hopkins University Press, 1982). Sussman uses the term "Romantic-Modern" to refer to this post-Hegelian discursive formation.

10. See Cottom's chapter on "Realism and Romance" in *Social Figures*.

11. On the "painful collisions" "between the outward and the inward" as an issue in Hegel's *Aesthetics* and as a prominent feature of the discourses of Romanticism, see above, Chapter 2.

12. Jacqueline Rose, "George Eliot and the Spectacle of Woman," in her *Sexuality in the Field of Vision* (London: Verso, 1986), 116, 117. See also Nancy Armstrong's situating of this scenario as an integral feature of history of the novel in *Desire and Domestic Fiction: A Political History of the Novel* (Oxford: Oxford University Press, 1987). Subsequent references to Armstrong's book will be included in the text.

13. We may in fact read this as an exemplary instance of a narrative desire that constitutes one of the principal conventions of the nineteenth-century novel. On this "narrative desire," see Peter Brooks, *Reading for the Plot: Design and Intention in Narrative* (New York: Alfred Knopf, 1984), 37–62.

14. George Eliot, *Adam Bede*, ed. John Paterson (Boston: Houghton Mifflin, 1968), 134. Subsequent references to this edition will be included in the text. It would be instructive to compare this scene with one near the end of *Middlemarch* in which Dorothea, standing at her window, affirms "sympathy." See D. A. Miller's excellent discussion of this latter scene in *Narrative and Its Discontents*, 175–80.

15. The same point could be made of Dorothea, whose sympathetic "effect on those around her" in *Middlemarch* is not to be doubted but who manages nonetheless to make painful mistakes of judgment.

16. Hertz, *End of the Line*, 224. This is another way of demonstrating how narrative procedures, such as the "double surrogation" identified by Hertz, underwrite and sustain what Armstrong calls the "sexual contract of the novel" in the form of woman's "double bind."

17. As Terry Eagleton points out, Hetty's actions in the novel have "unwittingly ruptured the class-collaboration between squire and artisan, turning Adam against Arthur; but once she is, so to speak, deported from the novel, that organic allegiance can be gradually reaffirmed." *Criticism and Ideology* (London: Verso, 1976), 114.

18. I am referring again to the distinction, developed in structuralist narra-

tive theory and discussed above in Chapter 1, between the story (*récit*), the progression of events and actions in the novel, and the narration of those events and actions, their ordering by the novel's discourse (*discours*). The closer we examine the distinction in George Eliot's novels, the more it affirms the observations developed by Roland Barthes, Gérard Genette, and others that story can never be independent of discourse, and that while story appears logically to precede its narration, from the perspective of the narrative story is the *effect* of narration. On the implications of this wavering distinction, see Brooks, *Reading for the Plot*.

19. See for instance the chapter devoted to George Eliot in Colin Mac-Cabe's *James Joyce and the Revolution of the Word* (London: Macmillan, 1979).

20. See in particular Raymond Williams, *The Country and the City* (Oxford: Oxford University Press, 1973), 165–81; D. A. Miller, *Narrative and Its Discontents*; and J. Hillis Miller, *The Ethics of Reading* (New York: Columbia University Press, 1987), 61–80. A now classic formulation can be found in Georg Lukács, *The Theory of the Novel*, trans. Anna Bostock (Cambridge, Mass.: MIT Press, 1971): "The aesthetic problem . . . is at root an ethical one, and its artistic solution therefore presupposes, in accordance with the formal laws of the novel, that a solution has been found to the ethical problem" (115).

21. On this relationship between story and discourse in *Middlemarch*, see Moretti, *Way of the World*, 222.

22. D. A. Miller, *Narrative and Its Discontents*, 164.

23. On the problems posed by this narration of sympathy for George Eliot's notion of realism, see Cottom, *Social Figures*, 195.

24. See J. Hillis Miller's elegant and compelling reading of this chapter in *Ethics of Reading*. Miller demonstrates that between the representation of the ethical and the representation of the aesthetic, there is a "groundless figurality" that catches both the ethical and the aesthetic in a perpetual and unsettling oscillation.

25. As D. A. Miller points out, "the narrator may pay humble compliment to Fielding's regularly spaced digressions, but he is implicitly proud of the fact that his own discourse is far more interwoven with the fabric of the story" (*Narrative and Its Discontents*, 156). Eliot's discussions of Fielding's narrative digressions stress moreover that the "leisure" that permitted such narrative discourse is no longer available given the "hurry of imagination" encountered in the historical wake of Romanticism.

26. On this assertion of the "needfulness" of sympathy and its ethical implications, see J. Hillis Miller, *Ethics of Reading*.

27. On the narrative effects of this "penetration of urban capital," see Eagleton, *Criticism and Ideology*, 115.

28. On the ideological valence of the "complex amalgam of fictional de-

vices" displayed throughout Eliot's novels, see Eagleton, *Criticism and Ideology*, 110–25. On *The Mill on the Floss* as a "pilgrim's progress" and a *Bildungsroman*, see Barry Qualls, *The Secular Pilgrims of Victorian Fiction* (Cambridge, Eng.: Cambridge University Press, 1982), 147–48.

29. George Eliot, *Daniel Deronda*, ed. Barbara Hardy (Harmondsworth, Eng.: Penguin Books, 1967), 111. Subsequent references to this edition will be included in the text.

30. See Cottom's discussion of this crisis of a social signification in *Social Figures*, 115.

31. Levine, *Realistic Imagination*, 259.

32. Williams's essay on George Eliot in his *Country and City* is titled "Knowable Communities"; the ideological and narrative issues posed by this phrase are the central concerns of Williams's critical and fictional work. Further references to Williams's book will be included in the text.

33. Cottom's "Education and the Transfigurations of Realism" (in his *Social Figures*, 33–57) is an important discussion of the matter of education and its relationship to discourse of realism, though Cottom develops his interpretation without much consideration of the rhetorical and structural features of the novels.

34. As quoted by Levine, *Realistic Imagination*, 258.

35. *Selections from George Eliot's Letters*, ed. Gordon S. Haight (New Haven, Conn.: Yale University Press, 1986), 318. Subsequent references to this book will be included in the text. The letter to Harrison is also discussed by Qualls, *Secular Pilgrims*, 139–40. For a study that discusses the thematics of teaching, see William Myers, *The Teaching of George Eliot* (Leicester, Eng.: Leicester University Press, 1984).

36. On the ideological functions of this disavowal, see D. A. Miller, *The Novel and the Police* (Berkeley: University of California Press, 1988), 67.

37. But to this it must be added, as Terry Eagleton remarks, that the act of renunciation is an authorized rejection of Stephen Guest, "an overbred product of the predatory capitalism which is ousting the old rural world of her father" (*Criticism and Ideology*, 115).

38. My argument is significantly at odds with Williams's important, if symptomatic, interpretations of Eliot as they are presented in *Country and City* and *The English Novel from Dickens to Lawrence* (London: Chatto & Windus, 1970), 75–94. Elsewhere, I have explored the intertwinings of culture and community in Williams's work: see "Raymond Williams and the Inhuman Limits of Culture," in *Views Beyond the Border Country: Perspectives on Raymond Williams*, ed. Leslie Roman and Dennis Dworkin (New York: Routledge, 1992), 260–74.

39. Implicit in the social and cultural discourses of community is the opposition between "community" and "society," a version of the opposition be-

tween *Gemeinschaft* and *Gesellschaft* developed in German social theory and explicitly formulated in the work of Ferdinand Tönnies. See Tönnies, *Community and Society*, trans. Charles P. Loomis (East Lansing: Michigan State University Press, 1957). The notion of community continues, of course, to have a strong critical and ideological currency. Discourses of nationalism, for instance, cannot do without some variation of this notion of community; see Benedict Anderson, *Imagined Communities: Reflections on the Origin and Spread of Nationalism* (London: Verso, 1983). The most sustained consideration of the problem of community in George Eliot is Suzanne Graves, *George Eliot and Community: A Study in Social Theory and Fictional Form* (Berkeley: University of California Press, 1984). For a treatment of the opposition between *Gemeinschaft* and *Gesellschaft* that introduces a brief discussion of *Middlemarch*, see Fredric Jameson, "Criticism in History," in *The Weapons of Criticism*, ed. Norman Rudich (Palo Alto, Calif.: Ramparts Press, 1976), 31–50. Jameson argues: "George Eliot's novelistic construction of a community or a *Gemeinschaft*, her doctrine of the secret interweaving of human existences, stands itself as a symptom of the increasing difficulty her contemporaries have in feeling their society to be an organic totality" (37).

40. *Community at Loose Ends*, ed. Miami Theory Collective (Minneapolis: University of Minnesota Press, 1991). Two crucial recent treatments of the endless problem of community are: Maurice Blanchot, *The Unavowable Community*, trans. Pierre Joris (Barrytown, N.Y.: Station Hill Press, 1988); and Jean-Luc Nancy, *The Inoperative Community*, ed. Peter Conner, trans. Peter Conner et al. (Minneapolis: University of Minnesota Press, 1991).

41. For our recognition of the narrative operations of these "present causes of past events," see Cynthia Chase's brilliant reading of *Daniel Deronda* in "The Decomposition of the Elephants: Double-Reading *Daniel Deronda*," in her *Decomposing Figures: Rhetorical Readings in the Romantic Tradition* (Ithaca, N.Y.: Cornell University Press, 1986), 157–74.

42. Readers of Eliot will recognize that this curious narrative two-step is not an aberration but a repeated feature of her work, one that her narrators will entertain, as in the famous commentary on *Macbeth* in *Middlemarch*: "For Macbeth's rhetoric about the impossibility of being many opposite things in the same moment referred to the clumsy necessities of action and not to the subtler possibilities of feeling. We cannot speak a loyal word and be meanly silent, we cannot kill and not kill in the same moment, but a room is wide enough for the loyal and mean desire, for the outlash of a murderous thought and the sharp backward stroke of repentance." We may well read the passage as commentary on "the clumsy necessities of action" that occur in narration, for her novels are indeed "wide enough" for the critical gesture, the "murderous thought" that is then canceled by the "backward stroke of repentance." For

Jacqueline Rose, who draws our attention to the passage, the staging of this contradiction is repeated throughout Eliot's novels, specifically in *Daniel Deronda* as "the spectacle of woman." See *Sexuality in the Field of Vision*, 107–9.

Epilogue

1. "Something's Missing: A Discussion Between Ernst Bloch and Theodor Adorno on the Contradictions of Utopian Longing," in Ernst Bloch, *The Utopian Function of Art and Literature: Selected Essays*, trans. Jack Zipes and Frank Mecklenburg (Cambridge, Mass.: MIT Press, 1988), 1–17.

2. Paul Ricoeur, *Lectures on Ideology and Utopia*, ed. George H. Taylor (New York: Columbia University Press, 1986), 1. Subsequent references to this work will be included in the text.

3. Gayatri Chakravorty Spivak, "In a Word: *Interview*," in her *Outside in the Teaching Machine* (London: Routledge, 1993), 22.

Index

In this index "f" after a number indicates a separate reference on the next page, and "ff" indicates separate references on the next two pages. A continuous discussion over two or more pages is indicated by a span of numbers. *Passim* is used for a cluster of references in close but not consecutive sequence.

Library of Congress Cataloging-in-Publication Data

Pyle, Forest.
The ideology of imagination : subject and society in the discourse
of Romanticism / Forest Pyle.
p.   cm.
Includes index.
ISBN 0-8047-1649-8 (cl.) : ISBN 0-8047-2862-3 (pbk.)
1. English literature—19th century—History and criticism.
2. Politics and literature—Great Britain—History—19th century.
3. Literature and society—Great Britain—History—19th century.
4. Political poetry, English—History and criticism. 5. Social
problems in literature. 6. Romanticism—Great Britain.
7. Imagination.   I. Title
PR468.R65P95   1995
821'.709355—dc20   94-20154   CIP Rev.

⊗ This book is printed on acid-free paper.
It was typeset in Monotype Bembo
on a Macintosh IIci at Stanford University Press.